Christ Commanding His Coronavirus to Covenant Breakers
by C. Matthew McMahon

Copyright Information

Christ Commanding His Coronavirus to Covenant Breakers by C. Matthew McMahon
Edited by Therese B. McMahon

Some language and grammar have been updated from the original manuscript. Any change in wording or punctuation has not changed the intent or meaning of the original authors, and has been made to aid the modern reader.

Published by Puritan Publications
A Ministry of A Puritan's Mind™ in Crossville, TN.
www.apuritansmind.com
www.puritanpublications.com

This Print Edition, 2020
Electronic Edition, 2020
Manufactured in the United States of America

ISBN: 978-1-62663-367-4
eISBN: 978-1-62663-366-7

Table of Contents

Introduction

Generally, in a work like this, I would expand and record numerous bibliographic citations that support both the biblical concepts, and reformed thinkers on the subject matter. I would expand it for the reader's study. In this case, I'm only going to refer you to a few resources that may be of extra-biblical help in the "relatively few footnotes" that are strewn throughout the chapters. For those that have read other works I have written, you know that they are often filled with an over-abundance of footnotes, and all kinds of citations. In this work, I desired it to be more readable, more of an exhortation and less encumbered. That means, practically, that when we begin with a text, we are going to allow that text to color and inform our ideas through the chapter overall.

Overall, this does not mean that the content in this work is devoid of biblical support, or further quotes and consensus from others. You'll see that it is squarely placed on key passages that are explained and applied. What it does mean is that this work is set up as an *exhortative* work. Yes, it is theological in nature, and yes, we will be covering what the bible says about *the plague*, and other afflictions. But sometimes, *we need to be exhorted,* and this is one of those times in the history of the world that we need *course correcting* exhortations that remain thoroughly biblical, and yet, are practical to our walk.

The title of the work speaks almost for itself. The rest of the work, all the pages between the title and the back cover, explain what that title *means* from a biblical perspective. There are a number of works and articles written in the last couple of months on the coronavirus that have been posted online. I've read *many* of them. They are, for the most part, typical "Americanized Evangelical" "stuff." That's not what we need today. It's never what the church needs. This work is not going to tread so lightly. It is going to keep Scripture in view, and outline, from a biblical point of view, why Christ has sent his coronavirus to covenant breakers in his church. Yes, the premise is that the virus (and other calamites now building) are here primarily for Christ's church; his disobedient, covenant breaking church across the globe that professes to follow King Jesus.

  This is most certainly a difficult and saddening time for many. At the time this work was written, almost 690,000 people have died worldwide from the coronavirus, (158,000 in the US) and the Lord is adding more and more calamity to our country on top of the horrors of prolonged and disease-ridden death; and it seems to be growing worse as the weeks go by. Aside from the economic strain, aside from the famine in many places, in America there is a growing sign of a Marxist revolution. It is a calamity of entirely another nature. And yet, God has sent it at the exact time that the plague is running its course, again, across the country and world. These Marxists have gained such a momentum in a short time period that it's, literally, surprising that it occurred so quickly. They want to remove every monument, and *shake the dust off* any history they hate, and they want to suppress all those that do not agree with them. And the political left is pandering to them, as well as some of the right. Defunding the police, desiring to destroy monuments like Mount Rushmore, toppling over statues of George Washington and Christopher Columbus, shootings that have escalated (killing small children in the midst of it), political rioting that has turned sinister, CHOP in Seattle; *all of it* is calamity upon calamity. It's actually "calamity" that God promises *his covenant breaking church* if they do not repent; and then, on top of it all, hurricane season is upon us.

What will the church do in a time like this? Since the calamity is growing and not subsiding, it doesn't seem like the church is doing much of anything collectively to stop the plague, much less those things that have not layered on top of that. Does that sound harsh? I don't think you will see it as so harsh once you read the texts we will deal with in this book. God deals very harshly with his people when they break covenant with him. Maybe you are completely unaware that the church has done that – broken covenant. That is part of the reason I set this work down as a book, and as an exhortation. I hope it will help you, and your church, to see the need for immediate, full, biblically non-negotiable reformation. That you would see the need for it *right now*, before we cross into lines that make it "too late." We may even be there in some respects.

There is a biblical reason that Christ is commanding his coronavirus to his church, to all his covenant breakers. Let's consider what and why that is beginning with Leviticus 26.

Chapter 1:
Pestilence is a Sign
From Christ to His Church

"And if ye will not be reformed by me by these things, but will walk contrary unto me; Then will I also walk contrary unto you, and will punish you yet seven times for your sins. And I will bring a sword upon you, that shall avenge the quarrel of my covenant: and when ye are gathered together within your cities, I will send the pestilence among you; and ye shall be delivered into the hand of the enemy," (Lev. 26:23-25).

The context of Leviticus chapter 26 surrounds rewards and curses in relation to God's covenant. The Israelites are to be a holy people because God is holy and he has commanded them certain duties that they must fulfill in his covenant as he prescribes if they are *to be* his people. What is the reason for this? The reason is, "I am the Lord, your God."[1] They must be holy, "because I, the Lord, am holy."[2] Here we see that the church must have a sound theology of walking. "Walk" (Lev. 18:3; 20:23; 26:3), in "my statutes and my laws," (Lev. 26:15, 43) (here it is then reversed), and you will "observe ... and do," what I command you (Lev. 18:4; 19:37; 20:8, 22; 22:31; 25:18; 26:3).

Chapters 17-25 give directions concerning sacrifices, instructions on worship, regulating the holy oil,

---

[1] Leviticus 18:2, 4, 30; 19:3, 4, 10, 25, 31, 34, 36; 20:7; 23:22, 43; 24:22; 25:17, 55; 26:1, 44.
[2] Leviticus 19:2; 20:26; 21:8.

the holy bread and aspects of blasphemy, times for worship, and chapter 26 concludes this section of the book with covenant blessings and covenant curses. All of Leviticus is set in the context of God's gracious covenant of grace. This gracious covenant is where Christ can be found if the people heed his prescriptions precisely in this administration of the covenant. Blessings and curses are joined with an evangelical grace, and it houses instructions on restoration if the people break God's covenant, (26:40-45). God begins, "Ye shall keep my sabbaths, and reverence my sanctuary: I am the LORD. If ye walk in my statutes, and keep my commandments, and do them; Then ..." (Lev. 26:2-4).

More particularly Leviticus 26:14–39 is a curse to the covenant breaker, or those disobedient. If the people do not uphold the covenant, in light of all the wonderful works of God's grace in their midst, by taking them out of Egypt to come and worship God, and if they think they are serving God where they in fact break covenant by doing their own thing, "if ye will not hearken unto me," proportionately, to the privileges of the covenant will be the criminality and the severity of judgment on them; even up to 7 times. In 26:15, "If ye despise my commandments." Despising or abhorring God's commands or judgments is doing anything not commanded, or not doing anything that he has commanded.

In verse 16 he says, "I will even appoint over you terror." This terror is famine, sword and pestilence, where pestilence is "consumption, and the burning ague," symptoms of disease, a plague.

In verse 17, God's blessing is no longer on them, his "face" is removed; pestilence may be defined as *a turning of God's face away from his people.* How shall one live in light of God's face if his face has turned?

In verse 18, "if ye will not yet for all this hearken to me, then I will punish you seven times more." He will bring more calamity, calamity upon calamity; calamity will *build.*

In verse 19 their might is broken; their high view of themselves, their privileged view, God will crush.

In verse 22, "your highways shall be desolate" where commerce will be interrupted; freedoms will be restricted.

In verse 31, "I will make your cities waste." Flourishing cities will not look the same. And, meeting places, places of safety, God will "bring your sanctuaries unto desolation, and I will not smell the savour of your sweet odours." Worship will be abhorred by God and he will close them down. The reference to *sanctuaries* refers to the various departments of the tabernacle and worship.

In verse 33, "I will scatter you among the heathen." The church will be mixed where they will not stand out as they ought; they go to take refuge in their cites, and God brings in calamity whether by sword, famine or pestilence.

And yet, even in the midst of the pestilence, verse 40, "If they shall confess their iniquity..." The passage still sets down the gracious promise of divine forgiveness and favor if they will repent. Who? The Egyptians? The Philistines? No, the church.

What will God do to his church? He will bring a curse on them for breaking his gracious covenant. "And if ye will not be reformed by me by these things, but will walk contrary unto me; then will I also walk contrary unto you, and will punish you yet seven times for your sins." Reformation is a term used as a starting point. God's direction here in Leviticus 26 is that reformation and amendment of life, sanctification under the curse of the fall, ought to be the common theme of the times; follow God's prescription for holiness. Peter, in the same light, quotes Leviticus, "be holy" (1 Peter 1:16). God is saying that your whole lives, your worship, your acceptable sacrifices are always to be done in the midst of reformation of life - *holiness*, because everything I have provided for you in a gracious covenant with me, in this covenant of gracious provision and all the means of grace, are to reverse the fall in you; but this will only work if you listen to me; you are to be constantly reforming and holy. But, if you don't want to be reformed, if you don't want to amend your life, if you don't want the fall of Adam reversed in you as I prescribe, if you did not want to do all things I command you precisely, if you do not want to listen to me, then *you don't want me*. And if you don't want me, in the same way that you act as the heathen, and walk contrary to me, so I will make no distinction between you and the heathen and I will walk contrary to you, not simply walk, but in fury, walk against you as I do them. I will bring a sword upon you, that shall avenge the quarrel of my covenant; for my covenant is most important in that it is the substance of my eternal decree (the blessed work of my Son for sinners no less) and I will not have it blasphemed.

God tells them, you will know this is happening when you are gathered together within your cities for refuge, that I will send the pestilence among you; you will know my fury when pestilence comes. And you will, in the midst of the pestilence, try to satisfy yourselves in so many other ways, and you will not find satisfaction in any temporary thing. And if I do all this, when you walk contrary to me, and I walk in opposition to you, bringing in the pestilence, and the pain, and the death, if you will not listen to me in this, I will do all I do to you in fury; and I will chastise you, discipline you, instruct you, admonish you, seven times for your sins, (Lev. 26:23-28) if needs be; it will be *calamitous.*

Pestilence itself is one of the armies that the Lord of Hosts commands at will. "If I shut up heaven that there be no rain, or if I command the locusts to devour the land,[3] or if I send pestilence among my people;[4] If my people, which are called by my name, shall humble themselves, and pray, and seek my face, and turn from their wicked ways; then will I hear from heaven, and will forgive their sin, and will heal their land." (2 Chr. 7:13-14). He will chastise those who provoke him by it. "... there was a plague *in the congregation* of the LORD," (Joshua 22:17). In this way, if you will "not be reformed by me by these things," (Lev. 26:23). If you will not amend your life, if you will not follow my word, if you will institute things I have not commanded, if you will disparage my commands, and my laws and my statues, and walk contrary to me, I will act in a hostile manner towards you, you will know it when the pestilence comes. He will be the cause of bringing in

---

[3] Have you heard about the East Africa locust plague, where there is the worst infestation in decades?

[4] Have you heard about the Covid-19 pestilence across the face of the earth?

misery against them to correct them, even to *wrestle against them*, as the Hebrew intimates.

God is saying, I will not treat you in those times in regards to the blessing of the covenant, but I will treat you as covenant breakers and it will be as though you will be indistinguishable from the heathen in outward calamity. People will not be able to make a distinction between you and them with what I bring you. The pestilence that will fall on you, the fever and consumption will treat all of you alike and I will punish you seven times worse if you persist as stiff necked. If one judgment is not enough, I'll send two, if two is not enough, I'll send three, if three is not enough, I'll send ... seven. I'll keep bringing it to you if you do not repent.

He gives them stipulated curses, a horrible effect of the fall that would make them miserable if they despise the covenant. God would bring them to desolation, and not reformation, if they were to act in rebellion against his covenant. Later on, he says to the church "You only have I known of all the families of the earth: therefore I will punish you for all your iniquities," (Amos 3:2). And it is interesting to note here in Leviticus that God has given them specific commands and laws which shadow the coming of the Christ, that they were to uphold these shadows and rites and ceremonies in such a way as to be precise. Precision was key. These were not sins of ignorance, but sins against what God had specifically said, where they decided, on their own, to do something else, something different. They would show a dislike of God's leading and instruction. Not hearing, not walking, walking in fact contrary to him. They don't merely miss the mark in a small way, but they despise what God's provision for reformation is, and instead would do what they want to do. God knew that if they rejected his commands, that it would not be beyond doubt that soon, they would reject him outright. In fact, rejecting his word is rejecting him. But would they then be corrected by God? Would they strive for reformation? He makes a gracious evangelical plea to them, "And yet for all that, when they be in the land of their enemies, I will not cast them away, neither will I abhor them, to destroy them utterly [key word], and to break my covenant with them: for I am the LORD their God. But I will for their sakes remember the covenant of their ancestors," (Lev. 26:44-45).

The doctrine to glean from the text here is that pestilence is a sign where God makes no difference in his temporal judgments between the church and the most depraved sinners in the world.

Consider why pestilence or sword or famine *exists*. Why is the plague here across this planet right now; why have there been plagues, why will there be more plagues? The pestilence is here because of the *real* pandemic, sin, "as by one man sin entered into the world, and death by sin," (Rom. 5:12). The reason that plagues exist is a result of the curse of God in the fall against Adam; sin is the perpetual and real pandemic that the church should notice always. Death is a result of the fall. Sickness is a result of the fall. Pestilence is an infection, a deadly disease, sent of God on men for their sins; it is part of the misery of this life. "The LORD shall make the pestilence cleave unto thee," (Deut. 28:21). The fall and sin are the reason there is pestilence. If Adam had not fell, there would be no plagues, no sickness, no disease, and no death. *The 1647 Westminster Larger Catechism* question 28 asks, "What are the punishments of sin in this world?" The answer is, "The punishments of sin in this world are either inward, as blindness of mind, a reprobate sense, strong delusions, hardness of heart, horror of conscience, and vile affections; or outward, as the curse of God upon the creatures for our sakes, and all other evils that befall us in our bodies, names, estates, relations, and employments; together with death itself."

Scripture calls *pestilence* many things. It is called in Psalm 89:23 a plague that is striking. Psalm 91:10 calls it a disease, a plague of death. Psalm 106:29 it means a slaughtering, a blow, smiting against God's people. The hand of the Lord, 2 Sam. 24:14, where David chose the pestilence at God's hand and 70,000 men died. It is called in various places in Scripture, the fear of the night, an arrow flying by day, the destroyer, destruction, ruin, a scourge, a whip to correct God's people, even a grievous beating. Pestilence exists because of sin.

It is revived by God's hand against the church because of their sin and rebellion against God first and foremost. People in the world, lost people, unsaved people, people who cannot understand the word because the carnal mind is at enmity with God, they think that pestilence is *not* the judgment of God for sin. They think that some breakdown in nature, some aspect of the laws of nature bring in disease. They are not thinking that pestilence is brought by God to his church as a judgment, or on the world as a judgment...where is that in the news?

Lost people who are self-absorbed with their own idolatry and self-love will never consider repentance in this light, and they do not want to call on God for salvation through Jesus Christ because of pestilence in the world; they call their doctor and go to the hospital. But pestilence brought *to the church,* or the world, because of rebellion and transgression and sin in God's rod, can only be prevented in the manner and means that God has provided. How does one stop the plague? "If they shall confess their iniquity, ... that ... they have walked contrary unto me;" (Lev. 26:40). "And Aaron took as Moses commanded, and ran into the midst of the congregation; and, behold, the plague was begun among the people: and he put on incense, and made an atonement for the people. And he stood between the dead and the living; and the plague was stayed. Now they that died in the plague were fourteen thousand and seven hundred, beside them that died about the matter of Korah. And Aaron returned unto Moses unto the door of the tabernacle of the congregation: and the plague was stayed," (Num. 16:47-50). "And David built there an altar unto the LORD, and offered burnt offerings and peace offerings. So the LORD was intreated for the land, and the plague was stayed from Israel," (2 Sam. 24:25). The way to prevent and remove pestilence from God's people was to remove their wicked sins out of Gods sight, the sins that made them in God's sight look like the heathen who did not follow the Lord's commands; and humble themselves; to turn and reform, to be reconciled to their God; to repent. But how will they do this when the flourishing cities are desolate, and the church's doors are being closed across the face of the earth? Is this an accident? Dismissive spirits say *yes.* How many times has this happened in the history of the world that the church's doors are closed to God's people? Do Christians care about that; or are they just looking on the bright side of the virus plaguing the planet that they get to stay home with their family for a time? I believe Christians should fundamentally care about *this messenger from heaven.* God has taken the word, and the means of grace, *away* from his people. They are not gathering together for worship where the dynamic motions of the Spirit of God are set in the midst of the organic congregation of the righteous during the preaching of the word and the right administration of the sacraments for the good of their souls and fall-reversing power of Jesus Christ ministered to them; they're at home. Do the churches across the country see it this way, or are they content to listen to a podcast, or read a sermon in a book, during self-isolation? God has halted the work of ministers to a certain degree, and closed up, shut up the sanctuaries of God's people. What did he say, "And I will make your cities waste, and bring your sanctuaries unto desolation," (Lev. 26:31). Are Christian's *weeping* over this? Pestilence is among the people of God and they are listening to the news on TV as their source of comfort. "Will the government give me some money in this trying time? How long can I go without visiting my favorite restaurant? When will life go back to the way it was, because all this is just so ridiculous?"

What happens when God in his chastisements treats saints like sinners in outward calamity? The Hebrew word "walking" in the text refers to walking recklessly by covenant breakers, without considering God. When Christian people cease to consider God, they walk without amendment of life, without a consideration to what God requires of them, they turn from God and despise his commandments. So, when the church does this, and continues to do it, and does it for a prolonged time, when they abuse the patience of God, ... the punishment by God upon them will be suitable to the sin they are committing against him; and judgment begins with the house of God. He will make no discrimination in his judgments between the church and the most depraved of men of the world; both kinds of people will die in the pestilence alike, or by the sword, or by famine. And in this pestilence that God has brought, he has made sanctuaries desolate, and flourishing cities bare, and closed the doors of the church against professing Christians.

God will be justified in his walking contrary to them. Now, in this passage in Leviticus, God tends to deal with his people in a manner suitable to their sin, but also shows them that when they rebel against him, he is justified in dealing with them in this way. But he gives them preachers and teachers and the word of God to direct them to find mercy in the calamity. This is so that in the pestilence sent of God, it may be taken away by true repentance worked by the Spirit according to the word. The real calamity here on planet earth today (as it has been through history) is not the coronavirus, it's the spiritual declension of the church; that is why the doors are closed. If they repent, God says he will not destroy them utterly. But if they do not repent, they may be made more inexcusable by the continuation of pestilence, death, the sword (are there wars), famine (is there famine), even things seven times worse; healthcare inability to serve the sick, economic and financial ruin? What else is coming against the church?[5] If God's people do not receive the correction ... what will God do if they are not profiting from the rod of his chastisement? A more painful and extensive outcome will occur for his people; God *promises* such in the text.

When pestilence comes, and ravages a city, when it comes and ravages a country, when it comes and ravages a whole planet, there is no outward distinction between the church and the most depraved of sinners in it. What a horrible thing it is for the church to be subjected to the same plight of pestilence as wicked men by the judgment of God. The religious pundits are everywhere that are dismissive of God's judgments in that way. There is no one on the news talking about reformation of life, reformation of the church; as a matter of fact, anyone who is saying anything about judgment on TV is solely directing that judgment to places like Hollywood, and the unchristian Laws in the US, and detestable practices of abortion, and gender issues, and America's decline; national sins. There is no one on the talk shows or podcasts telling the country to repent and believe the Gospel of Jesus Christ because God is angry with his church and that is why the virus is worldwide because his covenant has been broken by them. There is no one telling people on TV that *the church* is being punished. Interestingly, many Christians are probably thinking about the coronavirus in a way that reverses why it's here. "Wow, God must be really angry at the wicked in the world to be bringing such a calamity on the world." Could it not be said that God brings in the pestilence because his people, his professing church, is

---

[5] Riots in the streets? Political upheaval? Famine?

lazy, asleep, rebellious, covenant breaking against his commandments?

In most churches in the United States, they have replaced God's worship with the world. Most churches turn their sanctuary into Bunyan's Vanity Fair, to attract more worldly people so that they can have big rallies, and music events, and hire celebrities to bring in a show; they gut the historic confessions, rewrite them, compromise with social desires and fall prey to cultural pressure on a variety of national sins which they usher into the church, not to mention, blatantly change God's worship to suit them, making the church look just like the world; is this not what God is doing directly back to the church, to make the church indistinguishable? All of that idolatrous work drives God from the sanctuary, because God is *in* nothing he does not prescribe, and when God is driven from the sanctuary for a time, he will drive the sanctuary and means of grace from the church.

The church in America, and I can only speak about the church in America, has lost its spiritual way; it has, in a great part, rejected God for convenience. Today's Christian church is no longer a spiritual guide in whose mouth the law of God can be found, or the sweet sounds of the Gospel can be heard. Where are the people seeking truth from the mouths of the priests, and to whom shall they go? They have turned into worldings now, false shepherds walking contrary to God, leading people astray and God is bringing a judgment against the church in pestilence. When God brings in pestilence against the church for their sin, he does it in such a way as to make no distinction between them and the most depraved wicked men. What a thought it is that the worst of sinners die as a result of the pestilence, and a Christian, in the same hospital, dies next to him or her in the same way; with no distinction. The church must consider why it is despising God's word, and why the doors of the church are closed in our country.

Why would God withhold grace from his people in that way? It is because they do not seek him in the way he has prescribed. What would so motion the God of heaven to bring pestilence to the entire earth to persecute the entire planet, but men's abominable sin, either in their depravity, or in irreverence and ungodliness in the professing church of Jesus Christ that have changed God's prescriptions into vain worship? "Therefore say unto the house of Israel, Thus saith the Lord GOD; Repent, and turn yourselves from your idols; and turn away your faces from all your abominations," (Ezek. 14:6). Today professing Christian churches are just looking to get back to the show. When will the church be open so we can have our parades and puppet shows again?

Sinning against God's covenant and his worship will bring in God's judgment of pestilence and sickness. I find it interesting in James 5:14, "Is any sick among you? let him send for the coronavirus experts ... the government ... the healthcare professionals ... no, no, let him send for the elders of the church." Where are they? Well, the doors are *closed.* But why the elders? Because pestilence, sickness, is a physical manifestation of the fall. Note, God directs his people to spiritual considerations in times of sickness; where most are looking to Advil and antibiotics before they look to God.

Leviticus 26 is very clear. "And I will make your cities waste, and bring your sanctuaries unto desolation, and I will not smell the savour of your sweet odours," (Lev. 26:31); the assumption of communion is gone until they repent. When churches remove God's worship, change God's worship, which is the same as despising God because they despise God's commands, he will bring in the pestilence. He will make their sanctuaries desolate. Think about the spiritual dimension and impact of taking away the Lord's Supper from the church. 1 Cor. 11 teaches that Christians ought to be examining themselves in light of the supper. What do they do when it is taken away from them altogether? Now some ignorant Christians will say, "well, when we get back together we'll take it again; I don't need it right now." These kinds of people are missing the entire point. If they are not deists, if they really believe that God looks after his people, they should be thinking: "God has brought pestilence and closed the doors of the church, has made the sanctuary desolate, and taken the means of grace from his people across the face of the whole world." There is nothing I can think of in this lifetime, in this way so far, that can compare to the bringing in of the virus, and the desolation of the sanctuary of God in our time.

If the church doesn't really care what they do before the face of God, what does it really matter if the sanctuary is now desolate? If they bring contempt on the word of God, and do not minister the word but their own fancy and imaginations, they hold the word in contempt anyway. How terrible it is when God treats the church without distinction to the heathen and places them indiscriminately in that kind of outward providence.

21

Consider pestilence in light of the coming of the Christ and it gets even more serious. Jesus said, "And great earthquakes shall be in divers places, and famines, and pestilences; and fearful sights and great signs shall there be from heaven," (Luke 21:11). The end is not yet when all these things come, but they are signs and messengers of Christ's return. Pestilence is a messenger to the church. How terrible is this pestilence? How terrible will it get? It is already dreadful in so many ways. I would hope the church sees it as serious, yet, it is but a *birth pang.* It is nothing in comparison to the coming of the Warrior Christ, the Lord in glory, where the sky will roll back like a scroll and he will come with the armies of heaven and his holy angels, with the sword of the word from his mouth to strike down the nations, where he will melt the earth with fervent heat, coming to tread the winepress of the wrath of almighty God. But events like this pestilence are signs of the times. How many times, in the history of the planet, has something this big, wide, far reaching, into the very houses of God's worship, into the homes of people all over the face of the planet, ever happened. Not that many. The Son of Man will return in glory, with revenging justice. And it is a most terrible thing, that now, one cannot tell the wheat from the chaff because he has made the sanctuaries desolate, and the flourishing cities bare, and has closed the doors of the church.

Pestilence is a sign where God makes no difference in his temporal judgments between the church and the most depraved sinners in the world, and that should concern you heartily; it should make you feel like Habakkuk that your bones are rotten as God has shown up, like Ezra, rending your garment and mantle and plucking the hair from head and beard because of sin (9:3).

What do you think of this pestilence? In the city in which I live, there are 11,000 people, and there are 200+ churches here and no revival of any kind, no ripple of it, no sign of it. That's obscene. The church here is an excuse to make religious play for an hour on a Sunday. Not to mention the cults here, and the Antichrist Papists. "My parents went to such and such a church and this is the pew he sat in, and this is where I go now with my kids." Church, here, in this bible belt, is a cultural phenomenon; they have no problem mixing the world and the church together in that; go to the big Baptist church on the corner or the PCA church and attend a service and they both look *exactly* the same. How did God begin Lev. 26? "Ye shall keep my sabbaths, and reverence my sanctuary: I am the LORD." (Lev. 26:2), otherwise I have a quarrel against you. Uphold the Lord's Day, and godly worship here? They wouldn't even know what it is. Where is the reformation of the church?

Are you being reformed by God? What will you do now that he has sent pestilence to your cities, maybe to your very door, and made no distinction between you and the most depraved men in the world, and taken away the means of grace from you that you cannot now, even partake of worship or have the communion of the Savior in the Supper? The doors of the sanctuary are closed and it is desolate. What did saints do in times past? In all the biblical examples, plagues and pestilence were all halted by actions annexed to repentance. Amendment of life, reformation of life, repent and believe the Gospel ends

23

plagues. Christians got together to pray fervently and repent and looked for a revival even in those times. We don't want a revival; we just want the government to fix this, and send us a check.

I bring up an objection here: preacher, you can't make the assumption that God is doing all this because of sin. They'll quote, "Now Elisha was fallen sick of his sickness whereof he died. And Joash the king of Israel came down unto him, and wept over his face, and said, O my father, my father, the chariot of Israel, and the horsemen thereof," (2 Kings 13:14). This is an individual account of the manner approved of God for the prophet's death; it had nothing to do with covenant or judgment. They'll jump to, "And his disciples asked him, saying, Master, who did sin, this man, or his parents, that he was born blind?" "Jesus answered, Neither hath this man sinned, nor his parents: but that the works of God should be made manifest in him," in John 9. Jesus says in this individual instance, with this one man, with a physical birth defect, that it was not due to any sin, but done to solely glorify God. This has nothing to do with pestilence, plague, covenant breaking, etc. But take notice, Peter's mind was programmed to think that something *must* have happened, some sin, that God would smite this man in this way. Why?

Job's friends, in that ancient book, those miserable comforters, were *programmed to think* that Job must have done something to cause the boils on him personally, and for his family to be killed, and his possessions in his house to be taken away. The Jewish mindset is that sin brings calamity; why did they think so? Because, *sin brings misery and calamity!* Jews came to Jesus in Luke 13 and reported

24

that Galileans were slaughtered by Pilate, and they must have been great sinners for God do that to them. They were programmed to think so. Jesus does not rebuke the programming, but he does rebuke their misapprehension to think that one sinner is so much worse than another; he rebukes *that idea.* There is a consideration to think about that in shutting down whole cities, and states, and countries, by pestilence that in response to God's providence, are we considering Christ's words "that unless we repent a worse thing will happen to us?" Are we or any others really, worse sinners than those crushed by the Siloam tower?

Jesus doesn't rebuke Peter, doesn't rebuke the news bearers for thinking that sin is the culprit, but does correct Peter and then brings them to the point where regarding isolated points of providential calamity are due not because one is a worse sinner or not; but used by Christ to preach repentance, or hell will befall people, that which is worse. Yet, where is that message that a worse thing might happen to you than the coronavirus on the lips of the preachers who are on all those TV news spots to the church? I don't hear anything of that. I don't hear anything about the church confessing their sins.

So, the whole objection citing passages concerning *individuals* won't disarm the force of Leviticus 26. The bible is filled with pestilence and plague due to sin. Paul is programmed to say, knowing the Scriptures, that in light of sin, *in the church*, many have died because they did not take the Lord's Supper the right way in 1 Cor. 11. They were programmed to equate times of wickedness and God's judgments together *in the church*. And are we considering

25

that in such mandates by the Civil Magistrate, which we are bound to obey for the public good in godly instances, that God may in fact be using the pestilence to cease giving his church the word of God for a time in public worship, to take away your covenanted means of grace from your church for a time, and in that case, the word, through fear of sickness and plague to shake the church up? Is the public worship of God not the place where God's voice is to be heard? Where is his voice crying in the city now? *Who has brought the rod?* What do you think of the Lord's Supper out of your reach? "Not a big deal, we can take that at another time. We have seasons of the supper anyway, so this might just fall perfectly with our schedule." Those are unholy thoughts from unthinking virgins, who may in fact be foolish ones.

What do we think of the church being incumbered in this way in Christ's ministry of the word to his people and the world? "Not a big deal, we can listen to sermons online, or read a book of sermons, or have access to all kinds of technological helps today that bring the word of God to us." Where are you? YOU'RE NOT IN WORSHIP. "Ye shall keep my sabbaths, and reverence my sanctuary: I am the LORD," (Lev. 26:2). ... "that they may serve me in the wilderness" (Exo. 7:16). ... for "true worshippers shall worship the Father in spirit and in truth: for the Father seeketh such to worship him," (John 4:23), but your church doors ARE CLOSED. Will it divide serious Christians from hypocrites to amend their life, in this time of pestilence, knowing that judgment begins at the house of God? What ... did you think the pestilence here, now, was for lost sinners who are so very wicked in their life?

You think that NY and CA are hardest hit because they are the worst of sinners in the US, or Italy because there are worse sinners there? It may be they *are* depraved sinners, but the virus is for *covenant breakers*, it's for the church, the sleepy church all around the world that has lost its first love.

The old puritans called times like these *strange providences*, but I think they are for us now a most solemn and grave providence that God is literally cutting off the church's ability to worship together. Who would have thought such would ever happen today? The Psalmist said, "The LORD loveth the gates of Zion more than all the dwellings of Jacob," (Psa. 87:2). God does, but what a strain this is putting on *the work* of the gates of Zion, and the availability of the ordinances of God for you as Christians, and truly, the conversion of souls or even lack thereof that the church is closed. We should take time to consider such things very carefully. I'm not saying, to be unwise in some way, if you are diseased that you ought to disregard the virus and meet together, infected, and pass it to others – violating the sixth commandment. No, all I'm saying is that you take time this Lord's Day to consider God's providence against his church in that way where he has made no difference between the most heinous of sinners, and his people; it has come that far in our lifetime. They both die in the same hospital under the same conditions in the same way. It is, I think profound, for those who love the gates of Zion to think about such things. Sweet Jesus is *skipping* on the hills, and *leaping* on the mountains, but unlike the Song of Songs, he seems to be skipping and leaping *further away from his church* for a time; and that should frighten you. How has it affected you? Has it brought you to tears? Has it caused you angst? God says, "I will make your cities waste, and bring your sanctuaries unto desolation," (Lev. 26:31).

You say to me, "where is the hope in this?" Just look to the Lord's words, "If they shall confess their iniquity," and the iniquity of their churches, with their trespasses which they trespassed against me, and that also they have walked contrary unto me ... "Then will I remember my covenant with them ..." (Lev. 26:40, 42). "Repent all of you: for the kingdom of heaven is at hand," (Matt. 3:2). "Surely he shall deliver thee from the snare of the fowler, and from the noisome pestilence," (Psa. 91:3). But stop looking at the pestilence in the world as something done to wicked sinners; God has sent *you* a message. Instead, *look in the mirror*, and point out the culprit there, and know that judgment begins at the house of God, and you are part of the church. The Lord is striking his people across the face with a grievous beating all over the earth in a pestilence. Yet, when you wisely consider and discern the causes of pestilence and sickness, then you will wisely turn to reformation and amendment of life.

Turn to God, look to him, look to Jesus the great physician, with all your heart, with fasting, with weeping, with sackcloth and mourning if you need to. Pray that Christ would minister his Spirit to you, praying for an increase of true faith and repentance, that you and the church would look to God for a true revival. You and your church should be thinking about repentance and revival; what a better time than this? Repent and God will revive us; will churches change? What ignorance are we settled in, or are involved with in our churches? What blasphemy have we spoken against him in worship, life or practice? What have we done in his sanctuary that would drive him out of it as he says in Ezekiel, and close up the doors of the means of grace upon us? How have we abused his holy name in our lack of godly zeal in serious walking? What contempt have we brought against Jesus Christ and his Gospel in our life and in our families and in our churches? Can the heathen tell the difference between you and them right now? They can't; God has made, through pestilence, *no difference between you and them.* Far reaching pestilences argue for far reaching sins against God and the need for the power of the Spirit of Christ to amend our ways and turn back to him.

What counterfeit teachings, perverted ministries, ignorance of the highest order, the revival of heresy, the acceptance of false doctrine in seminaries, adulteries in churches by ministers, usury, deceit, oppression, discontentedness, malice, backbiting, unwholesome dress and clothing in the sanctuary, social compromises, doctrinal indifference, unqualified ministers filling the pulpits, filthy communication out of your mouth, anger, diverse lusts, hatefulness, envy, evil speaking, blatantly false worship, women teaching and preaching in the church, sin of all kinds, which ones are among you and in your church? Why is God closing the doors of *your* church? How will you amend your life and doctrine before God? What will you do, what will your church do to "stay the plague before King Jesus who commands the wheels of his providences even down to the tiny cells of the virus?" Who has spoken about that? Who has laid out a strategy to repent? What has your church done to think through, stopping the pestilence through reformation? "Just wash your hands more, we'll be together soon." *Souls* need washing by Christ's word – he has sent a messenger, and the church must listen.

Truly, there is this wonderful grand promise of King Jesus in this text; the silver lining of the virus is repentance. "If they shall confess their iniquity," it does not get more gracious and wonderful than that and its consequences; in the midst of judgment the Lord provides a way of escape. This is the same as saying, "repent ye, and believe the Gospel," (Mark 1:15), as Christ preached. This Good News is in light of the pestilence, so that the church might be restored to walk in holiness before God's face. It is only through Jesus Christ, the only Savior, planned from before the foundation of the world in covenant with God; is this covenant not what God was concerned about in this text; having a quarrel over his covenant with his church? It is founded upon the grace of God, and the purpose of God and it is God's only manner of amending souls and reversing the fall in sinners. It is by way of covenant, in Jesus Christ, which is why God is so angry when he has to quarrel with his church about the particulars of his covenant. But he will bring blessing, and remember his promises in Christ, if they shall confess, turn, reform, repent, walk with him again, instead of walking so blatantly against him. God is not looking for you to amend your life in one part like people do with some kind of new year's resolution. There is no comparison on such a serious notion as this, at a time as this. Your church is closed and pestilence is flowing across the face of the earth.[6]

God is not interested in your partial reformation, which is a full offense to him. Nor is he interested in gradual reformation over a few years, for that is intolerable to him. God commands of you full reformation, amendment of life, and a dedication of all his people to King Jesus in all their ways right now; Christ demands instant and full reform of all church sins; and national sins as if we had time to name all those; an overhaul in your church and life. But, I wonder, what the church will do at large? Will they plan out their next event just a few months down the road? Will they just take this time to refresh the maintenance of the building? ... Or, will they call for solemn prayer and revival and repentance and contrite hearts with fasting? What will you do in this time of pestilence? Are you indifferent to it, or moved to repentance by it? Can you hear the messenger of pestilence from the throne room of Christ's power? Or will you remain apathetic?

Pray that it is not too late. "When they fast, I will not hear their cry; and when they offer burnt offering and an oblation, I will not accept them: but I will consume them by the sword, and by the famine, and by the pestilence," (Jer. 14:12). "O LORD, I have heard thy speech, and was afraid: O LORD, revive thy work in the midst of the years, in the midst of the years make known; in wrath remember mercy. God came from Teman, and the Holy One from mount Paran. Selah. His glory covered the

---

[6] Maybe your church is now open, and the virus is still flowing across the face of the earth. What shall you say of that?

heavens, and the earth was full of his praise. And his brightness was as the light; he had horns coming out of his hand: and there was the hiding of his power. Before him went the pestilence," (Hab. 3:2-5).

I give a final word to you who are sinners, even the most depraved of sinners. To keep it simple, God is angered by sin ... and the pestilence that he has brought upon his church should cause you to quake. If God will chastise his people, making no difference between them and you in this temporary life to discipline them and correct them and cause them to repent, what will he do to sinners like you that are unrepentant in this life and then go to Christ's judgment seat? What will he do to you personally? What will the eternal, almighty Christ do to you when you come before his judgment seat in all your sins, exposed and open to his eye after he kills you by the pestilence, or some other means? In contemplating this it should cause you to shudder and quake now, amend your life now, look to Christ now, for this life is but an entrance into eternity. Whichever way you go out of this life, with all the miseries that are attached to it while you are in it, it will be the worse for you in hell forever if you do not repent and believe the Gospel. It will be a perpetual existence of the wrath of God in the worst kind of pestilence never to be removed on you forever.

You should actually take note here in these times if you are wise heathen, filled with desires of self-preservation. Take note of the sins that the Christian church has committed against God; surely even point them out them if needs be; be Pharaoh to Abraham or Abimelech to Isaac, read the bible once with just a little thought and all the sins of the church should not be too hard to point out at all. If God will bring pestilence, and remove the means of grace from his people for a time, truly, what will happen to you will be far worse unless you take a hearty interest in Jesus Christ. Yes, the church has committed idolatry against God of the worst sort. But you are a worse idolater who loves self with all your might. Yes, the church has profaned God's worship. But you are a worse one by worshipping yourself in conceit. Yes, the church has become ignorant of so many foundational Christian truths. But you are far worse in rejecting them all for in them you reject the only Savior. Yes, the church has lost the fire of its fervency in loving Christ as her first love. But you are far worse in being a God-hater. Yes, the church, in this pestilence, has now tarnished its testimony before the face of the whole world in their sin against God. But you are a rank heathen, who despises the word of Christ, which will be the sword that comes from his mouth to cut you down in the end, unless you repent. Yes, the church is ungrateful to God for all his blessings, and they have abused this grace; feeling entitled. But you are filled with ingratitude and overflow with the most stinking and vile aversion of all God requires of you in his gracious covenant. Yes, the church has been obstinate and are following the dictates of their own fleshly desires in false worship, and so God has closed down their sanctuaries. But you, you are obstinate to give God the glory he deserves in all things, even in eating a meal; you go to eat food like a dog or pig without giving him glorifying thanks. Yes, the church has had its many benefits removed even now during this time of pestilence, being forsaken, having God's face turned aside for a time, where he has turned his blessings away from them. But you, unless you repent, and believe on the Lord Jesus Christ alone for salvation, that you amend your life, that you walk according to his commands, he will forsake you withholding all his eternal blessings, and you will remain under his wrath forever along with all unrepentant sinners, and the devil and his angels in the fiery torments of hell if you die in such a state; for soul-sickness is far worse than a temporary pestilence which lasts temporarily. To live in a land where the Gospel of Christ can be found, or a bible can be read, and yet still to sin against God and live in it willfully, is to abuse the mercy of Jesus Christ and his Word of grace. What can you expect from all this but his wrath on you, which is far worse, than mere pestilence for a time? Repent and believe the good news that God has a Savior that will forgive you of all your sin, and usher you into his kingdom upon repentance. Consider it today, pestilence is a sign where God makes no difference in his temporal judgments between the church and the most depraved sinners.

Chapter 2:
Christ's Remedies
Against the Plague

Luke 5:27-32, "And after these things he went forth, and saw a publican, named Levi, sitting at the receipt of custom: and he said unto him, Follow me. And he left all, rose up, and followed him. And Levi made him a great feast in his own house: and there was a great company of publicans and of others that sat down with them. But their scribes and Pharisees murmured against his disciples, saying, Why do ye eat and drink with publicans and sinners? And Jesus answering said unto them, They that are whole need not a physician; but they that are sick. I came not to call the righteous, but sinners to repentance."

The calling of Levi, son of Alpheus is found in this passage. Levi also called Matthew as the three Synoptic accounts show. Luke calls Levi a "publican" (5:27), and in the list of the Twelve as recorded in Matthew 10:3 there is mention of "Matthew the publican." Levi was a tax-collector, a "publican," those held in very low esteem.[1] "Publicans" and "sinners" are synonymous in this way; deplorables, the worst of society. Jesus calls this hated individual to follow him, in order that this publican would come to know the healing virtues of the Christ. When Jesus said, "Follow me," Levi immediately followed him; in both Matthew and Mark, Levi *immediately* obeys. Luke

---

[1] Luke 5:30; 7:34; 15:1; 19:7; cf. Matt. 9:10, 11; 11:19; 21:31, 32; Mark 2:15, 16.

5:28 also shows us that Levi "left everything behind, got up and followed Jesus." Levi's sacrifice was much greater than that made by the four earlier disciples (Simon and Andrew, James and John) as recorded in Mark 1:18, 20. He gave up his livelihood to follow Jesus (Luke 5:11). Would it not have been easier for the fishermen to return to their fishing than for Levi to become reemployed as a collector of taxes for the Romans? Levi here rejoices publicly over what Jesus has brought into his life (*cf.* 15:6, 9, 22–24; 19:6) and he throws a party.

At this party, some grumbling occurs, murmuring (verse 30) against his disciples. Interestingly the Pharisees follow Jesus and the disciples to a feast that is being thrown by Levi for this blessed event. They went because they could deny they attended the deplorable's party for their own happiness, but instead, to follow this supposed Rabbi and catch him in something. This something raises its head immediately. They asked the disciples why does your master, why do you all, eat with the unsavory people who live beyond the edge of respectable society? The Pharisees felt contaminated by being with these kinds of people. The disciples did not answer, but instead, Jesus intervenes and answers. Jesus does not say in his answer, "no, no, these are not unsavory people." No, he doesn't do that; certainly, he was among and ministered to unsavory people. What he does is give them a simile to the whole idea to explain not only his actions (along with the disciples) but his position, power, and ability to minister to those God brings into *his* kingdom over *their* kingdom. He likens these sinners to those who are sick.

Christ answers their murmuring challenge. The question was not given directly to him, but to his disciples as a kind of backbiting. Yet, knowing his opponents in this, he answers for them. Such a Savior is ready to stoop down and answer the most terrible blasphemies against him, even if they were to come from despicable people like the Pharisees, or even the devil himself. He looks to stop the mouths of those who call into question how righteousness is viewed and possessed, or how one is to live in light of the righteousness of God. The Pharisees thought they knew exactly how to do that in the face of a troubled society which was rejecting God and his word. In his answer to them, he blames them of hypocrisy, thinking they were so just and righteous, and that they were not sinners, at least not like others were. They did not need a Physician. They would have never thought of themselves as sick. As it is with all wayward religious pundits, *others* are the problem; others, not them; never them.

He defends himself in this simile, in a proverb of sorts; sick people need a physician to come close to them in order to heal them. Jesus did not come to raise people up and set them high in their own eyes; he came to help them, and to heal them. Being the Physician of sick-souls, he was and is to be among sinners, where else should the Christ be? Where should this Great Physician be, but near to his patients? This shows the patients (sinners who know their sin and that they are sinners), the Physician (Jesus Christ), the remedy or cure of their ailment which he prescribes, (repentance).

"They that are whole need not a physician; but they that are sick," (Luke 5:31). Luke, the doctor, shows Jesus' comparison between the publicans as sinners, and the sick who need a physician. People who are not sick, do not need a physician to care for them. People who are sick, need a physician to take care of them, in this case, to heal them. But it is a spiritual idea; which is why it works so well as a simile. Those who believe themselves to be righteous, do not need a physician to heal them of their soul-sickness, so to speak; though they really are sick; but they are not aware of it. Those who know they are sick need a physician to heal them.

Pause here to consider that this simile, this proverb of sorts, is not to disregard the depravity of the soul, and make men who are dead in sin merely sick in sin instead of dead in sin. Christ knew men were dead in sin. Christ knew they needed to be born again before they could perceive anything worthy of the kingdom, or even repent, John 3. Jesus' words to those who think they are worthy show they have no sight of their sin, and they are not even called by a Physician to be healed if they do not see their sickness. So when the term "soul-sickness" is used throughout my explanation here, or further in the sermon, I am in no way denying total depravity, but simply using the simile that Christ's sets forth of those who know that they are sick, and that they have a soul-sickness of which they must repent.

Jesus says, "I came not to call the righteous, but sinners to repentance," (Luke 5:32). The conclusion to the simile is that Christ does not call those who are righteous to do those things that sinners must do, and know they must do them. People healthy in their own eyes do not need a physician. They are not *called* by the Physician to be healed. Sinners, who know they are sick, need a physician. But the clincher here is that *they know* they are sick. What is the prescription to these sickened souls who know they are sick?

Sick people are called to repentance. They are called to a new idea, a new change of mind, a new change of heart, to do new things for the kingdom of God and king Jesus. In fact, a publican is called to leave off his livelihood and come and follow a rabbi, and he does so, seeing his need he has of such a physician because his soul is sick. Also note that the calling of Christ, is the calling of the sinner to repentance, which is something only God does. Christ calls sinners to repent and God calls sinners. These are both the same thing; for Christ is God. This was also something that the Pharisees often chided Christ of, "Who is this that can forgive sins?" But, until the sinner is convinced of sin, he can never be completely converted from sin. Christ's coming was as a Savior to die for sinners; and the Spirit's coming is to convince men *as* sinners, that they may repent and turn to Jesus Christ as a Savior; in fact, turn to the Great Physician to be healed by his remedy. If sin is not seen, then Christ is not needed. So as long as sin is hidden, Christ will never be sought out. "They that be whole need not the physician, but they that are sick," (Luke 5:31). This applies as much to an individual sinner as it does a whole church of sinners, or *vice versa*. The church is in fact made up of individuals, and the church is in as much need of the Great Physician to minister to them on a regular basis as they were the first time they saw their sin and came to him for healing. Christ's words, "I came," shows he was referring to himself in the call, and that likened to a Physician that tends to a sick person. The Pharisees did not want to get close to people that were unworthy of their company. To socialize with them would be to partake of them in whatever degraded ideas society had about them; they may be contaminated by such socialization; they were afraid of getting something, that in God's eyes, they already had as sinners. They were practicing both a physical and a spiritual kind of social distancing to their own demise. But Jesus tells them that he is the Physician, and physicians must get close to the sick in order to help them. He does not mind coming close to the sinner. He does not mind showing them the remedy they need. He does not mind prescribing certain remedies for them to draw close to him. He does not mind doing everything he can to save their life. This spiritual sickness, so to speak, is a call from darkness to light, to call for sinners to repent, those that find themselves in sin, and in need of the physician to care for them.

This Great Physician treats all kinds of sickness. Physicians are of many kinds, that treat many maladies. But often Physicians have certain specialties. Jesus heals all disease; he is the Great Physician who deals with all the effects of sin in every way. But, Jesus centers on the principal malady of sin, and requires all his patients, those that see their need, to repent, which is his prescription for them to be holy, be at peace, be near to God, and be reconciled by his work as Savior. Sin is the foundation of all plagues and sickness in the world, *for through one man* sin and death *came into the world* as a covenant breach – that is Adam when he fell in the Covenant of Works.

Sicknesses might be of various kinds, may be gangrene, a plague, a fever, or consumption, or leprosy, or an issue of blood, coronavirus, or any sickness, and the Great Physician knows the treatment for the underlying soul-sickness; and all remedies ultimately lead back, as the simile instructs, to the Great Physician in repentance. And so, as a good and Great Physician, Jesus can command remedies that will stop the sickness, and make a person whole. Knowing that Christ is the Great Physician, he knows what remedies are to be prescribed for whatever ails sinners in their soul-sickness, whether inward as original sin, or outward as all the miseries of this life as a result of sin. So, the doctrine to be pulled from the text is the following:

The doctrine to consider from the text is DOCTRINE: The restraining of a plague can only be accomplished through the Great Physician, Jesus Christ, who knows and prescribes the best remedies against sin.

Plagues are of two qualities: physical and spiritual. Sin is a plague as applied by the fall of Adam. It is the root of all plagues, the main wickedness in the heart against God in original sin, which all men are conceived in at conception, and they break forth into the world speaking lies; under the curse of God for which they must repent. We will call this a soul-sickness. It is not the heretical notion of being merely sick in sin, but as the bible teaches it is being dead in sin; men are born under the curse into the morgue when they are conceived, so to speak. Jesus equates soul-sickness with those sinners who recognize they are in trouble. They may not be converted like Felix, and yet tremble. They may in fact be born again, and see

41

their need of Christ in a way as Levi did to press into the kingdom and take hold of the promise. In either case, those who do not see their sin (like the religious leaders of Christ's day) are excluded from this.

The coronavirus is a plague, as is a plague of locusts. These kinds of plagues are not the root of plagues. Plagues stem from the curse, from the fall, from sin in the world; and the consequences and miseries of sin that are still present in the world. The coronavirus is a physical plague that has, at its root, the spiritual dimension of sin. It is here because people have sinned against God, and God in judgment against them has sent a messenger to them, a messenger to alarm them of his displeasure against sin because his church has broken his covenant; he has a quarrel with them.

Sin is a spiritual condition with both spiritual and physical affects. Sin always has both spiritual and physical affects to it; spiritual death, and physical death; and all the miseries attached to those things. The physical virus causes misery and death (aside from other consequences). But spiritually, it heralds God's will in that it warns against sin and his ultimate judgment on sin in hell if one does not repent.

When any plague is sent across the face of the whole earth, or against a people for their sin, God is sending a spiritual message that demonstrates a need to seek his remedy to escape that physical judgment. It is a very sad time, as I mentioned in the last chapter, that when God is silent, this shows he is more angry with men for their sin, and he leaves them in their sin with no recourse. He does not warn them, correct them, bless their means of grace, nor does he reside close to them, but turns his face; they don't even know he has left the sanctuary. Jesus said of the Pharisees, "Let them alone: they be blind leaders of the blind," (Matt. 15:14). But in a plague God is speaking and wise Christians discern his meaning there because of his directives in Scripture. There are remedies that Christ can prescribe which cure both the spiritual plague of sin, and the physical plague going forth across the face of the earth.

The best remedy against sin or any plague is repentance. Repentance is sight of sin, sorrow for sin, confession of sin, shame for sin, hating of sin and turning from sin. This is true no matter where repentance is applied. Whether it is true of a first convert (general), or sanctified holiness in a church (constant), or whether it is true of a confessing church against a plague (occasional); repentance is made up of those points.

Repentance is a supernatural grace, where believing sinners, one who is sensibly and discernably affected with and afflicted for his sin as committed against God, freely confesses, and fervently pleads for pardon, turns from all sin to the only Savior Jesus Christ. Being born again by the Spirit precedes repentance, or repentance will be like that of Esau, tears without change. Esau sought the blessing with tears, doing more than what most Christians will do; how many Christians will cry over this sin today? Repentance is *supernatural*, and part of the renewed ability of the believer.

Repentance precedes God's pardon. Justification does not come before repentance. Men must turn and repent, and then they are declared just in the sight of God by believing in Jesus Christ alone for salvation. It houses in it, a turning from sin to God. Again, this would apply to the person first converted, to sanctification, and to a church in a time of plague in that both turn from sin to God. But for the first converted sinner, it leads to justification. For a church, it leads to holiness of life and service in worship to God. For the repenting church, it leads to the stopping of a judgment on them. In all cases, people are to be made more holy.

There is no room for repentance in a person's life if they don't see their sin. "What? Me? An evil sinner? Hitler is an evil sinner. Islamic Terrorists that murder people are evil sinners. I'm not like them." In speaking to the disciples and the crowds in Matthew 7, in Christ's famous *Sermon on the Mount,* Jesus calls people evil. "If ye then, being evil..." (Matt. 7:11). Yes, that means everyone. Jesus knows what is in the heart of man. In the same sermon, he said, "But if thine eye be evil, thy whole body shall be full of darkness," (Matt. 6:23). By nature, men are evil, and according to the Christ, by nature all men are full of darkness. Once a person is converted, if they see their sin, and repent, that means that then, as a professing Christian, their life should be constantly concerned with the exercise and act of biblical repentance to be further sanctified; killing sin and living for God. Sanctification, holiness, is the result, which allows sinners to draw closer to Jesus Christ. This repentance that Jesus speaks of is a sense of, and sorrow for sin, as committed against God. The sinner, who understands that he is evil in the sight of God and commits all kinds of atrocities against God's holy Law, must spread himself before the Law of God to survey the entire course of his own life in light of God's character. He needs to weigh himself in the balance of God's perfections, which is found in the ten commandments.

It doesn't take long to figure out where he stands in relation to God's requirement of being perfect. Yes, God requires everyone to be perfect. Jesus Christ in that same sermon said, "Be ye therefore perfect, even as your Father which is in heaven is perfect, (Matt. 5:48). Perfect? Yes, God requires perfection. That means imperfect people, according to God's Law, are evil because they are imperfect sinners who are cursed with original sin, and delight to disobey God's word. And again, yes, that means everyone. In the process of conversion, and repenting, the sinner knows he is imperfect, and in view of God's Law, which shows him his sin, he comes away not just lacking in some spiritual and moral goodness, but sees the utter viciousness of his nature against God's prescription for holiness; if people don't think they are vicious against God, they have never been converted; malicious, brutal, spiteful, savage, wild. Such vicious sinners then sentence themselves as accursed of God, agreeing that his Law is right and good, and they know that they are "bound" to experience God's Divine fury for their sin in hell by God's justice which is just and good, and that forever. Yet, they do not despair. Why? The soul that perceives it is evil before God, knows its fate is an eternal punishment in hell for his original sin nature and inclination to further sin. It knows that hell will be all the more unbearable due to his aggravation of that state of sin as he continually does evil works in the sight of God. But his fear of God's wrath will turn to hope, knowing that he is afflicted for the guilt of his sin. He not only sees that he is a true sinner before God, but sorrows under his understanding of sin, and is ashamed of such a sad and sinful state. He comes to learn that repentance is a supernatural gift given to him from God, and that he must turn from sin and confess his sin by the power of the Spirit. This is not an option, it is necessary, for this is whom Jesus came to call to repentance. This kind of repentance is necessary to remove the wrath and judgments of God and to, "answer the call of the Gospel," which requires everyone to repent. God, "now commandeth all men every where to repent," (Acts 17:30).

The characteristics of true biblical repentance are sight of sin, sorrow for sin, confession of sin, shame for sin, hating of sin and turning from sin. This is the Savior's prescription for conversion. This is also the Savior's prescription for a wayward church that must repent due to a pestilence, famine or war to walk in holiness when they break his covenant and he sends them consuming plagues. Churches and individuals must contemplate whether or not they have a counterfeit repentance which emulates Esau, Judas and Saul, or a biblical repentance that emulates Moses, David and the Apostle Paul. Repentance is God's gift, "if God peradventure will give them repentance to the acknowledging of the truth," (2 Tim. 2:25). "Then hath God also to the Gentiles granted repentance unto life," (Acts 11:18). It is Christ's purchase, the covenant's promise, and may be sought with boldness and confidence before God's throne of grace as a gift to be given. Jesus Christ is exalted to give repentance; so all must go to him in faith. All the means of grace are ineffectual without God's blessing. God must bless the repentance, and people must pursue the supernatural grace of repentance. Why repent? In light of the plague, consider ...

Sin has a twofold affect on men. Sin either makes men miserable *and* damnable, or, miserable. Sin makes most men, lost men, miserable *and* damnable. If both miserable and damnable, this applies to sinners who are not yet converted, and will be miserable under such sin, as well as made more damnable for hell, unless they repent. When lost people are both physically plagued with some miserable disease, and spiritually plagued with original sin, they are eaten up with diseases, and deadly pains, and yet feel nothing spiritual; they do not see their sin or feel its weight. The painfulness and misery of sin is like the pain and misery of sickness: the less they are felt, the more dangerous and deadly they are. When the word of God is bitter, if their mind rises against it, and the mouth of their soul does not like its taste, if they do not place it in their memory, if they despise the doctrine of God, if they do not by meditation digest it and work it into their soul, if they do not take the word and send it into all the various parts of their life, they are lost. By not using the word as they ought, as God prescribes, these soul-sick people will have no strength in themselves to do anything profitable before him. They are open to the works of the devil, they are, as Scripture says, to call him father. They do not see what grace is, nor care for it. They have no discernable sense of the heinousness of sin, unless it profits them. They think themselves worthy enough, and good enough for their own tastes. They point the finger at others who are worse than they perceive themselves to be. They do not care about the lusts of uncleanness, drunkenness, covetousness, swearing, lying, malice against God, indifference to the church and its ordinances; honoring superiors or inferiors. In fact, they do not despise any of these things, but rather rejoice in them and wonder why Christians do not rejoice in them as well, as the apostle says in 1 Peter 4:4. Such lost people do not hear the voice of God in the minister's preaching. They do not and cannot really pray to God because they do not even know how to beg him for mercy, grace and help which is only done by the Spirit. Their very prayers are an abomination to him. They do not know that Christ alone has the only remedy for them.

Repentant sinners are awakened with certain impressions of the Spirit to know their sickness, and that this sickness must be healed by the Great Physician. When such people feel and groan under the pain and burden of their sin, they are made sensible by the Spirit to God's holy word. They know that sin is the most dangerous sickness in the whole world. Such a one knows that he is not healthy, but sick. He knows his nature has been poisoned by sin. He knows that sin brings forth more sin. He knows that all the sins he has committed are his fault. He knows that the plague of sin cannot be taken off by his own strength. He knows it has made him weak, and it has given him a darkened mind, a corrupted will, and disordered all his affections towards God. He knows, that like a plague bringing in a torment on the body, that sin, which is deep seated in his soul, is bringing in constant misery and the hints of torment, both now, and to come into eternity if he does not have it remedied. He has, as a result, a haunting suffering of mind knowing that one day he will go to judgment and be judged for both his original sin and all his actual sins. Sin will press him to consider the torture of the second death; which he knows is justifiably certain. Equally, a physical plague will also press him to consider the spiritual side of the torments he will face if he dies in his sin. He knows he is not curable except by the Great Physician and his remedy alone.

It is interesting, that in a world-wide plague, how careful men are to keep their health in times of sickness against physically getting ill, who are not careful at all against spiritual sickness; that is directed to Christ's church. This was also a problem that the Pharisees had. Those who do not know they are sick, are not aware of it, but they will be very aware, as the Pharisees were, to wash the cup, to keep things clean. That spiritual discernable sense is not present because sin is only discernable by the working of the Holy Spirit in men. These kinds of people think they are all okay, and Jesus said to such, there is no remedy for them; Jesus said he did not come to call them.

Sin, as a plague in the church, generally speaking, which is what the messenger of a plague often is, is that which makes Christians miserable but not damnable. Sin in the church is a misery, and will inflict misery in plagues; people will even die in it. This misery is applied to the church under any distress sent to them by God for rebellion against him, breaking his covenant, as well as Christ having a quarrel with them. It is interesting that in either case, Christ's remedy to stop the plague of sin, or to stop any physical plague, is repentance, whether in the church, or by individuals who need to be converted. God gets angry by the sin of his people, he is provoked by them, and sin then comes into an outward experience in some way; by famine, sword, or pestilence. It may be by silence and desertion, which is most terrible for them, but born again sinners are sensible of their sin. They know that sin is displeasing to God, it needs to be mortified, killed, and when they persist in doing what they ought not to do, God may in fact wake them up by some outward calamity that makes them even more miserable, depressed, physically endangered, desolate, melancholy. They need a remedy in times of plague; what might that remedy be for the church?

The Great Physician Jesus Christ prescribes repentance. Jesus says he is the Great Physician in the words "I came not to call..." Christ is the one who heals; he is Yahweh Rapha the healer, Job 5:18, "He maketh sore, and bindeth up: he woundeth, and his hands make whole." Exod. 5:26, "I am the Lord, that healeth thee." He is the marvelous comfort for afflicted souls, those under the burden of sin either inward or outward. He knows all their diseases, and their remedies so that sinners may safely commit themselves to him, in sincerity. They know he is able enough to cure them, because he is the Omnipotent God, able to work an infinite cure through his blood, for his blood is the sacred remedy for all sin.

He is a skillful Physician. He knows what is in man. In John 2 he could not commit himself to men who were trying to follow him for selfish and worldly reasons, because he knew what was in a man; the depravity of their heart. Jesus does not merely look at the outward part of man, as most physicians do when they inspect a person, nor does he only look at the physical effects of a plague or pestilence, even as physicians do when they read a test, but Christ looks at the heart – sin is a heart issue. His gaze is one that knows the malady perfectly because he is God. And no matter what effects of sin might be on a man, or ruining his walk, Christ knows how to cure it; initially, he cures it by regeneration and in holiness; later on, he may do so in a time of plague. He knows what men need who are sick in sin in this way. He knows the disease and its remedy. Physicians do not have the general ability to know any person perfectly. Jesus Christ not only knows the malady, but the cure, and both quite perfectly. And, he knows the work that the remedy will make on those that take up his prescriptions. He even says, "I have lost none" whom the Father gave him; he has a perfect record in saving men from the plague of sin and death and outward misery if he so chooses. How many men and women, physically speaking, have Physicians lost today under the virus? Jesus loses none that he saves from the plague of original sin, and he is able to rescue his people from under the misery of any outward plague due from sin if they repent.

Christ knows the best remedies for all soul-sickness. What do men have? Pride, envy, covetousness, lust, a troubled conscience, murderous thoughts, heinous thoughts, wayward thoughts, lying, backbiting, ignorance, filthiness and uncleanness, uncontrolled passions, sinful indifference, well, Christ knows that the remedy for all those is by his blood, and under the doctrine of repentance which he calls his people to.

Christ makes the soul sensible of sin, for his remedies *work*. Only he is able to cure all sin. The cure of sin comes from his work and merit, his life and death, his exaltation and intercession for sinners, for souls that are sick. He pardons sins through repentance, but pardons through the cure of his work. He came and lived a perfect life in the flesh. He willingly died on the cross as the sin-bearer. He rose from the dead in the power of God. He is exalted at the right hand of God to intercede on behalf of soul-sick sinners. He took the infirmities of his people, and bore all their sickness, both bodily and spiritually, and now is at the right hand of the power of the Father where he dispenses the work of the Holy Spirit who applies the power of his cure, as the sacred elixir and medicine of his remedies.

In his cure of the soul, he does this freely, requiring no payment; he does it perfectly, requiring no other remedy to come in; and he does it diligently, that all which is needed to be done is done in whole, and not in part. This is the Physician all sick souls should seek out. Whether sinners come to him initially to be cured of their sin, or when the church has become so heinous in their sin that they need a physical malady and remedy for their covenant breaking, Christ can remedy both.

Jesus Christ tends his church as a Physician; he makes house calls. It is in and through the church that souls are made sensible of their sin; there is no salvation outside the church – that is where all his remedies are found; that is where his ordinances are found, his voice in the preaching of the word, his work in the sacraments in the church by lawfully ordained men. His promise is to be with his church by his Spirit and grace, to the end of the world, "I will be with you." And he will be with his people in both a gracious working, as well as in chastising afflictions.

This is where a shift in thought takes place, to see Christ as the Physician of his church, but also the Judge of his church. It is not a one and done kind of thing, to heal once. He is the Great Physician who heals them all the time; and he is to be sought out by his church in that way. He shows them in plagues that instead of following him as they ought, instead, they are returning like a dog to its vomit, and casting aside the sound qualities of his gracious covenant, and so judgment comes to the house of God first. In this, the church now must deal with their Physician, who, as Lord, sends them plagues, that they may again be shaken up to come back to him as the great Healer. Christ desires to fulfill his work as a Physician for his church, until they are taken to heaven, and so, in order to do that, there must be maladies sent for remedies to be given. And when they come back to him as the Great Physician, they come to him as they did at first, and look to his remedies and his cures and his prescriptions that they may be made whole, and the plague would be stopped by repenting.

The church should be coming to Christ daily to lay open their sins, and their very hearts before him. They should be looking to him for reformation of life, amendment of life by the Spirit in godly repentance. With David, the physical plague was stayed immediately on repentance. With Moses and Aaron, the physical plague was stayed immediately on repentance. With men today the plague is ... continuing... What, will wicked, sinful, Pharisaic men stop the plague? How can blind guides stop the plague? They are blind. The plague is continuing this week in America. What is needed? Where are the penitent Christians? Where are all the penitent churches? Where are they called out of their lapsed estate by the Physician who prescribes repentance, and they take heed of it? Where are all the warnings of the word and the preaching of ministers? Is the plague stopped yet upon the face of the earth? Where is the earnest entreaty to heal the church by the great Physician through hearty repentance? Maybe the church does not realize what is happening, no doubt that is the case, and maybe they are unaware of his prescription and remedies for the plague to be stopped, that too is tragic. They do not know how to lay open all their sores and sicknesses to the Physician and they are unaware that they have broken his covenant and he has a quarrel against them, even making their sanctuaries desolate. One cannot confess their sins unless they know what their sins are.

What is his Script, but to repent? Christ takes this idea of repentance, a sensibleness of sinning against God in a time of plague, and requires his church occasionally to consider it in four ways as it concerns them at such times. This means that Christ demands full repentance, not repentance in part. If the church merely confesses their sin, without shame or sorrow or turning, without actual reformation, that would be useless; God already knows what they did. To repent in part is not really to repent; nor to repent in part is to be serious about repenting. If a church repents together and yet does not change what they are repenting of, they are not really repenting.

This also means that they cannot repent with some sin, but they must hate all sin. Constant repentance by the church is a sanctifying of their life, but in special occasions, they are to repent at those times heartily, so sins of worship, sins in leadership, changes have they made that have departed from the Christian faith in doctrine, ceremonial additions have they added, things they have forgotten, strange fire they are bringing in, indifference plaguing them, everything must be repented of, or the plague will not be stopped. They have to confess all of it against themselves. They have to put themselves, as it were, completely into the hands of the Physician and his remedies; holding nothing back, and turn from it. They lay all sin at the feet of the Savior, that they may be washed by the crimson flow down from the cross of the sin-bearer who died that they might live righteously as his people.

They must besiege heaven with a holy fervor in this repentance until they have been delivered by Christ's cure to the sin plaguing them. How will they know they have repented in such a way as Christ desires his church to repent at such strange providences of plagues at such a time as this? The plague will be stopped – those entertaining unbelief in this will say, "What?" What do you mean he will stop it? I mean what Scriptures says, he will stop it. Do Christians really believe that? They must confess their blindness and beg the Lord that their eyes may be opened; and then amend what is faulty, trust in the Physician to heal them, and Christ will stop the plague. That is a very hard one for most to swallow, because it implies a physical event to occur for a spiritual reality, where dismissive cynics who claim to be Christians really do not believe the Scriptures.

The church must use the cure that Christ has provided. The cure to all pestilence, spiritual or otherwise, is the blood of Jesus Christ applied in repentance by the power of the holy Spirit. His blood purges away all sin, and can stop the plague. But, 1 Peter 1:18, "Ye are not redeemed with corruptible things, *[m95 masks, ventilators, malaria drugs, z-packs]*[2] but with the precious blood of Jesus Christ." His precious blood cures the soul of the church, removes the stains that have built up on the soul, the spots that tarnish its standing before God and its testimony before the world. It reaches that far down and has many powerful effects communicated by faith to believers. In our church we partake of the Lord's Supper each week because there is no week in which we have not sinned, and in it we are reminded that such a remedy we take is the very blood of God for us, (Acts 20:28); he is the cure all.

Interestingly there are many things that cross over here. Jesus is the Physician that heals, but the Judge that sends the messenger of his plagues that need to be healed which shows his displeasure at his church in which he quarrels over his covenant, but this covenant is the covenant in his blood, which is able to heal, yet he sends these plagues upon breach of his covenant to his church, whom he's bought by his blood, to stir them up to come to him that he might heal them through the grace of repentance, which he grants them by way of his covenant, which they are breaking, by the Spirit as he so wills, yet they can take hold of the virtue of his work to stop the plague against them which costs them nothing but

---

[2] This is not to say we should not use all, wise, constituted means to fight the temporary affects of such things. Avoiding the serpents when God sent them to the Israelites is a constituted use of "sense" against the plague. But if one wants to stop the plague, these temporary things will never do it.

obedience to his prescription, that they can be made whole again and in his favor looking to him as the Physician of their souls. He is the Judge, the Physician, and the Remedy. Christ's work and person were put into the mortar and pestle of God's wrath and churned and smashed and mixed until God was satisfied with it. It is there that the sacred elixir and medicine may be taken in full by repentance through faith in his deeds.

But what if the church does not repent? Are they not then like the Pharisees who count themselves worthy, point the finger at others and really, are blinded by the soul-sickness of sin? It is everyone else's fault but ours. It is the wickedness of the world's fault, the country's fault, the government's fault.

It is important to note that the application of such a cure cannot be made after one dies. The medicine that Christ offers, the cure that he gives, the remedy that he prescribes, even in a time of plague, will do no one any good if they do not run after it in this life. There is no cure for men in the grave. They cannot afford to let it pass by, simply to hear that there is a remedy, but they must seek to have it applied through Christ now. How will one know if it is applied rightly? Whenever one takes the right medicine for the job it cures them. Remedies in Christ's blood to sinners initially converted show forth a change in their nature. It is rightly applied and they are new men. IF the remedies of Christ are used, taken in repentance, under the blood of the great Physician, by the church, they will in turn see the cure in the literal stopping of the plague and a revival. For the elect's sake, we pray that such plaguing days are shortened.

What should you do if you find you have a sick-soul? You must discern and be sensible of your sin. This is where you must apply yourself to Christ, the great Physician of souls. Christ comes to those like a Physician that makes house calls, to your door, but only to those that see they are sick. And he will heal you by his wounds, and cure you by his stripes, (Isa. 53:5).

Jesus is your Great Physician if you believe it. He is very skillful in that he knows what the nature of every one of your sins are. He knows the virtue of every spiritual remedy for your soul-sickness; the nature of his word, the power of his Spirit, the wonderous workings of his ordinances and such things that minister his blood as the cure. He is authorized and appointed as the Physician to work good for your soul. He was tried many ways, and gloriously approved and exalted, to be in every way able to undertake the care and cure of your soul. He knows all your inward parts, for he knows the heart. He knows the causes of them, and the cures for them. He cures all those he undertakes to make a cure, cuts the heart open like a skilled surgeon, implants the power of his Spirit, and effectually cures what ails you. As it was initially said of the Jews at Pentecost, "They were pricked in their heart."

Jesus heals the plaguing sin of your heart. Jesus has the whole cure for sin, if you see your need. He does so without money and without price. He does it with compassion and tenderness. Some remedies are bitter, others sweet, some hard on the body, others easy to endure. Christ deals tenderly with sinners in every way. Whether it is spiritual, he deals tenderly. Whether it is physical, he deals tenderly, though it may not be easily. He will be near you and with you and by you always; that he will be sure to heal your soul-sickness thoroughly and effectually if you desire it. So, if it is initial, call for the Great Physician and he will come and heal you. Believe on him by faith and he will make you whole and heal your plague of sin.

What of the church in a time of plaguing? Christ the Judge has sent a plague to you his church. How will you have this treated? What remedy will you have Christ give you? Do you want deliverance without repentance? You're a Pharisee if that is the case. Will you follow the contemporary wayward church and blame others for the plague? Will you point the finger and murmur? If you do not think your church needs the Physician, so certainly the Physician does not need you. He did not come for those who do not need him. They have as much help as they seek. If your church is looking at the world because of the plague, the pestilence that the Judge has sent to them as a messenger, they are thinking quite wrongly about the how to stop it; and this will color your whole church and your attitude about the current pestilence. He came not to call the self-centered pious religious pundits of the day. He calls and cures only the sick, and heavy laden with the sense and burden of sin. Plagues are never stopped by carnal men, ever. And when he has a quarrel with his people, his church, by way of his covenant, he requires them to repent, that they may be healed. Exercising that supernatural grace, by which the believing sinner, sensibly affected with and afflicted for his sin as committed against God, freely confess, and fervently begs pardon, and turns from all sin to God. Is that what your church has done because of their covenant breaking? Calling you to repent? I hope so. Religious people that are senseless of their sin, have no remedy in Jesus Christ. What remedy can Christ make for them? There are two kinds of people that can never have the remedy: those who do not see their sin, and religious people who do not think they need to repent. "I hearkened and heard, but they spake not aright: no man repented him of his wickedness, saying, What have I done? every one turned to his course, as the horse rusheth into the battle," (Jer. 8:6). That's useless in a time of pestilence against the church.

If you would be healed of your soul-sickness, you must follow the directions and prescriptions of Christ your spiritual Physician. He has told you what to do, repent. Here is the rub – does the church actually believe Christ that true repentance can stop the plague, a plague, any plague, any judgment? You go to church, involve yourself with all the functions of the church, involve yourself with all the personal devotions of the Christian, and all those things seem, most of the time, to be ordinary. What about the extraordinary providence of God to intervene during a plague to stop it? Will church-wide repentance stop it? Let that hang in the air for a time ... will church wide repentance stop the plague? Or are you so cynical to what God said to his church and covenant people that you are really engaging in unbelief? Will God really do it? Does repentance stop the plague? Hopefully you believe by faith in the Son of God who can stop the plague in a moment if he so desires. And yet still in that, Christians will snicker, they will laugh like Sarah did under her breath but the Lord knows whether you believe that or not. You ask, then, what are the strategies for repentance that the plague will be stopped if such is successful?

I will give you some initial general thoughts about the remedy of repentance to stop the plague prescribed by the Great Physician. First, only Christ's remedy of repentance will stop it. Whatever will stop the plague, must be the means used. David humbled himself, confessed his sin with a penitent heart, and offered sacrifice to God; he repented and the plague was stopped, (2 Sam. 24:25).

Second, be careful at the beginning of a plague (which is right now) not to lessen God's anger against his people. Is God really provoked to anger by your church? Well, the whole earth is covered in plagues. I'd imagine so, and it is not by accident. William Gouge said, "And that you may be more conscionable in this, know that plagues do not come by chance, they do not come by any ordinary course and means. They come from Gods wrath." Lessening God's anger in such things brings calamity upon calamity, even up to seven times as Lev. 26 told us. It is not something to be taken lightly, and all of you should be sure not to lessen the severity of what God is doing, but to be as serious as God is, and he is taking thousands of lives and souls to the judgment seat of Jesus Christ right now in the plague.

Third, Christ must be sought speedily in repentance. How long will the physician be in town when he calls the sick to come to him to find rest, by way of comparison? If your church is to be healed of your soul-sickness, you cannot afford to let time slip by; redeem the time.

Fourth, if your church is to be healed of your soul-sickness, you must take heed of all those things that will continue to bring judgment. You cannot dismiss the reason the plague is here, and you cannot try to fix it yourself. You are not the Physician, your church is not the Physician, only Christ's remedies will work. It requires amendment of life, and true repentance, and walking in circumspection before the Lord of glory in all he has prescribed in his church. Refusing this, is really refusing Christ as offered in the Gospel. It is to become and act in a Pharisaical manner. Is not refusing Christ in the Gospel the great condemning sin of the whole world? It is the ruin of sinners. It must not be the ruin of the church. Because unbelief and slighting Christ as both Physician and Judge, defeats the whole design of the Gospel to bring peace to the soul; and there is no peace for the church when God turns his face from a religious people and closes their doors so that the means of grace are out of their reach because of a plague, because of their sin.

Fifth, that Christ's prescription for repentance is not an easy thing for most Christians and churches to deal with. He has prescribed rules and preservatives and directions for his church to heed in reformation of church life and private life. But if the church or individuals in the church see more importantly what they like and do, than to sit calmly under repentance and the misery of a plague, they will not experience change; they are not really seeing their sin; and that will make a time of plague hard and prolonged.

Sixth, repenting of any soul-sickness is a return to God's prescriptions. Occasional repentance rightly employed receives the church back into that abundant life they need in order to gain health and vigor, for godliness will always dispel the wickedness and miseries of sin; always. It is a denial of former sins. If the church is sinning against God in their dispensationalism, in their non-confessionalism, in their false corrupted worship, in their skew of the Gospel, in their lack of love, in their unsound practices, in their lack of sound leadership, in their misuse of discipline, in their imperfection as his people, they must deny those sins, and repent of those sins and change whatever it is that makes up those sins. It is not merely about confession, it is about change due to confession, and when the bible uses the phrase confess one's sin, it is taken for the whole of repentance, which again is made up of all those various parts; and there, amendment of life must be discernably seen.

It is only by doing the will of God as it is prescribed in his word that the church may stop the plague. From the will of God comes the favor of God. Which is why Christ's medicine is repentance. Where are all the ministers in the church today diligently calling upon all their people to repent? Where is reformation? If we will walk in his ordinances, he will send peace in our land, but if we despise his commandments he will send a sword, a pestilence, a famine, economic trouble, the dominoes that will fall with be a harbinger of judgment which go out from the mountains of brass and the chariots that fly across the face of the earth in his decrees against us.

Seventh, be watchful that you do not rob Christ of the honor which is due to him as our Great Physician. If you try and make a cure of your own, when you attribute it to yourself, your duties, your skill, your power, you steal from Christ which is rightly his work; and that will further the calamity among us; believe that his remedies alone will work. These seven are all general principles, yet, in the next chapter we will consider the first of specific actions that flow from repentance that the church can take in stopping the plague of sin as Leviticus 26 directs, and the plague encompassing the earth at this very time, the first of which is godly humility.

Chapter 3:
Christian Humility Needed During Times of Occasional Repentance

"If they shall confess their iniquity, and the iniquity of their fathers, with their trespass which they trespassed against me, and that also they have walked contrary unto me; And that I also have walked contrary unto them, and have brought them into the land of their enemies; if then their uncircumcised hearts be humbled, and they then accept of the punishment of their iniquity: Then will I remember my covenant with Jacob, and also my covenant with Isaac, and also my covenant with Abraham will I remember; and I will remember the land," (Lev. 26:40-42).

Be reminded, this chapter explains rewards and curses for God's gracious covenant. God's people are to be a holy people because God is holy and he has commanded them certain duties that they must fulfill in his covenant as he prescribes if they are to be his people. There have been and are many religious people in the world, but not many holy people. Speak about religion in a church and many people will weigh in. Speak about holiness and all the hypocrites will scatter; or they will have nothing to say because they are unfamiliar with what it means to be holy and separate for God. They must be holy, why? "because I, the Lord, am holy," 19:2; 20:26; 21:8. All of Leviticus is set in the context of God's gracious covenant of grace and God's holiness.

In Lev. 26:14–39 is found curses to the covenant breaker. In 26:15, "If ye despise my commandments" If they do not do what God has commanded, or add to it or take away from it, God says he will appoint terror over them. This terror is famine, sword and pestilence. Their (v. 22), "highways shall be desolate." They will be punished seven times if needs be to learn their lesson. Their (v. 31) "cities waste." Their meeting places, places of safety, God will "bring your sanctuaries unto desolation ..." Worship will be abhorred by God and he will close them down. They will be (verse 33), "scattered ... among the heathen," The church will be mixed where they will not stand out as they ought among the heathen.

In verse 40, even in the midst of the war, famine and pestilence sent to them, "If they shall confess their iniquity..." "If they shall confess their iniquity, and the iniquity of their fathers, with their trespass which they trespassed against me, and that also they have walked contrary unto me." This is deep seated sin. It not only suggests that they are sinning against God, but that their fathers sinned. This sinning has been going on for a very long time. The church here needs to make a tally of what it had done for a generation. People are often so myopic, thinking that what happened just last week is what God is only concerned about; God stretches what happen twenty-five years ago, thirty years ago, forty years ago all the way until today. This covenant breaking, is a walking that is contrary, not for a minute, but for a span of time, even a generational span, up to 40 or 50 years. In some churches such generational sin might be present from the very founding of the church; starting off in theological and liturgical error; men ordaining themselves to start a work they think erroneously, God has called them to. God gives these wayward covenant breakers a call to a time of prayer, which is attached to the phrase "confess their iniquity." This phrase is taken for the whole of repentance; all parts of repentance are taken up in it. Yet, there is annexed to this repentance the mode, which is prayer, and the manner in which it is to be done in verse 41.

In verse 41, "And that I also have walked contrary unto them, and have brought them into the land of their enemies; if then their uncircumcised hearts be humbled, and they then accept of the punishment of their iniquity." In verse 19 they are said to have their pride broken by God, humbled. Those stiffnecked are to be made pliable by breaking. "Ye stiffnecked and uncircumcised in heart and ears, ye do always resist the Holy Ghost: as your fathers did, so do ye," (Acts 7:51).

In verse 42, "Then (if they are humble, will I remember my covenant with Jacob, and also my covenant with Isaac, and also my covenant with Abraham will I remember; and I will remember the land." God will bring back covenant blessings to his people, if they are humbled and repent. This covenant, this gracious covenant of God to his people, is filled with Evangelical promises, and centers in on the Lord Jesus Christ. Shadows of Christ in the law are found, and the faith that those have at this time look forward to the Messiah to come.

The passage sets down the gracious promise of divine forgiveness and favor *if they will repent of their sin.* Repentance is twofold for these church goers. On the one hand, those who have uncircumcised hearts, those who are in the church and not regenerate, need to repent. They are hypocritical covenant breakers. On the other hand, those who act like they have uncircumcised hearts in the church, yet are born again in the church, need to repent of their wayward walking. Whether a man acts like Judas or is Judas, repentance is the prescription of the Great Physician. In a time of occasional repentance, a time when special repentance is needful due to sin and wayward walking, God's direction here in Leviticus 26 is that reformation and amendment of life, sanctification under the curse of the fall, ought to be foremost on their minds; it is there first "go to." They are to follow God's prescription for holiness, the theme of the entire book. This is the same exhortation given in multiple places in Scripture, as Solomon prayed, "If my people, which are called by my name, shall humble themselves, and pray, and seek my face, and turn from their wicked ways; then will I hear from heaven, and will forgive their sin, and will heal their land," (2 Chron. 7:13-14). Would they strive for reformation? The evangelical plea to them, "And yet for all that, when they be in the land of their enemies, I will not cast them away, neither will I abhor them, to destroy them utterly, and to break my covenant with them: for I am the LORD their God. But I will for their sakes remember the covenant of their ancestors," (Lev. 26:44-45). There is a quality to repentance that is needful, without which repentance cannot take place, and this is the doctrine we will pull from this text.

DOCTRINE: Humility is a non-negotiable divine virtue to be exercised of every Christian especially in times of occasional repentance.

When God says they will confess their sins, when the Great Physician says that those soul-sick will repent, God attached onto repentance a non-negotiable quality. He told them that they must do certain things, but how they are to do those certain things is set in a particular quality. And that quality is humility. It is such an important quality for the church in times of occasional repentance, that when Rehoboam and Manasseh repented in their narratives, they are only said to *humble themselves,* (2 Chron. 12:6, 33:12). To humble one's self comprises the whole of repentance, and the quality of the heart during true repentance. And under the Gospel, repentance for sin, as well as from sin, is described as "godly sorrow," which, "worketh repentance," (2 Cor. 7:10). This, then, is in contrast to those who are not humble, those who are a Judas in the church, or those who act like Judas in the church. It is, at its base, a heart issue. Humiliation makes way for true, biblical reformation. It presupposes a conviction.

To repent, is to exercise all those qualities of divine virtue that stem from having true faith. What are those qualities? They start with humility, reverence, obedience, patience, love, fear, zeal, hope, and confidence in the Great Physician and his prescriptions. Conviction (which is the reflex stage of being born again) works humiliation, and humiliation presses the soul to reformation; so humility is very important in salvation. Pride alienates the soul from God but humility unites it to him in adoration. Humility and confession go together, but humility is larger than confession and repentance, and is a distinct affection. Repentance is an exercise of sight and sorrow for sin. But humility acknowledges all men's wickedness. Original sin, guilt, weakness, unworthiness, and such.

. What is humility? Humility is a divine quality and grace by which the Christian completely denies himself and carries himself before God and men in a lowliness of heart; and it houses in it the repentance of all pride. It is a deliberate inclination of the mind, grounded on a true and sincere knowledge of the soul's condition before God. It accounts one's life before God and finds one's life lacking in God's balance of holiness. Gregory said, "He that gathers any divine virtues without humility, carries dust against the wind." Of all such Christian qualities, the hardest is to be humble. It is to be subject to God's will. "Submit yourselves therefore to God," (Jam. 4:7). How? "Humble yourselves in the sight of the Lord, and he shall lift you up," (James 4:10). One of the best pieces of armor of the Christian mind is humility. Godly sorrow, humility, works repentance, but is not itself repentance; it leads there, and is so important in its leading that it is given for the whole *process* of repentance. It is where the tender conscience grieves for its sins, not out of a servile fear of punishment, from which Christ has freed one from death and hell by his death, but because they have God who is their good, bountiful and blessed Lord and Master. God gives grace to the humble, therefore submit to God, that is, come humbly before him to seek grace for help in time of need. "Submit yourselves therefore to God. Resist the devil, and he will flee from you. Draw nigh to God, and he will draw nigh to you," (James 4:7-8). It is a lowliness and modesty of mind; being subject to God and his will. Such who have humility cultivate a voluntary devotion that is sparked by the Spirit of Christ to submit to the will of God in all things. It is, as many divines have said, "the ornament and jewel of the Christian religion."

Qualities of humility must be considered. It is a grace given by the Holy Spirit. It is only found in a renewed Christian. No carnal person ever persuaded God for mercy through enmity. No carnal person ever set forth in reformation of life by their own power that would have been acceptable to God. The qualification of repentance is to humble one's self. Humility must be present, and it cannot be a mere going through the motions. When such a thought is considered, and knowing the rather extensive ignorance that the Christian church has today of almost all Christian doctrines, it is a very sad consideration to think that Christians must know how to be humble before they could ever repent, and in times of occasional repentance, before the plague is stopped. Those who are symptomatic under God's divine fury are those with the curse on them, who are plagued with hypocrisy, luke-warmness, self-conceit, a lack of humility, because they have not fled to Christ, are not born again, have not truly been convicted of the truth of the Gospel. Those with such spiritual problems need the Great Physician, and they need him to change their hearts and make them tender. But a born-again Christian has humility as a grace of the Spirit instilled at their conversion. Where the Spirit of Christ dwells, there one finds humility. Humility is only by the Spirit and through Christ. This is particularly important in occasional repentance where the church must confess their iniquity to God as covenant breakers, specifically. Repentance that is ineffectual is not humble and does not have the Spirit. Christians do this all the time. Rattling off sins committed is not repentance, nor does such have humility attached to it simply because one goes through the motions of confession. One cannot repent, if they are not in the Spirit, and one cannot have humility if they are not in the Spirit and one cannot pray if they are not in the Spirit. All these require the Spirit. "be clothed with humility: for God resisteth the proud, and giveth grace to the humble," (1 Peter 5:5). Those who are filled with grace, filled with the grace of the Spirit, are endowed with the ability to be humble before God.

Humility is submissive. Humility teaches men to submit themselves and all their affections and faculties to Christ alone. "Serving the Lord with all humility of mind," (Acts 20:19). Such Christians believe God at his word. They are satisfied in Christ to suffer anything God brings; no matter what the affliction or blessing might be. Such a disposition has power to make prayer itself effective. Confess while humble. And the outcome is a power to cultivate divine contentment. If humility is so important, and God has joined it to this work of repentance, without which repentance cannot take place ... then

What practical exercises can the Christian church use to cultivate humility during times of occasional repentance? Consider the Word of God first. Humility disposes a man to give attention to the truth. It always resolves a Christian to a ready conviction and a quick but sound repentance. It is there, as it is in this passage of Leviticus, that God subjugates his church. King Jesus rules his people with the word. The word of God is not manifested to all people indifferently, but only to those endued with the true faith, who have a humble heart, and are therefore spiritually persuaded by the work of the Spirit to know its truth. The carnal mind is in opposition to this and is at enmity with God. No carnal man will ever stop the plague then. Their ideas about the plague are to stop shaking hands. Without humility and lowliness of heart before God, who would ever submit themselves to God? The true sense of the Scripture, the true Spirit of God are present to those who submit to his word in humility; without which holy Scripture will never be plain, clear and manifest to direct them.

Humility calls to mind the work of sin. Far reaching, back a generation. Calling to mind, in humility, is a Christian virtue so developed in this act, that it is impossible to think about one's sin effectively for repentance without it. This is not *dwelling* on sin. But stirring up one's self that all one does is tainted, is imperfect, is not acceptable. Sin is any want of conformity or transgression of God's law. It is to break its covenant stipulations. Christians are doing this all the time. The church must consider what it does. Leviticus is filled in this chapter with ideas surrounding worship, so are they worshipping God as God desires in humility? Or is it will-worship? Is it false worship? "Which things have indeed a shew of wisdom in will worship, and humility," (Col. 2:23). False worship that is religious, or what people think has a religious flavor, is expressly linked to false humility and vain will-worship by the Apostle; it is what God hates. If a church does not do what God wants them to do, they are idolaters. How long will God put up with idolatry? Look back to the last plague. Measure back, 1917-1918?

Measure back to a war? Measure back to a famine? Consider it. What was the warning in Leviticus 26? Don't change what I tell you, be holy as I am holy. Don't break my covenant by changing it to your liking; don't change my covenant in any way because it is about my Son. Do what I want you to do because I am the Physician who prescribes what is lawful for you to do. Anything less, changed or indifferent is idolatry. Which is why the whole chapter harps on the first verse of having no idolatry in their midst and to keep the Lord's commandments. What is the church doing perfectly before God? Nothing? Then they have reason to contemplate where they lack this godly humility for their sin.

Humility presses the church to call to mind the work of Christ. The ground of holiness comes from Jesus Chris alone. The entire foundation and all its parts of a believer's acceptable stance before God is set in the righteousness and salvation of the Christ. The fulfillment of the law, the destruction of sin, the overthrow of the curse, is from the nature, office, work and merit of Christ for his elect. It is his imputation to them that reconciles their nature to God's law. The church in Leviticus could do nothing without Jesus Christ and his blood virtually applied to them, by faith looking forward to the Messiah. Christ intervenes on behalf of all his people clothed in their nature, between God and man, and in that with all the sins of believers on him, God having laid "on him the iniquities of us all." In his work he obeyed, suffered, satisfied, and offered up himself, and now stands as a Mediator at the right hand of power, to perpetuate or make his sacrifice, obedience, suffering, and righteousness everlasting. He alone brings in everlasting righteousness. In this God accounts, reckons, imputes all that Christ has done in human nature as the God-man, as if it was done by the believer himself, calling things that are not as if they were.

Is this not an encouragement to promote humility? No one can stand before God on their own. People will say "I was a good person. I tried my best. I led a good life. I was not so bad as Hitler, so let me into heaven." Hell is filled with people who have given such self-placating and irreligious answers. To enter heaven, there is only standing at the throne of God's justice in the righteousness of Christ on the day of judgment. He is *made sin* for all believers, he who knew no sin, that they might be made the righteousness of God in him. And such people must have more done for them than Judas had or Esau had or Saul had. The evangelical grace of repentance and humility in Leviticus 26 is set and bound by those who have faith, who have the Spirit, who exercise it in Christ. It makes little difference whether one looks forward to Christ or back to Christ. It is the same covenant, the same Lord. This is why God was so angry, and had such a quarrel with those that broke his covenant stipulations.

Humility calls to mind the need of the Spirit. What can anyone do who does not walk in the Spirit? It does not matter whether one looks to the Old Testament or the New Testament. Jesus said all those who go to heaven are born again; read John 3, born from above by the Spirit, an Old Testament idea, not a New Testament one. "Searching what, or what manner of time the Spirit of Christ which was in them did signify, when it testified beforehand the sufferings of Christ, and the glory that should follow," (1

Peter 1:11). "Can we find such a one as this is, a man in whom the Spirit of God is?" (Gen. 41:38). "The Spirit of God hath made me, and the breath of the Almighty hath given me life," (Job 33:4). Is there any virtue accomplished without him? Is there no humility promoted in this where there is no work of humility without the Spirit?

Humility calls to mind the work of grace. All the works of the Christ, and all the works of the Spirit are of grace. Grace is unmerited favor of God. This is what a person does not deserve or better yet, should not get. God bestows graciously in Christ, by the power of the Spirit. Does this promote humility? Meditation plays a large part in this. As with John, Ezekiel and Jeremiah, to eat this book of God, to find it sweet in the mouth. To hide its knowledge in the heart, and to digest it by godly meditation, Rev. 10:9, "Take it, and eat it up." The effect of this meditation should be sweetness (like the sweetness of honey) in the mouth, but bitterness in the belly. To know it and believe it, brings delight to the Christian mind; but the earnest desire to vent and publish it to others, the heaviness and sorrow for its condemnation makes it often like gall to God's Servants. Ezek. 3:3; Jer. 15:16; Job 32. But this is where the humble are directed by God. It is not a feeling that directs people, but knowledge of the word of God.

What are the signs of humility in a church's repentance? Humility is joined to the fear of God. There is a developed understanding of what it means to be imperfect before the sight of God's law. Psa. 30:2-3; Isa. 40:6; 1 Peter 1:24. Pride never does this. The word humility has connotations attached to it that mean to shrink in light of the fear of God which is the beginning of wisdom.

Humility is joined to confession (repentance), which is the acknowledgement of sin and sinfulness. Humility is serious under God's judgments.[1]

Humility lays itself in the dust while in the presence of God and in worship, (Rev. 4:10). It is a holy discretion in worship, (Eccl. 5:1-3).

Humility is necessary that the church may seek God and turn away his anger, (2 Chron. 12:7). It is true that it is required in every single duty that the Christian performs. "He hath shewed thee, O man, what is good; and what doth the LORD require of thee, but to do justly, and to love mercy, and to walk humbly with thy God?" (Micah 6:8).

Humility is laying all the Christian's supposed honor in the dust. Set in the context of a national lament, the Psalmist says, "For our soul is bowed down to the dust," (Psa. 44:25). Such a humility will adore God, and bring honor to God, and give all glory to God, and none to themselves. It is to bring a man out of his own of pride, and to cause him to set his whole life, and all its facets before the Christ. He sees himself as vile in his own judgement, which takes a great amount of thought. This isn't a *one and done* thing. A person is told to repent, they are humbled for a moment, lay down into the dust before the almighty, and confess generally that they feel bad about what they have done; get up and go their way thinking all is right and fine now. Humility is not once, it's constant. But it is a necessary ingredient to be pointed out in times of

---

[1] Psa. 39:5; Rom. 3:18; Job 1:21, 39:37.

occasional repentance for things like the plague. Imagine a man who has the blessing of God only within his reach if he would ask for it? There he lays himself in the dust, cries out to God, confesses his sins, and opens up his heart to asking God to forgive him, and to bless him abundantly, and this, with great earnestness and even with tears; what will he gain by this? One might think, he will gain salvation. Esau did this, and what did he gain? Esau does more than most Christians do. It must not be a kind of selfish pride which does not travel from the mind to the heart; as Esau's was. Will superficial confession turn away the plague of God's wrath? The repentance of all those like Esau's will fail in this. False humility is a devilish disease which will never stop the plague.

What about forced humility? This was the plight of Pharaoh. He was humbled, but in a forced way, which did not bring forth true humility. While God was plaguing him, and he discerned the plagues, he promised to let the people go, but when the plagues ceased, he hardened his heart. "And Pharaoh said, Who is the LORD, that I should obey his voice to let Israel go? I know not the LORD, neither will I let Israel go," (Exod. 5:2). Make bricks without straw instead you slaves.

What of the plagues sent to the church? Are not plagues, as God states in Leviticus 26 a motive to nurture humility? The very stopping of the plague requires humility and repentance to be combined. Repentance without humility does nothing. There will be no virtue in it, and it cannot be true repentance without it. Lancelot Andrews (1555-1626) (who oversaw the translation of the KJV) said, "The first outward sign of true humility is on our tongue."[2] Humility speaks in the language of guilt. It is in repentance and confession where God places humility. It is to place a high value on God's prescription of mercy in that light.

Humility in this way is one of the foundations of the entire Christian Religion. Soul-sick people need a physician, those who see their need. Mourners are humble. God orders plagues for the church when they sin, and if they repent sincerely of sins, where their scarlet sins are confessed in true humility and lowliness of mind and heart, they will find God being merciful. That is where Christ is found. And nothing is a greater injustice to God's covenant mercy, than to persevere in a sinful course without an eye-sight of sin and wickedness before God. Whole denominations have deemed good Friday and Easter as days of humiliation and prayer for the plague. They think that Papist Holidays will somehow get God's attention. They are simply following the same problem God has sent them for being idolaters. In their pride, they are not listening to God and not worshipping God as he instructs. God has not declared pardon in vain, Isa. 1:18, "Though your sins be as scarlet, they shall be white as snow; though they be red like crimson, they shall be as wool." He has declared it to be so for all those who humble themselves before him.

Jesus was lowly in heart, and the pattern of humility for all men. The greatest motive to humility in the Christian life is the example of Jesus Christ. He says, "Learn of me for I am meek and lowly in heart." "Pride

---

[2] Lancelot Andrewes, *The Pattern of Catechistical Doctrine at Large*, (London: Imprinted by Roger Norton, 1650), 135.

turned Lucifer into a devil, and humility exalted the Son of God above every Name, and placed him eternally at the right hand of his Father."[3] All his works, all his actions, all his speech, all he did was in humility before God. Now Christ does not have need to repent, for he was without sin, and it may be confusing to consider the Lord Jesus in humility for the church during a plague, who must confess their iniquity in humility. But the Christian can have nothing Christ did not fulfill. He fulfilled all things in humility before God as far as his sinless nature would allow. Is this humility the same thing in Jesus as it should be in the church? Lowliness of heart is a submission to God. Being humble does not mean that one must be a sinner to be humble. Humility is joined in unconverted sinners to *confession*, but in Jesus Christ it is joined to his obedience; he was perfect, perfect in humble obedience always. That person which has the most holiness, has the most humility. Christ was subjected to God in all things.

So, all Christ's acts on earth testified of him as humble before God. He was humble in his birth, being born in a manger, he was humbled in his life, in his preaching, in his death, even the death of the cross. Was he not made flesh, God clothed with flesh, *a stooping down and condescending* in humility? "But made himself of no reputation, and took upon him the form of a servant, and was made in the likeness of men: And being found in fashion as a man, he humbled himself, and became obedient unto death, even the death of the cross," (Phil. 2:7-8). As Christ was made flesh, his glory was veiled from

---

[3] Jeremy Taylor, *Holy Living,* (London: Printed for Richard Royston, 1656), 121.

human sight, until his works showed his quality, and even this in his transfiguration. Christ took all the infirmities of man's flesh, yet without sin. Hunger, tiredness, sorrow, fear of God, to his very death, all in what is called his humiliation. Thomas Watson said, "O look on Christ, this rare pattern, and be humbled! It is an unseemly sight to see God humbling himself, and man exalting himself; to see a humble Savior, and a proud sinner."[4]

In a time of plague and judgment, humility in confession of sin is non-negotiable. The Physician's prescription is repentance, but repentance is tied to humility. In times of the plague this should move the church to greater heights of humility. If the church by the Spirit ties humility and repentance together, so that confession of sin demonstrates the qualities of real Spirit-filled occasional repentance, what should that look like? How will one know that they have repented well? The humbled church of Jesus will see the plague stopped.

At every point, in any sin, with humility, repentance and confession, the church ought to be happy that Christ is calling to her to amend her way and her doings. If by careful repentance and sincere humiliation they come boldly before the throne of the Savior, their sin will be removed which is the cause, and then the plague which is only the effect, will stop. But without this, all the medicines in the world, all the masks, all the hospitals, all the data, and everything along with it will be in vain. Until God is pacified by his prescriptions, the plague will never be appeased; or that he has decreed a certain end of it at a time if the church does not repent in godly humility. Until

---

[4] Watson, Thomas, *Body of Practical Divinity.*

the church is humble before him, he will not heal his people. Unless the church by faith flies into his hands, and lays themselves in his care completely, wholly and without reservation, he will not protect his church from the pestilence, or any of its consequences. I ask you, is the church still closed? Are the means of grace still out of reach?

The plague has deprived the church in the world of its means of grace. Judgments like these seldom move along the face of the earth without other things accompanying them. Famine, poverty, depopulation, domestic abuse, suicide, economic ruin for countless businesses, loss of life in a number of ways, (Jer. 22:6-9, 28:8; Ezek. 14:21). Do you think the world will go back to the way it was? Do you think the world will look like it did just a few short months ago? Plagues like this robs the church of many blessings. Just consider, as I have belabored, the freedom of worship in God's house and ordinances. That is the saddest of all the afflictions I believe; or indifference to it. "My soul longeth, yea, even fainteth for the courts of the LORD," (Psa. 84:2). It even has deprived many in the church (and others outside of the church) of our vocation. Men without purpose, without finances, not able to serve God in their vocations? It deprives the church of friends. Where is the contact? Where is the fellowship? It has killed thousands in a relatively short period of time. It is an arrow that flies speedily, (Psa. 91:5).

The humble church will have, a sincere repentance, not forced nor counterfeit. The true penitent confesses his sins with much candor, ingenuity, and freedom of spirit.

He is as free in his confession of sin, as he has been free in the commission of his sin. The church will not be looking for the plague to be stopped because of outward pain, but because of the inward affects of the heart before God. Carnal men always murmur at outward miseries. Christians always look to their heart sins.

The humbled church will not reform in part but in whole. This is an exciting prospect to see and expect. God's church reforming to the full. Wouldn't that be a sight? Revival. If the church is not sincere, the plague will not be stopped, and if their confession is not full, the plague will not be stopped; does God work on halves? They confess all their sins in particular, and this, to the full. The church must know their sins; things they have left undone, and things they have specifically transgressed against; but does the church even realize it is doing anything wrong, or are they still pointing the finger? "And the children of Israel cried unto the LORD, saying, We have sinned against thee, both because we have forsaken our God, and also served Balaam," (Judges 10:10). "If they shall confess their iniquity, and the iniquity of their fathers, with their trespass which they trespassed against me, and that also they have walked contrary unto me;" (Lev. 26:40). God is very specific about what he wants them to confess, and they have to know these things. "And the second time the cock crew. And Peter called to mind the word that Jesus said unto him, Before the cock crow twice, thou shalt deny me thrice. And when he thought thereon, he wept," (Mark 14:72). Peter did not weep generally over him being a sinner, but particularly about his sin against Christ. Thomas Brooks said, "there is nothing more common to a wicked heart, than to keep close his sin, than to cover and hide his transgressions."[5] This is what Adam did on his transgression, hid himself behind a leaf. Not only futile, but stupid; which is what sin makes men do. Wicked men never engaged in a humble sincerity in confessing their sins. There is nothing in the bible of that because they are not subject to the law of God nor can they be.

Is this merely a removal of sin? One cannot think in that way. It is not only a removal of sin. It is not only a taking away of outward difficulty. Humility goes far deeper because of the fact that Christ is not a sinner, but was yet the most humble man who ever walked the face of the earth. What did humility do for him? It is the same thing that is promised in the drawing of God's people close to him. What does it mean in Leviticus 26:42 that God will remember his covenant with them upon their repentance, humility and confession of sin? All the covenantal benefits are bestowed in experimental fullness.

It is not merely a removal of sin and then a removal of outward misery; that's self-centered if it is only that. Thomas Manton said, "... in our distresses the main thing we should look on, is not so much the removal of God's anger, and the removal of the evil, as the renewed sense of his love, to be reconciled ... It is an easy matter to be sensible of the evil of trouble. Nature will teach us that."[6] Humility is more than the carnal man would want. He wants the plague to stop. Christians should want the

---

[5] Brooks, *Works*, 398.
[6] Manton, Thomas, *One Hundred and Ninety Sermons on the Hundred and Nineteenth Psalm*, (London: Printed for T.P. &c. and are to be sold by Michael Hide, bookseller in Exon, 1681), 903–904.

plague to stop. Christians should want whatever course of pride to be struck down, reformation to occur, revamping of their worship before God, and for the plague to cease. It is commanded they be humble, repent and confess their iniquities, and that thoroughly. But to merely look to the stopping of the plague in order to stop outward misery is to miss the whole idea of being at peace with God.

Consider what it means for you to have a proud spirit and not a humble spirit. A proud spirit wants the plagued stopped. A humbled spirit wants his humility to lead him to repentance for his sins, *that* the plague would be stopped. What carnal man will stop a plague and promote a lively sense of God's love? He is never brought down for the depth of his sin. All his duties are for show. The evil heart of the proud man is not going to engage in humbling duties. Can he enter a penitent confession for sin? Can he be humble? Can he give a serious prayer for grace and pardon in Jesus Christ? All he can do is give some kind of lip-service, or the Pharisees self-grandeur, "I thank thee that I am not as other men, nor as this Publican." The Great Physician came for such publicans. Proud men are involved in lip-service to God, like the Pharisees, who did much, and said much, but with insincere and proud hearts; like a day of humiliation on a papist holiday. Their spiritual peace is fabricated conjecture and supposition.

Proud men do not see their sin, really, and do not think they are too sick with sin, to need the Physician in the way Leviticus describes. The proud are not acquainted with God, or the Physician of souls. If he is, it is superficial and merely by way of knowing, but not experimental. He has no work of the Spirit in his heart.

Proud men have sins they deal with, but do not deal *with sin*. He thinks that not abusing his wife, or not getting drunk, or any moral leaps are put in place of humility and confession in sincerity towards a godly repentance, makes him a better man, where they really make him deceived. Proud men have no experience with soul-sickness. Do they think their hearts are desperately wicked?

Proud men are always irritated with outward afflictions, and will do all they can to stop the annoyance; just watch the news for five minutes. They do not have humility in it; we will get through this if we wash our hands, if we don't gather together, we will push through it together; no they won't. Will they pray, "God, deliver us, but, thy will be done in it?" Lord, if you so deem it necessary for our repentance to bring back godly worship, to leave off sins, and the cultivation of our humility before you, then prolong the plague you have sent to us? Will the people on TV say or even think that? Lev. 26 is echoed in Micah 7:9, "I will bear the indignation of the Lord because I have sinned against him." They will never put up with living humbly under the sovereign hand of God in anything, much less a plague. These do not see their need of a Physician, confession, repentance in humility and subjection before God.

Are you humble? How do you answer that? If you say *yes I am humble*, is that humble? Don't be fooled into the oddness of the question of humility. Christians that have the most holiness, have the most humility as they follow the Christ; there is your answer. Humility is the highway in which all exchanged between you and God exist in righteousness. Humility is the way that self-denial occurs as it implies obedience to God's commands, and submission to his will in all things that you do. When we sit humbly under God's correcting hand, and bear it patiently, and say, God is just in all this, then it will succeed well with us and our church. Does the church see this? Will they say this in this time of occasional repentance? Lev. 26:41, is literally called "accepting" of a man's due punishment, putting yourself into God's hands, and looking wholly to Christ while the chastisement falls on you and those around you.

When God afflicts you, will you profit by his blows? Will you do it with humility, which turns rapidly into confession, which turns rapidly into repentance, which turns rapidly into an other-worldly joy. Our hope is in Jesus Christ, and our sin against Christ, should not make us not only to bear God's blows patiently, and thankfully, but also to be exceeding humble which then will cultivate joy in God. Hannibal Gammon said, "We must not measure our afflictions by the present pain we feel, but, (Hebrews 12:11), by the benefit that follows after them ... therefore, let us kiss his rod, not struggle and strive under the mighty hand of God, (1 Peter 5:6). The quicker we do this, the sooner we shall be delivered. Bear you, (St. Bernard says), the rod of correction, lest you feel the hammer of confusion."[7]

Is your church humble? Are you humble? Are the times evil? How are they made evil? What is your answer to that question? Worldly people make the times evil. Others make the times evil and perilous. Others are at

---

[7] Gammon, Hannibal, *God's Desertion of the Unjust and Other Works.*

fault. Then, at that point just say the next line, "I am not at fault." Are not the times made evil by our sins; are they not made perilously evil times? "This know also, that in the last days perilous times shall come. For professing Christians shall be covenant-breakers (truce breakers) ... having a form of godliness, but denying the power thereof: from such turn away," (2 Tim. 3:1-5). What church, what Christian can show his face and say, "I have not committed any sins that may be in part a cause to bring down the spiritual and physical plagues that are now among us?" Who will say that?

People are so busy to complain of the times, and so careless to complain of their own sins. But that is a trick of the devil. To be so keen to spy out the sins of others, but to be blind to your own sin. Will you, out of a humble heart, confess and repent of all your sins? Are you cognizant of the fact that as much as anyone else in your church, that your sins have made the times worse than they would have been otherwise? That the times would be better if you did not sin? You have a divine directive, for the plague is here, and God requires the church to be humble and confess their iniquity, and think heartily on committing them, as far back as they can remember, and you are part of that church. No one is exempt. That does not mean that you rehash the sins that you have already repented of in times past for. That was not what God was directing in Leviticus 26. But things left undone, things which were not seen, where there was no real sight of sin, and that reformation had to ensue. It may be old sins that you were not contrite for. It may be that you didn't even know they were sins; where are all your secret sins housed? What time will you take this Lord's Day and consider it? Do you have better things to do to occupy yourself at this time of plague?

Will God bring an instantaneous fix? It is one thing to do all God requires by the Spirit in humility, and another to see the consequences of it. "Humble yourselves therefore under the mighty hand of God, that he may exalt you in due time," (1 Peter 5:6). God will stop a plague, but the consequences left in the time it was enacted may have dire consequences.

God has humbled in a physical way, many in your great cities, wherever you live. It started with sickness, it's going to move to a decay in the economy, loss of jobs, loss of finances, desperation, homelessness, and it will flourish without godly humility, confession and true repentance. Are we humbled by this? There is no waiting in this. Jesus stands at the door where he knocks to his church to open it so that they may have fellowship with him. It is true, if we do not learn our lessons quickly, he will continue to cast us all down; with as many chastisements as it takes.

If God is your Physician, even if you are at the gates of death, as so many are today, he can bring you back. Yes, you use all the constituted means to get well, but you look to God first. He can heal a physical plague with a spiritual remedy. He can heal a whole kingdom of sickness, of pestilence. He is both a physician of the body and the soul. This should encourage us in this plague, to actually have a path and remedy to God, through Christ in humility. Will it cost you anything but time? It does not matter how low God brings us, he can stop the plague and raise up people back to health. We ought, then, to use the means he has set forth, that in a time of plague though other means are far from us, these means of humility, confession and repentance are at our grasp. Humility is a non-negotiable divine virtue to be exercised of every Christian especially in these times of occasional repentance.

Yet, know, that in all this, humility, repentance and confession of our iniquities are housed in those means God has provided in prayer and fasting which are taken for confession, as much as for repentance. So, Prayer and fasting in this context are what we will consider in the next chapter as suitable to Leviticus 26.

Chapter 4:
Humble Prayer and Fasting

Again, in remembering Leviticus 26, the chapter explains rewards and curses for God's gracious covenant. God's people are to be a holy people *because God is holy* and he has commanded them certain duties that they must fulfill in his covenant as he prescribes if they are to be his people since he has saved them from bondage. They must be holy, why? "because I, the Lord, am holy," (19:2; 20:26; 21:8). All of Leviticus is set in the context of God's gracious covenant of grace and God's holiness.

In verse 40, even in the midst of the war, famine and pestilence sent to them, "If they shall confess their iniquity, and the iniquity of their fathers, with their trespass which they trespassed against me, and that also they have walked contrary unto me." This is a confession of deep-seated sin, long standing sin. God sends a sword, famine and plague to his church because they are *sinning* against him, and even that their *fathers* sinned. This sinning has been going on for a very long time. This covenant breaking, is a walking against God, and in this way consequently his walking against them in light of his holiness. It goes on even for a generational span, 40 or 50 years. God gives these wayward covenant breakers a call to a time of prayer, which is attached to the phrase "confess their iniquity." This phrase is taken for the *whole* of repentance; all parts of repentance are taken up in it. Yet, there is annexed to this repentance the mode, which is prayer, and the manner in which it is to be done in verse 41, *humbly*. If they humbly entreat God in prayer by way of confession in times of occasional repentance, God will remember his covenant. They are to, in point of fact, stir God up to remembrance of his blessings. Verse 42, "Then *(if they are humble)* will I remember my covenant with Jacob, and also my covenant with Isaac, and also my covenant with Abraham will I remember; and I will remember the land." God will bring back covenant blessings to his people, if they are humbled and repent. This covenant, this gracious covenant of God to his people, is filled with Evangelical promises, and centers in on the Lord Jesus Christ.

This repentance is twofold for the church. On the one hand, those who have uncircumcised hearts, those who are in the church and not regenerate, need to repent. They are *hypocritical* covenant breakers. On the other hand, those who *act like* they have uncircumcised hearts in the church, yet are born again in the church, need to repent of their wayward walking, idolatry and covenant breaking. Remember, there is general repentance, when people repent for the first time being born again by the Spirit; there is constant repentance in light of holy living, and there is *occasional repentance* when the church has broken God's covenant and he requires them to come back to him in reformation. Humility leads to confession, confession is part of prayer, and they are to do it in a manner befitting God's holiness toward amendment of life. Would they now desire reformation? Would they exercise humility? Will they repent in whole? Will they come back to God that the afflictions God has placed on them would be stopped?

Here, we consider the DOCTRINE: the fruit of humility before God in times of occasional repentance (such as the plague) is holy prayer and fasting towards an amendment or reformation of the church.

Humility is seen in confession and repentance which implies humble prayer before God at the breaking of his covenant. "If my people confess," and are "humble" is the requirement. This is not a general confession. It considers and searches out sins even back to their father's sins. It is a complete repentance, and a whole reformation. Partial reformation, reformation in halves, is not something God desires, nor blesses. What does the Christian think? "I will repent of some of my sins. I will change part of my life." This is not a humiliation before God. This is not a reformation and such will never lead to revival.

To humble one's self comprises the whole of repentance, and the quality of the heart during true repentance. *Humility* is a divine quality and grace by which the Christian completely denies himself and carries himself before God and men in a lowliness of heart; and it houses in it the repentance of all pride. It is a deliberate inclination of the mind, grounded on a true and sincere knowledge of the soul's condition before God. It examines one's life before God and finds one's life lacking in God's balance of holiness; such people are humbled in this.

The fruit of humility before God is holy prayer towards a reformation of life. First, to understand godly humility is to understand that the church is absolutely subjugated to God in all things, and wholly opposed to the world. Unconverted men do not like the idea of resting in a godly submission under God in humility. They believe themselves to control their life and desire to do so. They will have nothing of yielding to Christ in all things. Oh, they may yield in things that cost them nothing, but they will not yield in all things. They are unable to demonstrate a truly penitent heart, though they might have a sorry heart once in a while. That's a phrase, "I'm sorry," which Christians ought to *eject* from their vocabulary. Being sorry with no recourse is not a biblical concept. Such people will not lay aside their pride and stubbornness, humbly acknowledging their sins, though, sins that offend them, they will cry out against. If something comes against their person, or family, or hurts them in some way that they do not like, they will cry out against that. They will cry out at neglecting saving the whales. They will start a foundation. They will give money to them. They will help them in whatever way they can. This may be good, but it is not humility, repentance and prayer that God speaks about in Leviticus 26. They are wholly unaware that increasing their eternal happiness is done by quickened obedience to Christ's revealed will, and that in total subjection.

Generally, church goers do not desire humility to God's divine religion in his law and government, by grace alone, through God's Christ. They reject God's law and in doing so reject God's Christ. They reject God's means by which they would be made truly happy. Humility to such things counteracts and crucifies the self-will and their desire of independence which dominates their fallen nature. That is the source of rebellion against God. They have no desire to be changed of that. Churches that miss the impact of the plague now on them will go back to what they have always done in the way they always do it; it will not *change* them. All Christians that understand Christ's commanding of his coronavirus against covenant breakers, will be *changed people* in the end. But the wicked, they have no desire to submit their wills to God's will. Only a change made by God in the heart of such people will create true humility, which is annexed to the fruit of the Spirit in being faithful to God and will bring them to submit to Jesus Christ. God must give that new heart and must apply all of Christ's crucified benefits to the changed sinner.

Second, humility in godly prayer is yielding to God in all his ways and governance. It is to give up one's self to God in every way; that dreadful word "all." Christians do not give God *lip service* on the Lord's Day and live like the devil the rest of the week. Those the bible calls *hypocrites.* To give over to God, in all things, no matter the affliction, is to remain under God's hand in a submissive manner in everything. Humble obedience coupled with the heart of a servant to confess one's sin in prayer and subjugate one's self before God begging for his grace and pardon in Christ Jesus is God's desire in Leviticus 26 of his wayward church. It is to completely disavow one's self; to *comply*. It is to lower one's self into the dust from where they came and yield to the government of King Jesus. Covenanted, legally bound Christian confessors, are humbled in their covenant breaking and desire to pray to God, for forgiveness, pardon and blessing. He entreats God, confessing his sins in humility to stir up both himself and God to remember the blessings of his covenant with them.

Third, humble prayer is the duty of every covenanted Christian in the church. It is submitting to God even in the little things, without question, without excuse and without delay.[1] Godly Christians act this way in light of God's revealed will for them; they hear Christ's voice and follow willingly, dependently. Humble prayer in times of occasional repentance for the plague is a fresh drawing near to God in humble service in light of his word, to seek the grace of Christ for God's glory and their good, to change their ways, and amend their lives and do right before the God who requires righteousness in them and for them. Christians are the covenanted and professed subjects of the kingdom of Jesus Christ, why would they not desire to submit themselves to the laws of his kingdom? His commandments for Christians are not burdensome.

Certainly, it is true, sometimes God must make people humble and send them a sword, famine or plagues; sometimes he must use the rod instead of the staff. Prideful hearts sometimes involve the long and painful process of breaking bones to fit them back in the right place, and this may be done up to seven times, or until the church considers its position and service to the holiness of God. He may send them a plague, a war, famine; have you seen the long lines at the food banks for millions of people who have no job and no money now, to buy food? Does this not all seem rather simple, as an exercise of a constant Christian virtue: humble prayer before God? But it is most difficult, is it not? Because it holds in it, the idea of debasing one's self, and a submissive contentment to God's will in all things. People hate change; but God *requires* they change and conform to his will.

---

[1] See the *Appendix* to this work for an exhortation to obedience.

Now, coupled with humility in this way, is humble prayer. Confession in humble prayer is the way Christians act. Strike Saul blind, later Paul, helpless on the road to Damascus and ... then what? "Behold, he prays," do you recall that? The church is to make a humble search, going back decades, to see their sins that they have hidden away, or those prescriptions that they fail to observe, or those directives they fail to employ in service to God as a whole church, throw them down at the foot of God's throne, and ask God to forgive them, and then have an amendment of life. Imagine all the wars, famines and plagues on the earth that could be avoided if professing Christians would simply humble themselves under God's providential direction and revealed will in Scripture and pray for his grace and forgiveness to worship him rightly. You might say, "You make it sound so easy." Well, what is hard about what God has said? As if God says, *My people are to come humbly, confess their sins with conviction, and amendment and walk with me, and I will remember my covenant.* But wait – *they too* must remember that covenant, because they are humbly confessing their sins against that covenant which they have broken and why the sword, famine and plague are here, and why further layers of cultural difficulty are also starting. Such humility in prayer and godly conviction will cause people to turn away from their parades and puppet shows in church, and turn back to God. You think I'm kidding when I use the term "parades and puppet shows." In South Florida, I was a member, years ago, of a PCA church pastored by one who you know very well as a reformed minister, who writes books and has conferences and such, and yet there were

97

parades and puppet shows in worship. Appalling. Again, I was a member of another PCA church where they had all kinds of things in worship, interpretive dance by young women, special music by worship teams, and such things. I'm not exaggerating when I say things that way to sound pithy or cute. Is the professing church going to turn away from man-centered worship, and instead, turn back to God? Will they turn back to a sound theology of walking, and will they walk with God again? Then, God will remember, as they have stirred themselves up to remember. And yet, look around, the plague is still here, and the famine is beginning; and other calamities are now building. What would the world of Christianity look like set within the bounds of unreserved trust in God's word and will for the church? What rods of chastening could be avoided? Yes, the church would be smaller, and with fewer people. But is this not what Christ said, that the road to eternal life is narrow and there be few that find it?

It is extremely interesting to look hypocritically at Leviticus 26 and the history of the church in the wilderness and compare it with the way Christians think today. You might say, "I don't follow what you mean by that." One reads many parts of the Old Testament and comes away with saying, *why don't these people learn?*

> They are constantly sinning before God. They are sinning so much that God brings wars and famines and plagues against them and he is constantly rebuking them in their waywardness. Is there no grace for them? Are there no blessings for them? Why don't they reach out and take the blessing? Is

there only chastisement for them? Why don't they just humble themselves? Why don't they just pray? Why don't they just reform and listen to God? Is it so hard to listen? Why don't they just look back at the old paths, and the highway of holiness and the righteous instruction that God blessed their fathers with? Why don't they listen to God in his word and remain faithful to worship him in truth?

There the Pharisee is speaking in asking those questions. How so? You might ask? I'll answer this way:

What? Is there no plagues among the church today? Are there no wars, no disease in the world today? Are there no great wars in the last 100 years? Are there no great disasters? Is there no famine? Is there political upheaval? Is there moral erosion? Is there a plague? Is the church listening to God and reforming in light of his word and will? Is there no grace for them? Are there no blessings to be had by them where they can't but reach out at them and grab them? Why don't they just humble themselves? Why don't they just pray? Why don't they just look back to the old paths, and the highway of holiness and the truths housed in the faithful providence of God's fatherly kindness of the days of old? Why can't they give up their parades and puppet shows? Why must they gut their confessions? Why must they change God's worship to look like the world? Why can't they just do what God says in his word?

One cannot look back to the Old Testament and say those things because they apply to the New Testament church too, and are being experience in this very day. When will the church learn? Will they desire the old ways? Will these contemporary Christians humble themselves and pray and seek God's face in confession with conviction? Will they humbly make a tally of their abominations before God and confess their sins? Will they confess them sincerely, will they reform? Are they even *teachable enough* to change? The Psalmist says, "You are good, and do good; Teach me Your statutes," (Psa. 119:68). God is the Christian's teacher; what a privilege that is that he sends plagues and famine to teach them in Christ's school of affliction. The question is if they come in humble obedience to pray in order to change. They must look to the source of spiritual knowledge (Divine truth is only found in Scripture and nowhere else). Christians are ignorant in so many spiritual things because they only know in part in this life. They see things dimly here on earth, and God wants them to search out their sins, and confess even the iniquities of their fathers; he wants them to make an effort!

Humble Christians, though, strive to see Christ clearly through the Spirit's spiritual persuasion of the truth. In opposition, ignorance and indifference are destructive like a virus that replicates itself and destroys good cells to make one exceedingly sick, even to death. Ignorance is *never* Christian, nor does it show forth humility to God. What will the covenant breakers fix? How will they know what to fix? Where is their safety amidst the preachers of truth in the church if they have cast away most of God's ordinances that they are to follow?

There is a great need to be constantly taught of God, refreshed in Gospel truths that Christians may grow in grace and the knowledge of Jesus. Such is the very prayer of the Christian in humble submission to God in confessing his sins so that Christ will be glorified and reformation may occur and the church changed.

The church may certainly have a Bible in their pews or their hands and still have blinders on their eyes. Such a knowledge is not saving, nor transforming in the eternal sense, for those people. Such a blindness in spiritual things shows emphatically, that they do not have the Spirit, and they are not spiritually minded. As Lamentations says, they "wandered blind in the streets," (Lam. 4:14). What will stop the plague for them? We'll just ride it out and social distance because it will take care of itself in the long run, the atheist says. Professors of this kind may be able to tell others all about the substance of the Bible, but without the humble heart and a true knowledge of the word to know their sins so that they may pray. This God grants through the Spirit, yet, they have no light in them if they are void of it. Where is all the humble prayer? Where are all the Christians taking the word and forming it into an argument and sending it up to heaven so God will be stirred to remember his ailing people? Or is it that the covenant breakers "just don't like the plague" and want it stopped?

The Lord Jesus saw God's house as what? He saw it as a house of prayer. God's house, his temple, is described as the house of prayer, (Luke 19:46). There covenanted

Christians come and pray together. It is the place that Christians come and confess their sins in humility to God. "It is written, "My house is a house of prayer," but you have made it a "den of thieves,"" (Luke 19:46). To oversimplify this, when people make church something else other than a house of prayer, they become thieves. Is it not interesting that God's house is not called a house of preaching or a house of doctrine or a house of ministry? Prayer is set at such a high priority in this way in the midst of the congregation because it teaches God's people about his sovereign providence over willing Christians submitting themselves to his word as those tainted with sin and in need of the blood of Jesus Christ constantly.

What do church people do at his house of prayer? They should pray. There his people met together to seek his face in humility and confession; subjugated to God for his glory and their good; ah, but, look what God has done in closing down your churches; and where is the prayer now?

Jesus explained God's house in this way. "Even them I will bring to My holy mountain, and make them joyful in My house of prayer. Their burnt offerings and their sacrifices will be accepted on My altar; For My house shall be called a house of prayer for all nations,"" (Isa. 56:7). This Scripture, speaking of Gospel times, speaks of people coming together from all around the world in their respective and providentially placed geographic areas, to pray together. This is why Leviticus 26 says they come and pray in a humble frame of heart and I will hear them and remember my covenant. It is true that Christians pray daily at home. They pray alone in their closets as instructed. They pray in the little churches of their home. But they most desire to pray in big meeting houses at stated prayer meetings, together at the gates of Zion; God loves to hear them there. What does that say for those churches who, 1) don't pray together because people just aren't interested, or 2) they don't pray because they have only a little turnout from their congregation at prayer meetings. "It is written, "My house shall be called a house of prayer,"" (Matt. 21:13). The humble church comes together to pray, and that not only regularly, but especially in times of occasional repentance. If churches are not humbly praying in confession of their sins to amendment of life, how could they be called churches; God's gathered and called out ones? Part of the five marks of a godly church is: sound worship and sound doctrine; both of those include a hearty section on prayer as a means of grace.[2]

Do not be fooled, when Christians don't gather together, well, not to be trite, simply, *they don't gather together.* They do not *assemble* as instructed and commanded. They are to be wise, yet, when they can't gather, or do not gather, there is a great means of grace taken away from them, a requirement that God desires where they are to confess humbly together.

God did not say if they have good intentions, I'll remember the covenant and stop the wars, famine and plague; churches are filled with people with good intentions. They go to the church, sit in the pew, and come with merely good intentions, without any real desire or

---

[2] See my works as part of the *5 Marks* series on the church, disciples and devotions.

purpose to engage in what they will confess. Lord, forgive us for our idolatry in our church. But then never change.

We stand for the truth of God. But they have heretical material in their foyer for people to pick up and read. Or they simply decide to take exceptions to their confession, and believe something else. We desire a purity of worship. But they have mime and parades and puppet shows and interpretive dance and choirs and worship teams and special music and poem readings and plays and skits in their church service; even women leading the church in those things. They don't *really* desire purity of worship; they are liars if they have a day of humiliation but never change; and how many denominations conducted that in light of the plague? How many Protestant churches this year celebrated Antichrist's Easter and Good Friday? They don't really want purity of worship. They don't really want to stop the plague. They just want to go back to the way things were and they are engaging in the very things he sent them the plague for in the first place! God hears that as, "We love you Lord but we don't want to do what you actually say. We're not that convicted about it. And we'll lose too many people if we take away what they like in our church. And then what, we'll not be able to pay the bills. And we'll lose the idols that we love."

God told his church that they must come humble, and with a confessing prayer, and repent, and change. Only that will stop the sword, famine and plague. Only that will cause God to remember his gracious covenant. Humble prayer in confession of *all* their sins. What Christian or church can give an excuse not to engage in that?

Fasting is not explicitly in the text. However, a kind of fasting is in the text, because it is linked to humility, which is given for the whole duty of lowering one's self into the dust. Cultivating a hunger for God, and a desire for true reformation is the heart of fasting, which is why fasting joined to prayer is powerful.

Fasting is vitally linked to humiliation before God. The aim of fasting is that the soul would be afflicted. The body is afflicted in the plague, but here the soul is voluntarily afflicted. Fasting is not famine, nor is it merely temperance in eating.

Fasting is a specific form of humility before God. It is a putting off of something in this present life which is regularly used for the Christian's life and happiness. There are various kinds of fasting, but linked to prayer, in occasional repentance, it is a spiritual application to the denial of physical sustenance. Laying aside nourishment of the body from its regular use is a sign of humility and an affliction of the soul; God blesses that in contrite spirits. "My clothing was sackcloth; I humbled myself with fasting; and my prayer would return to my own heart," (Psa. 35:13). Prayer and fasting are linked in humility. It is done in dangerous and perilous situations. When Daniel was in the lion's den in Dan. 6:18, Darius fasted. How about a worldwide *plague,* is that dangerous and perilous? It is used for approaching danger, Esther 4:16 and the eradication of the Jews by Haman, where they fasted and sought God. How about a *plague* that is an approaching danger? It is used for a demonstration of humiliation to God. Moses said, "And I fell down before the LORD, as at the first, forty days and forty nights; I neither ate bread nor drank water, because of all your sin which you committed in doing wickedly in the sight of the LORD, to provoke Him to anger," (Deut. 9:18). It was a habitual practice by those who professed to love God by John's disciples, Matt. 9:14; by Anna, Luke 2:37; by Cornelius, Acts 10:30; by Paul, 2 Cor. 6:5; 11:27. Even by hypocrites who pretend to love God such as the Pharisees did, Matt. 9:14; Mark 2:18; Luke 18:12.

Fasting is used in light of humiliation, confession and the affliction of the soul in prayer. Keep it simple, fasting in humility supercharges prayer in extraordinary circumstances supernaturally by the Spirit. Why extraordinary? People would die if they don't eat. It can't be done all the time.

What is its purpose? Having more of God than just having things that God can provide; cultivating a hunger for him, generally speaking. It surrounds spiritual power and enablement in the Spirit to pray effectively. It surrounds the coming of the Kingdom. It surrounds true spiritual power. This is why fasting is called in Scripture, *afflicting the soul.* Power in affliction? "Why have we fasted," they say, "and You have not seen? Why have we afflicted our souls," (Isa. 58:3)? Humility and self-denial are specifically tied to this idea of fasting. Fasting cultivates that self-denial. It is critically attached to prayer in times of occasional repentance. The Spirit uses that affliction to make prayer *more effectual.* "The effectual, fervent prayer of a righteous man avails much," (James 5:16). How much more in times like these when fasting is attached to it?

There are myriads of Biblical examples of fasting and prayer linked together. Ezra, "So we fasted and entreated our God for this, and He answered our prayer," (Ezra 8:23). David, "My clothing was sackcloth; I humbled myself with fasting; and my prayer would return to my own heart," (Psa. 35:13). Daniel, "Then I set my face toward the Lord God to make request by prayer and supplications, with fasting, sackcloth, and ashes," (Dan. 9:3). Paul, "that you may give yourselves to fasting and prayer," (1 Cor. 7:5). Robert Leighton said, "Fasting, which is a necessary help of prayer, unclogs and frees the wings of the soul to fly to heaven."[3] So, be reminded, that the fruit of humility before God in times of occasional repentance, such as the plague, is holy prayer and fasting towards a reformation of the church.

The goal of humble prayer and fasting is your amendment of life and your church's reformation. Biblical Reformation will be only accomplished through the Word of God and what Christ as the Great Prescription prescribes; it will never happen any other way. It will never happen in exceptions to historic Christian doctrine. It will never happen in mediocre Christianity. It will never happen if you or your church ever compromise on the truth. God is "in" no compromise. Then you might say, "well if that's the case, God is in few churches because most churches compromise somewhere." I'd answer, *you have it right*, and is that not a sad thing to have a church profess God, and yet compromise to force him out of the sanctuary, in fact, to close it down. It is seen in the very plague, now famine, now political unrest, now assault of morals, across the face of the whole earth.

---

[3] Leighton, Robert, *The Whole Works of Robert Leighton*, Volume 3, (London: Hatchard and Son, 1830) 48.

The things that interest a theologically disinterested contemporary American church is not right worship, and it's not conformity to God's Law. There is too much "Jesus loves me this I know because my heart tells me so." "I know it's right worship because it feels so good." "I know it's a good church because the pastor is friendly. I know it is God-honoring because so many other people feel the same way I do."

What is amendment of life? What is reformation by the word? It is to be chastened, admonished or corrected by the Bible, and to conform to that chastening, that correction or that admonition. To reject that is to have a form of religion while denying its power; to have a worship service but fill it up with "stuff."

You could have a big church building – one of a kind. Grander than the Mega church with its restaurants, coffee shops and snack bars, or the Crystal Cathedral with its towering glimmers and columns of glass. You can have it looking its best. You can have an affinity of agreeableness, to think religion is important with stuff in the church, yet be *utterly devoid* of Christ's power. What shall we do to be more spiritual in this time of plague? Paint the sanctuary? Get some new carpet. Install new pews; add a new sound system or whatnot. Those things are not bad in and of themselves, but not now; that is not what the church needs. Covenant breaking by the church is linked to religious syncretism, the mixing of unbiblical elements with elements of God's worship. Yet remember, to mix worship in this way is to *destroy it*. Religious people can have a zeal without knowledge like this; the question is ... do you? People can be religious and not ever see any hint of biblical reformation leading them back to the Word of God; do you see that leading? People all over the world are religious, but that does not mean God is pleased nor does it mean he accepts their worship, nor does it mean he's "in" it. People in America are so used to what they want, they forget and are numbed to what God's commands are, or simply, they've never learned them. It's sad that I could not have merely said to you, "let's have a day of humiliation, fasting and prayer and stop the plague." But, who knows what any of that *actually means?* Churches don't think that way. And even if they do something like have a fast, or pray, most of their people have a shallow understanding, or no idea, what that actually means; they just go along with what everyone else is doing. Many churches have religious instructors who can teach people how a person can have purpose in 40 days, or how one can pray a magic prayer and increase their borders like Jabez did; but reformation and amendment of life in searching out the church's sins, is only going to be accomplished through holding the Word in humility. There are no shortcuts to reformation. Pithy quotes, magic prayers; corporate strategies for the church do not matter to God. They are satanic distractions formulated by a cunning devil in his attempt to neutralize the power of God in the church at large; and God has sent a plague, famine, sword as a result of their acquiescence. It does not matter how popular or charismatic a preacher may be in the 21st century, and how many people he can persuade to visit his church. How many popular preachers are there across the United States alone and how degraded has the country become without so much as even a ripple of revival across the nation? In fact, it's quite the opposite; God has closed their doors and sent them a plague, and now the beginnings of famine and political unrest have started and heightened in America. Who would have thought? And people think they are being blessed where "Ichabod – the glory has departed," has been written across their church doors, and they don't even know it; yet their doors are closed. Do you think the devil wants those doors open? He will try to keep them shut as long as he can.

When Josiah had his reformation, after hearing the law read, he read Leviticus 26, what did he do? He was struck down in lamentation and bitter weeping, he tore his clothes. He lamented almost immoderately. Sackcloth? Ashes? Isn't that overdoing it a bit? Not remotely. After his repentance, he made the people gather and covenant together. He pressed them to be careful to do all that is written in the word. Such an amendment of life is always joined to a solemn resolve to continue to follow God's Word.

Would it not be foolish for the church today to have a time of solemn prayer, fasting and humiliation, and not change? It's not only foolish, but plain stupid. Play the hypocrite, God says, you want to continue to neglect my word, you want to continue to worship me falsely, I'll cover half your country in the midst of your adulterous religious celebration with a disastrous storm, that stretches across from the North to the South, kill more than 3 dozen people, cause homelessness, more famine, more difficulty, no power to millions, no money for those out of work so no recourse against it, the other half of the country I'll divide up, and I'll send half of them into a fresh deep freeze, and a third I'll cause severe drought. Multiple denominations had a Papist Good Friday day of humiliation.[4] What did their prayer and day of humiliation do, done in the wrong way? Amos 3:6, "Is there any evil in the city, and I have not done it, saith the Lord?"

The 1647 Westminster Confession of Faith says, "A lawful oath is a part of religious worship, wherein, upon just occasion, the person swearing solemnly calls God to witness what he asserts, or promises, and to judge him according to the truth or falsehood of what he swears." Will they swear to amend and reform? Will they vow on it upon pain of death? Will *you* swear and vow to change for the better? Deuteronomy 10:20, "You shall fear the LORD your God; you shall serve Him, and to Him you shall hold fast, and take oaths in His name."

Such a solemn resolve in humility, by prayer and fasting before God, in godly worship, confessing the church's sins is the only real catalyst for reformation. Where do we find the follow through past good intentions? In churches all across the globe today the solemn setting apart, or covenanting, has been abandoned because failure to uphold the covenant would result in discipline, and discipline is just not something trendy pastors want to get involved with. Churches don't feel safe by installing some kind of vow to covenant obligations. Keeping the peace is much more important, than amendment of life in the church because keeping the peace in a church keeps the members happy and pays the bills. It keeps the people in the church. Because it is so easy to not

---

[4] In the current news, all these things happened in the course of the "Easter Weekend."

like something the pastor said or did, and simply walk down the street to another church. Don't require too much of the people, don't have them commit themselves too much at church, and keep them placated and happy so they don't leave.

Without a solemn vow to God in the things of religion, it's just talk; it's just religiosity; it's not humility with fasting and prayer. Your theology must incorporate Christ's prescription for holiness, otherwise it is eternally useless. "...to follow the LORD and to keep His commandments and His testimonies and His statutes..." But HOW? With all your heart and soul! How could you or your church truly be on the road of reformation by humility, prayer and fasting in this time of occasional repentance without a solemn resolve, a fruit of humility, to uphold the Word of God towards amendment of life? "I'm not going to make any promises Lord, but, I'll do my best. You can count on that." *Wink, wink.* That's not holy tenderness in humility. Francis Whiddon, one of my favorite writers of the Westminster Assembly said, "He that has such holy tenderness in him will readily yield to God's precepts. Whatever God commands, he will do it circumspectly; warily and with solemn attention."[5] Would it be that we would *all* do it.

Such an amendment of life resolved in humility through prayer and fasting is always a thorough reformation. It is an oxymoron to say "partial reformation". What is partial reformation? It's nothing! In any

---

[5] Whiddon, Francis, *A Golden Topaz, or Heart-Jewel, Namely, a Conscience Purified and Pacified by the Blood and Spirit of Christ*, (Coconut Creek, FL: Puritan Publications, 2012), section on <u>Holy Tenderness</u>.

sanctifying act you must have a hearty resolve to thoroughly change, or its hypocrisy; confession without change is nothing but sin. One cannot "kinda have" reformation. "I want chastity," says Augustine, "but not yet." (Before his conversion). I want to change, and change a little, but not in every area. Think repentance – is it just confession of sin? No, it's sight of sin, sorrow, shame, confessing, hating, and turning from it. "I'm only going to take care of some things, but not all things Lord." "The church thinks, I am not resolved, just yet, to take care of it all, but I will do some of it; some is better than nothing right?" Churches say – "we want to worship God, but let's add all this other stuff, so that we can attract more people to the church and make it entertaining; what will that hurt, we'll get people in the door?" Religious syncretism of this kind has always been the downfall of the church. It was God's quarrel with his people in his covenant in Lev. 26. God alone determines the manner in which sinners are to approach him, that's why he's sent the plague, and famine.

The church, through a thorough humiliation, fasting, prayer and confession, must look to reform everything, immediately. Why immediately? Such will stop the plague, stop the locusts, stop the economic distress, *etc.* Because gradual reformation is intolerable to God. It's tiresome to God to hear his people say, "I want holiness but not yet." Anything less than full reformation is hypocrisy. It is not reformation – it is compromise.

What are the hindrances to your humble confession, prayer and fasting? I'll give you four hindrances to avoid in your church's humble confession of sin in prayer.

The Hindrance of Sin. You cannot walk contrary to God and his word then expect him to listen to you. Blessings are attached to God's covenant and they are stifled by sin, which is God's quarrel with his church. Again, and again, and again, carnal men cannot stop the plague. And, Christian men cannot stop the plague unless they take the remedy that Christ the Physician gives them. It cannot merely be a going through the motions.

The Hindrance of Insincerity. One does not have faith exercised in the right way to pray something he does not believe will come to pass. This could also be called a hindrance of hypocrisy. Will you change, will the church change if needs be? You might be thinking, I'm just waiting for all this be over so I can get back to normal. Well, if that's the case, you need King Jesus to save you. You do not have the things of God in mind and have missed the point of God's judgment on the whole world.

The Hindrance of Confusion. What should I pray for? Well, what have you searched out? What have you considered? What sins are you involved with? What sins is your church involved with? The word will direct you.

The Hindrance of Being Lukewarm. Cold prayers always freeze before they get to heaven. Christ does not want his people luke-warm, or cold, but on fire. He wants them zealous. I'm sure there were some people in Leviticus 26 that moaned and groaned over their humiliation that needed to occur. What good would they have gathered out of moaning over God's means to restore them?

Is your amendment of life from a humble heart, proceeding out of a submissive prayer and affliction of soul? It is dangerous to be left in any part of our duty to ourselves. Duty in your own hands is a terrible thought to Christians. Imagine if God said to you as he said to the church of old, "Ephraim is joined to idols, let him alone." I'm not going to help them because they aren't sincere and they are knee deep in their sins and they don't really care; so I will leave them there. Doing things in our own strength, not relying on the Spirit of God having tasted that the Lord is good is a scary proposition. We ought to have no desire to work any work without Christ's help. He's the one who sends the Spirit to produce fruit in us.

Humility ought to be your whole disposition to God; you pray to him, boldly coming to Christ for grace, the ascended Son of Man and high Priest, and then you resolve to walk as becoming a Christian, every day, all the time as your Lord instructs. Will you die for Christ in holy submission, so to speak, as Christ died for you to do the Father's will that you be saved? You are not only instructed by Christ to follow him, but also, Jesus says that unless you bear his cross, you can have no part in him; your life is to be characterized in humility. Amendment of life, constantly, is part of what it means to enter into covenant with God. This is God's right over you yielding to him, or your humility to him. He is look for you to be humble, pray and fast to seek out his favor and grace through Christ.

It is a far sweeter thing to obey Christ and taste the kisses of his mouth which is much more sweeter than wine, as the bride who yields to her husband in all things, than to rebel against him; having the omnipotent God in quarrel against you and his church is a frightful thing. It comes in plagues and wars and famines of various kinds. The Fruit of humble submission to God is prayer and fasting with amendment of life both in you as an individual and in your church. In these, all Christians are resolved.

Do you expect, then, spiritual revival? Do you expect personal reformation to occur? Do you expect to see something spiritually grand occur in your church and among your people, among the church in America? In the world? I do. I hope you do. But, will God withhold reformation and continue the layers of difficulty? Will he add to it famine? Will he add to it more natural disasters? Half the country experienced tornadic activity where a three-dozen died, with other catastrophes on top of that. There is a great duty to press into amendment of life, confession, repentance, humility, prayer, fasting for the plague to be stopped. If there is no reformation it gets worse. This was the doctrine of Stephen Marshall's work we published a few years ago, called, "Reformation, or Desolation." You *cannot put up with* compromising ministers, or bad preaching, or unbiblical worship, or poor theology, or a hundred other problems in the modern church and expect God to act in the midst of a people to stop the plague, sword or famine. It cannot be done; God will not allow it. There must be a humbling of ourselves before King Jesus who is commanding his coronavirus to covenant breakers right now. He is pressing the whole world very low. Don't listen to the atheists who hate God and just murmur, these things will pass, we'll get through it when it runs their course.

Do you follow the pattern of the Christ in humility?

He was zealous for God's honor and name at every point of his entire earthly existence. John 2:17, "Then His disciples remembered that it was written, "Zeal for Your house has eaten Me up." They could see it in his resolve, in his mission, in his desire to see his church reformed. His disciples saw it in his life, teaching, zeal, miracles, death, resurrection, and knew it continued in his present intercession. And in his present intercession he's sent the rod to his church; and it isn't even the hammer (more on that later). Christ is the great radical where you in all humility must be pressed down and squeezed for the honor of God's name and worship.

But as tender as Christ is, as he will not break a bruised reed or quench the smoking flax, though he carries his people tenderly in his arms, "So then, because you are lukewarm, and neither cold nor hot, I will vomit you out of My mouth," (Rev. 3:16). Jesus is a harsh; zealous, radical, humble, obedient reformer. Humphry Hardwicke (Westminster Divine) in his work on Reformation, said, the church "must be willing to do what they can to help themselves, to carry on the work of reformation to the uttermost; and you have a requisite willingness to remove and part with all things which may hinder perfect reformation."[6]

What hinders your perfect reformation that God requires? Rid yourself of it. There will be myriads of churches all across the world that will not change. There must be plowing, sowing, planting, a humble prayerful affliction of the soul in you and the church if a work of full

---

[6] Hardwicke, Humphry, *The Precious Seeds of Reformation*, (Coconut Creek, FL: Puritan Publications, 2015) 32.

reformation will ever be brought about. Have you ever been in a church where God was pleased to allow his Spirit to break out in a spiritual revival? The church is primed for it right now. Did Christ purchase so little for you that You are content to have so little reformation in your life? Does he not want abundant life for you in the Spirit? Is it not interesting that in historical accounts in church history, even biblical ones, of the Holy Spirit falling on the church toward amendment of life, and the return of covenant breakers, surrounds two things – conformity to the word, and affliction of soul? How will the plague be stopped? Now, how will the plague, political unrest, and famine be stopped? Now, how long will it be until the plague and the beginning of famine and financial ruin be stopped? Is God ready with pen in hand to write your name down in his book as a reformer? And your church as a catalyst for reformation? Conformity to the word, and affliction of soul in repentant humility with fasting and prayer. Our lives are to be given over to Jesus wholly, completely and without reservation. This is what is expected of you if humility is worked to bear fruit in real spiritual revival. Then, the plague will be stopped.

The fruit of humility before God in times of occasional repentance such as the plague is holy prayer and fasting towards an amendment or reformation of the church, ... with zeal.

Chapter 5:
Humility and Godly Zeal

"As many as I love, I rebuke and chasten: be zealous therefore, and repent," (Rev. 3:19).

By way of reminder, let's recap Revelation. This book was written by the Apostle John, in a type of language used all throughout the 22 chapters of the book, called "Apocalyptic Literature." This unique style of writing was not foreign to the readers in John's day, those 1st century Christians. No, there are no such things as big red dragons. No, there are so such things as large chains that can wrap around Satan, an immaterial being. No, there is no woman big enough who really sits on seven hills. No, there is no Lamb, an animal, that is able to open sealed documents. Revelation is written in fantastical language, *i.e.* apocalyptic language. Other books of the bible have this kind of language and imagery, such as Daniel (where the Christ is found in the courtroom of God with books and attendees riding on his glory cloud), as well as such visual portrayals in portions of Joel, Amos and Zechariah. There are real truths in those places conveyed in a fantastical manner, while producing a sacred meaning.

Revelation emphasizes the fight of the church militant against the world, the flesh and the devil, the establishment of the Christian faith in Christ, and the ultimate triumph of Christ over all his enemies. The theme of the entire book of Revelation points to the intention of the author. It is a covenant document from God himself involving a divorce from Israel, and the establishment of the Christian church in Christ. The Bible is a covenant document, from beginning to end, demonstrating God's establishment of true religion in the Messiah, the Christ. This is why Covenant Theology in its central message is set in the context of the work of the Trinity in bringing himself glory in redeeming a church out of the mass perdition to be his covenant bride.

The book of Revelation is *structured* as a covenant document. The number seven, for example, is used 54 times in the book. It is the number of "covenant." In the opening of the book, we find it written to the 7 churches and has: Seven Spirits (Rev. 1:4, 3:1, 4:5, 5:6) Seven candlesticks (Rev. 1:12, 13, 20; 2:1) Seven stars (Rev. 1:16, 20; 2:1, 3:1) Seven lamps (Rev. 4:5) Seven seals (Rev. 5:1, 5:5) Seven horns (Rev. 5:6), *etc.* John intended his book to be an opening up of divine truth for his original audience that meant something specific to his readers in covenanting with God's Christ. This covenant was made in Christ's blood; "even they who pierced Him," (Rev. 1:7). And judgment and warning come against the generation, or tribe, that pierced Christ, "Assuredly, I say to you, this generation will by no means pass away till all these things take place," (Matt. 24:34). "And all the tribes of the earth will mourn because of Him."

Revelation also holds eager expectation of things to occur. Rev. 1:1, shortly; Rev. 2:16, quickly; Rev. 3:11, quickly; Rev. 22:6, shortly; Rev. 22:7, 12, 20, quickly, quickly, quickly. John clearly expected the imminent occurrence of the events of Revelation. What is the occurrence? It is a certificate of divorce from Israel and the setting up of the way of Christ; that the scroll in Revelation

5 would be a bill of divorce. "And I saw in the right hand of Him who sat on the throne a scroll written inside and on the back, sealed with seven seals," (Rev. 5:1). Covenant seals where all manner of judgment flows forth as the seals were broken. Revelation depicts two women opposed to one another. The wicked harlot of the beast (Rev. 17-18) versus the pure bride of Christ, (Rev. 21). The earthly Jerusalem, where Christ was pierced (Rev. 11:8) versus the heavenly Jerusalem, which is holy, pure and undefiled, because it is covered by the blood of Jesus Christ, (Rev. 21:10). Christ divorces the harlot and takes on the bride. Ezekiel 16 prophetically shows Israel as God's covenant wife who became a harlot. "Son of man, cause Jerusalem to know her abominations," (Ezek. 16:2). In contrast, the new bride comes from heaven (Rev. 21-22). She comes out of the covenant work of the Messiah. She comes out of the Covenant of Redemption between the Father, Son and Spirit.

The main image found in this covenant document of the Revelation of Jesus Christ is "the blood, the crucified one, the Slain Lamb." Christ's blood is that which gives victory to his church. In Revelation there are 52 references to the cross of Christ throughout the book. They utilize a wide range of visual images and circumstances to describe the manner in which sinners have been redeemed in God's covenant and how that redemption surrounds the death of the One who is worthy to establish them by his death, resurrection, ascension and present intercession and reign.

In Revelation 3:14-22, we find the "AMEN," the Word of the Christ, to Laodicean church. Apart from this text, the name Laodicea occurs only in Colossians (Col.

4:13). Antiochus II (261–246 B.C.) fortified the earlier city of Diospolis as a Seleucid outpost between 261 and 253 B.C., naming it after his wife or sister, Laodice. "The city was called "Laodicea on the Lycus" to distinguish it."[1] It was near Colosse, where it may be that Epaphras was the minister preaching to it in Laodicea (Col. 1:7; 4:12–13). Paul had sent a letter to this church, and he requested that the Colossians arrange that their letter be read in the church of the Laodiceans and they in turn read the Laodiceans' letter (Col. 4:16).

The proclamation to Laodicea is given in Rev. 3:14–22, where it is addressed to the angel of the church in Laodicea (verse 14a). There is a command to write (verse 14a) Christ speaks to her (verse 14b), He who is the Amen. the faithful and true witness, the very *origin* of God's creation. "I know your conduct" (verses 15–17). The "cold" and "hot" metaphors (verses 15–16) are found here. You are neither "cold" nor "hot" (verse 15a). I wish you were either "cold" or "hot" (verse 15b). I will vomit you from my mouth (verse 16) because you are halfhearted, indifferent, unenthusiastic, apathetic, and lackadaisical. Because they are neither "cold" nor "hot" the church will be thrown up. The water supply for Laodicea came from a distance of six miles at Hierapolis by way of an aqueduct. Its sources were hot water springs; when the water arrived in Laodicea, it was lukewarm. Christ compares the lukewarm waters near the city to the lukewarm spiritual life of the Laodiceans.

---

[1] Aune, David E., Revelation 1–5, Vol. 52A, *Word Biblical Commentary* (Dallas: Word, Incorporated, 1997), 249.

They had a false view of life. Their imagined condition was "I am wealthy (verse 17a) I have become rich (verse 17a) I need nothing (verse 17a)." Their true condition is set within denouncing them (verse 17b) "You are wretched. You are pitiable. You are poor. You are blind. You are naked." Interestingly, Christ uses shopping metaphors (verse 18) here. Buy purified gold from me that you might be rich. Buy white garments from me that you might be clothed, that the shame of your nakedness might not be public. Buy medication from me to apply to your eyes to regain your sight.

The exhortation to repent is set in looking at how Christ deals with his people (verse 19). "Those whom I love (verse 19a) I chastise." "I discipline." Because of this love (verse 19b), because I love you my church in this way, be "zealous, repent."

The metaphor of a visitor is found in verse 20. The visitor calls: I stand before the door knocking (verse 20a); a visitor, not a resident. Will the church acknowledge him? Do they hear him knocking (verse 20b)? "If any one hears my voice If any one opens the door." If the Christ is admitted into his church (verse 20b) he will come in to visit him (verse 20c) will sup with him. He will share a meal with him (verse 20c); this is very gracious in light of their position.

Then we find the victory of Christ and those he sups with (verse 21). They will sit with me on my throne (verse 21a). Just as I sat down with my Father on his throne (verse 21b). The proclamation formula (verse 22) is then given, and the "Amen" conveys the idea of that which is true, firmly established, and trustworthy. Jesus takes this

Hebrew title as "the God of Amen," "the God of truth" (Isa. 65:16; compare 2 Cor. 1:20) for himself and interprets it in the next clause as "the faithful and true witness" against these things.

If the Laodiceans had never heard the Gospel, they would have been cold in a spiritual sense. But this church is *warmish*. They had little to no interest in godly things. Interesting that Jesus looks at these people *as his church* and warns them, a place that most stalwart reformed Christians today would not even visit. Jesus stands outside their door and knocks for them to answer if they hear him. They have their bible, yet, they were apathetic, indifferent, and unconcerned about the things which the AMEN of God cares about. Jesus said, "I know your works," with the inference that there were none; they were a church, though, doing churchly things. "So because you are lukewarm and neither hot nor cold, I am about to vomit you out of my mouth." Does the AMEN of God have any interest at all with lukewarm Christianity? None. Why? Because it is worthless rubbish; there are no good works in it.

Christ's desire is to ignite the church by the power of the Holy Spirit and work with a bride that is set ablaze with supernatural vitality to work righteousness in his sight. Lukewarm water laced with calcium carbonate induces vomiting. Covenanted Professing believers who are void of spiritual works are to be vomited out. Make a note here, though, they are *not yet* spewed out. There is much grace in the work of Christ for his church. His will corrects them, chastens them, instructs them, and warns them. He does not want them to be utterly ineffective as a church. His church is to be Spirit-filled and Spirit-enlivened.

These Laodiceans were infected with Ephraim's malady. "And Ephraim said, Yet I am become rich, I have found me out substance: in all my labours they shall find none iniquity in me that were sin," (Hosea 12:8). And what, these people, this church, does not need anything from the Origin of creation itself? To be self-sufficient is idolatry. It is worship of self. So, Christ says to them, those whom I love I reprove and discipline. Be zealous, therefore, and repent. These are taken from Proverbs 3:12 and also demonstrated in Heb. 12:6, "Because the LORD disciplines those he loves." "Those whom I love," to show that love and discipline go together in a humble repentance before God for those who have been brought back to him.

What is his prescription in all this? It is the same prescription as he said before about how Physicians treat sick people, (Luke 5:31-32). They are to see their sin, and repent. But he adds here to the church, a new quality. "Be zealous, therefore, and repent." The healing of this covenant breach is made by being zealous, and repenting. Zeal is a necessary part of true love for God.

Christ is there waiting for his church to repent in the metaphor of knocking. It's not to the world he says this, but to his people. He stands at the door and even knocks at the church. He is currently shut out of the spiritual life of the Laodicean church. They've driven him out (much like the churches of America today) though they think they are fine. He would like to come in, but they have *forced* him out. Will they hear him knocking? Will they even know it is a knock they hear? What chastening will they need to endure for him to wake them up? He loves them so intently that he will rebuke and chasten them, stand at the door and knock for them, and wait for them, and promise all kinds of blessings in what he prescribes.

Here now is the point, how quickly will they perceive this is happening to them? How zealous will they be in this? Do they have the spiritual optics to know what's going on? Will they come to themselves quickly and repent quickly and open the door quickly? Will they find the beloved standing at the door knocking? Will they wait too long and need to go searching for him? And there is again the Evangelical grace "If anyone hears my voice and opens the door, I will come in to him and I will dine with him and he with me." Jesus desires to fellowship with his church, do they desire to fellowship with him? Will they be overcomers? Will they rule and reign with him? Will they receive Christ's message of praise, rebuke and promise?

The DOCTRINE: the exercise of humility before God in times of occasional repentance for the reformation of the church, is to be done zealously for King Jesus. Take everything learned so far in these last four chapters, and place it in the context of zeal; covenant breaking, repentance, godly humility, prayer with fasting and confession of sin, and now add zeal. Can any Christian duty or work be done without it?

The church should be zealous, the Greek word ζήλωσον (Rev. 3:19), and they should burn with fire, the word itself *meaning* to burn. What does that mean? Hot? Burn? Ablaze? What does *that* mean? Jesus is directly instructing the church to be zealous and he's quite serious about it. What does being zealous to King Jesus mean during a time of occasional repentance, during a plague or famine or sword because of his chastening to the church? What does that actually mean or what does that look like? He says don't be lukewarm. The water traveling from one point far away from the city towards the city made the water warm, and its warmth with the calcium carbonite in it makes a person puke. Jesus doesn't like that taste in his mouth. What is hot water in this light? How is one to be zealous in this way, in a church-chastening, in a church rebuke, by humbled Christians looking to make amendment with God and have their covenant blessings restored?

There is a very famous picture of what this looks like in Numbers 25:6-11, which I was torn to use as a main text for this chapter.

> "And, behold, one of the children of Israel came and brought unto his brethren a Midianitish woman in the sight of Moses, and in the sight of all the congregation of the children of Israel, who were weeping before the door of the tabernacle of the congregation. And when Phinehas, the son of Eleazar, the son of Aaron the priest, saw it, he rose up from among the congregation, and took a javelin in his hand; And he went after the man of Israel into the tent, and thrust both of them through, the man of Israel, and the woman through her belly. So the plague was stayed from the children of Israel. And those that died in the plague were twenty and four thousand. And the LORD spake unto Moses, saying, Phinehas, the son of Eleazar, the son of

Aaron the priest, hath turned my wrath away from the children of Israel, while he was zealous for my sake among them, that I consumed not the children of Israel in my jealousy," (Num. 25:6-11).

Sin was in the church and the narrative explains the church's failure on the border of the land at Shittim. There, they were involved with Moabite women, and, inevitably, with Moabite cults, religious syncretism, mixing worship with things that are not worship, mixing the world with worship – God sent a plague to correct them. They did this with things connected with Baal. God tells Moses, "execute the offenders;" imagine if we *implied* such a thing today to execute all those in violation of Scripture. Adulterous worship to God is a capital offense in God's book; it is deserving of death and eradication – how many churches would be left standing today who are deviant in their worship? But, in relaying this information, the historical narrative turns to the specific sin of an Israelite Zimri, and a Midianite woman Cozbi. It seems there was a marriage arranged, but Phinehas son of Eleazar, the priest, takes the initiative upon hearing this judgment of God against this sin, and kills them both in the woman's shrine by thrusting a javelin through them. Phinehas is also noted in Psalm 106, the one who killed Zimri, who had entered into this marital relationship with Cozbi, and who together were engaged in wicked and sinful observances at a Baal shrine. God sends a plague, it starts to kill people in the camp, and Phinehas, zealously takes charge of the incident; this incident is written with a pen of iron, inscribed in Scripture for all time – Phinehas and his zeal are noted by the Holy Spirit. God writes it down in Scripture and says, "And he went after the man of Israel into the tent, and thrust both of them through, the man of Israel, and the woman through her belly. So the plague was stayed from the children of Israel." Make note here, just of the moment, the plague was stopped by Phinehas' zeal and the execution of just judgment. Interestingly, the word used of Phinehas' just judgment, or intervention, is the word for prayer. As if the action was interposed with prayer, or a kind of intervention on behalf of the people; an interceding, as a priest intercedes on behalf of the people before God. It screams loudly towards a very practical application to this as it is considered: can you stop the plague? Can your church alone stop the plague? Ah, but I digress, I forgot, the church is closed right now; such a question may not even be practical at this time. "And those that died in the plague were twenty and four thousand." Not as many as the coronavirus, "And the LORD spake unto Moses, saying, Phinehas, the son of Eleazar, the son of Aaron the priest, hath turned my wrath away from the children of Israel, while he was zealous for my sake among them, that I consumed not the children of Israel in my jealousy," (Num. 25:8-11). The word here, *zealous*, means *envious for God's name*, even *jealous* for it; intervening, in fact, praying, so to speak; which is why God said he was jealous for his name. Jesus said, *be zealous*, to the Laodicean church, envious for God's name, repent, and so, what is bound up in that? Humility, confession in prayer, repentance, zeal and such things; they all fall on top of one another, like a layered cake. The removal of the cause takes away the effect, and here the execution of judgement

129

removes God's anger; this has happened in other scriptural places. While Achan lives, Israel is troubled; stone Achan to death, burn the accursed wedge of gold, the silver, and the Babylonian garment, "and the Lord turns from the fierceness of his anger," (Joshua 7:26). While Jonah is in the ship, the, "sea rages," casts him overboard, and there the sea is calmed (Jonah 1:15). Will zealous justice, impartially considered, stop this plague today?

Holy zeal (ζῆλος) is found throughout all of Scripture, though it may not be found throughout all of Christendom today. It is to be a common, basic, religious characteristic found in every true Christian believer, imitating God's jealous desire for purity, but it is not found in connection to holiness in many professing churches, though Christ commands it, "be zealous and repent." The bible speaks about holy zeal repeatedly and gives dozens of examples of Christians who exemplified such genuine distinguishing behavior. Moses was zealous for God, as was Phinehas, Joshua, Gideon, Jephthah, Samuel, David, Elijah, Obadiah, Jehoash, Asa, Hezekiah, Josiah, Ezra, Nehemiah, Jeremiah, the Shepherds who heard the angel's announcement, Anna, Andrew and Philip, and many others. Notably, consider all that the Apostle Paul wrote about this subject which was extensive in seven letters to the churches.

Zeal means being vigorous in the work accomplished, as in the Hebrew word קִנְאָה (*qinah*), meaning to have jealousy about it. It is joined with the idea of *God's jealousy for his holiness*. It is *solemnly* guarded. "Zeal is a mixed affection, it consists partly of love, and partly of indignation; and so when I am zealous of a thing,

I love that thing, and shake off and hate all that ... hinders it." Thomas Manton said rightly.[2]

God desires his people to understand that in relationship to holy action, such an action must be constant, and zealous relative to God's constant zeal in remaining consistent with his nature. "I am the LORD: that is my name: and my glory will I not give to another, neither my praise to graven images," (Isa. 42:8). God is fiercely protective of his nature, rights and possessions, and so must the Christian be. Christ commands it, and requires it of his church, "be zealous and repent."

Zeal is a heart enflamed for the things of Christ. It is a non-negotiable command that makes a difference between the world and the believing Christian. It shows a difference between hypocritical covenant breakers, and all true Christians. Where are all the Phinehas' today? Are they all Laodiceans instead?

It is the duty of every Christian to be zealous for Jesus Christ. The heart of the Christian is to be heated with great fervency for the honor of God's name and nature, and the means of grace by which he should grow more into the image of Jesus Christ. It is to be important to them. Do churches believe this? Where is the evidence of this, during the plague when their churches are closed? Where is the spiritual javelin striking sin at its center and purging it from the life of the church that the plague be stopped? Where are all those like Phinehas today? Are we plagued more, by luke-warm Laodiceans in the church? Are minister's in Christ's church more like the Laodiceans,

---

[2] Manton, Thomas, *One Hundred and Fifty Sermons on Several Texts of Scripture*, Volume 4, (London: J. D., 1693), 185.

compromisers, than zealous for his name? Where are those who are so in love with Christ that they are zealous to repent, and zealous even amidst their chastening and rebukes?

Sound repentance and godly zeal go hand in hand. John Dod said in his work, *The Affects of Sin on the Soul*, "In this way, the holy man of God (Phinehas) was touched, yes, tormented with the things by which God's glory was impaired, as if he had been laden himself with reproaches and disgraces."[3] He felt what God perfectly experiences. Such a virtue is necessary for the honor of God's name; very necessary for all Christians. It is treasured where it is found, being the very life and soul of all sound Christianity, and one of the principal roots where many other virtues of the Spirit grow and come forth. It stops plagues and satisfies God against covenant breaking judgments if exercised in faith.

The Lord Jesus in his directives to the church tells them in this regard, if you are looking for a cure, to your luke-warmness (Rev. 3:19), he instructs them, be zealous, and repent. That was their sin, that they were as cold as ice. Truly the frozen chosen, so to speak. They were hardly exercising themselves in various righteous works and godly duties. Therefore, the Lord urges them toward a reformation, directing them to be zealous, and repent to amend their lives. Such goes hand in hand, or, not at all. How is a person "kind of" zealous? This should be seen by Christ's instruction as a means to do them good during their chastening and rebuke from him. To be zealous in

---

[3] Just read that whole book!

those things he specifically requires of them in their separation from the world, and their drawing close to him.

The motive for this zeal revolves partially around being chastened and rebuked by King Jesus. The opposite of zeal is negligence; and the King does not take kindly to that. It is the omission of that which God requires of the Christian who is in his militant army while in this world. And if they stray, and if they go wayward, they are chastened in the world that they may not be condemned with the world in the end; this is even seen as a grace from Christ. It is found in Rev. 3 that those who overcome sit with the enthroned Christ to rule and reign as kings and priests with him, but only if they *overcome.* He will dine with them. He will attend them with blessings. They will sit with him on his throne. Yet only if they do not despise him and his word and will, "My son, despise not the chastening of the LORD; neither be weary of his correction: For whom the LORD loveth he correcteth; even as a father the son in whom he delighteth," (Prov. 3:11-12). In such chastening, to such churches that break his covenant and enact a quarrel against them, such a motive of chastening in this way should prompt the church to humble repentance and prayerful confession of sin.

There is a bitter cup of affliction that the church must drink if they are chastened by the Lord. No matter how bitter the cup is, which they are to drink, and in whatever way God sends such bitter affliction, the comfort is in this, that the church receives this by the command of the Christ. It is of their heavenly Father, through the Son of His love, by the power of the Spirit, that they are given a cup of affliction in whatever form. This is Christ

133

commanding his coronavirus to covenant breakers; or famine, or tornadoes, or economic disaster, or poverty, or political unrest, or all manner of affliction. "The church must confess, it is of my heavenly Father's mixing, and I am sure he would not put anything poisonous in the cup for us to drink, although it may be filled with bitterness to the taste, it will be sweet in its sanctifying affects for his church." Will you hear that on the news? Did not Christ, in all humility and obedience before God say, "The cup which my Father has given me, shall I not drink it?" (John 18:11). And though it may be bitter, and it may be a hard affliction, it is connected to Christ's love for his people.

Chastening and rebuke are connected to Christ's love for the church. "As many as I love, I rebuke and chasten." Though he loves the church, the words following here show that he requires their zeal and repentance. Yes, he loves them, and he chastens them, but he requires godly duty as a result of the rebuke. Christ shows his love for his church in being afflicted for them, but also by afflicting them that they would be better instructed in the love of God. "In all their affliction he was afflicted, and the angel of his presence saved them: in his love and in his pity he redeemed them; and he bare them, and carried them all the days of old," (Isa. 63:9).

Affliction for the church does not argue God's eternal anger against them, or an individual Christian, but a love sent from God for their good, and ultimately their sanctification. He desires to wash them thoroughly and prepare them thoroughly for the wedding banquet. He does leave his church to themselves eternally, for as many as he loves he will rebuke and chasten.

Christ has infinite love to the church, sent of an infinite Christ, and infinite work on their behalf to save them from an infinite torment in hell. His love is so infinite that it shines in places where the church is least likely to see it, such as in a famine, or a plague, or the sword. Even in some kind of judgment, he still remembers mercy in Christ. Even when the church looks to King Jesus and sees him as the roaring and revenging lion of the tribe of Judah, or the warrior on the white horse coming with glory in the clouds of heaven, even when they think about him as most angry and to be feared, when he strikes his church in chastening and affliction and rebukes, he is in fact expressing his love. He is reproving them for their sin. He is taking sin away by the power of his sanctifying Spirit. He is really sending some misery to take away the core of misery in sin; he longs for their repentance, and that they do it zealously. And this love of Christ, sent to his church, calls, then for them to be zealous in seeing this truth, to repent, and not to lose their first love. They are now obliged to love him back, wherever he shows his love to them. And it is there, that hypocrites are divided from the Christian, for if they do not find love back to him, when he loves them, even during affliction, they see themselves in the mirror of sin and wickedness, and they see they are more of a Judas than a David.

Christian zeal must be set down in the context of this love he has for them. The church sees that they do not merely love him only because he takes away the plague. Such would be mimicking the world. The world wants the plague stopped so they can get "back to normal life," as they call it. The world sees the plague just as a horrible invisible enemy. How do Christians view it? Do they view it as Christ's *love* to them? Do they view it as Christ's love to them to enact holiness? Do they see it as an evil thing that brings about a good thing? Is it a cup they desire to drink since Christ has sent it? It does not mean that things revolving around death are necessarily, in themselves, good. Christ was murdered, and that was not good, but it was the cup that the humble and obedient Savior fulfilled in the joy set before him. What will the church do?

The church must not love Christ merely for deliverance. The world loves *benefits* in that way. They must love him *for who he is*. Yet, they must also love him for what he does for them. They must love all his providences, and count them as joy, even when they face trials of many kinds, knowing that the testing of their faith produces perseverance in them.

Christ loves his people and in the midst of that love, he showers down mercies on them. This can take various forms depending on their spiritual state. He is not revenging against them in a plague. God is delivering them from sin and death through the death of his Son, who was sent to die and suffer for them. It is not a revenging act on them. That revenge was placed on the Christ at the cross for all *believers*. But what shall they think about God making the church suffer under affliction, because he afflicts them *out of so much love* in order to deliver them from some kind of sin? Does he not place zeal and repentance hand in hand in this if they see it rightly? Are both of them not set in the context of his love, which may indeed show forth rebuke and chastening to those whom he loves? David Clarkson said, "Oh he has not such a love

136

for the world, as he has for his children, when he seems most severe in afflicting them."[4] And does he not do this to churches in places that any stalwart reformed Christian would never even walk into? There are churches all over the world that sound Christians will not attend because they find some erroneous fault in their doctrine, or their worship, or their practice. Is this not an interesting thought in light of Christ's rebuke, his afflicting providences and his standing at the door of those places knocking to them? Jesus says he loves his church. Jesus says he came to die for his church. Jesus says that if they are lazy, blind, poor, naked and miserable, he will send forth his love to them *via* chastening that they may be zealous and repent. They have not depreciated into a synagogue of Satan just yet. Christ has no love for such places as the synagogues of Satan. But to his wayward church, he sends them chastenings and rebukes to wake them up and cause them to consider what it means to love Christ in affliction and be zealous to repent. Did he not look to that great city Nineveh and send his prophet Jonah to preach to them, that they would be saved? Did he not say to Jonah, "And should not I spare Nineveh, that great city, wherein are more than sixscore thousand persons that cannot discern between their right hand and their left hand; and also much cattle?" (Jonah 4:11). Does he not say to the church, I stand at the door and knock to you, and I long to come in and sup with you and you with me, if you would be zealous and repent? Jesus cares about people, he cares about his people in his church.

---

[4] Clarkson, David, *The Works of David Clarkson,* Volume 2, (Edinburgh: Banner of Truth Trust, 1988) 240.

"Be zealous," he says, or Christ will remove their candlestick from its place. Christ never promises to allow geographic churches to remain in place for all time. His promise to the continuation of the church is not tied to a specific geographic region. This was part of the point of his rebuke to these churches. How many of the seven churches that this letter was written to are still intact? Where is the Laodicean church? You can visit three of seven today. Well, you can visit three *ruins* of the seven. Sardis, Philadelphia and Thyatira have ruins of the church in modern Turkey. Does this not shed a greater light to be zealous and repent in light of that fact? What will happen to the churches around the world today that remain lazy and lukewarm? They will be vomited out of the mouth of Christ.

Consider, the zeal of Jesus Christ. There is no better instance of holy zeal found in all of Scripture than that of Jesus Christ. Zeal about Christ is mentioned in Psalm 69:9, "For the zeal of thine house hath eaten me up," where Christ was all consumed for the purity of God's worship, (John 2:17). His zeal was an excitement of mind, and fervor of spirit. The word in John 2:17, ζῆλος, (zaylos), of Christ being zealous for God's house also holds in it the fierceness of a holy indignation, and a desire to see a punitive demonstration accomplished. That God would be revenged against all that opposed his name and character. Interestingly, this occurred in the temple, in the place of worship, in the place where prayer is to be had.

Christ had an absolute zeal for the truth of the word and a desire to see God's true worship followed. Isaiah 59:17 speaks of Christ being, "clad with zeal as a cloke." Even from a young age Christ must be, "about my Father's business?" (Luke 2:49).

His ministry was characterized by zealous work for the kingdom, "And Jesus went about all Galilee, teaching in their synagogues, and preaching the Gospel of the kingdom, and healing all manner of sickness and all manner of disease among the people," (Matt. 4:23, 9:35; Mark 3:20-21, 6:6; Acts 10:38).

He said of his covenant obligations to the Father, "I must preach the kingdom of God to other cities also: for therefore am I sent," (Luke 4:43, cf. Mark 1:38; Luke 8:1, 9:51; John 4:32-34, 9:4).

He was intimately aware of his mission to come and die for the sins of his people, in which he remained zealous to the end, (Luke 12:50; Luke 13:32-33; John 2:17; Rom. 15:3), and so exalted to the right hand of power to now intercede for them and tell them, to be zealous and repent.

The theme of holy zeal is closely connected with all of Christ's covenant-obligated work on behalf of God's glory, and for his elect people. He is the *epitome* of being zealous for the glory of God. He knows what it means to be zealous, and can command zeal of his church to be that in every situation. In the case of Laodicea, he was making the difference between a true church and a false one; between true Christians and false Christians, between zeal in accordance with godliness, and negligence, or false zeal.

What is false zeal? False zeal lacks the truth, and lacks sincerity. Any professing American church that says it does not need anything from Christ, lacks the truth and sincerity in its profession. It pretends to think God and his glory are important, but really, some other end is more important. This is why the word hypocrite literally means pretender; they pretend to be a church. It is merely a show of zeal, like those who wanted to commit themselves to Christ, but Christ would not commit himself to them in John 2. It is because he knew what was in the heart of men. They were not really sincere. Such a false zeal is blind, not according to the word of God. God would have his church to be zealous in all Christian duties, and never to do the work of God negligently. "He also that is slothful in his work is brother to him that is a great waster," (Prov. 18:9).

As much as there are numerous biblical examples of holy zeal, there are also many examples of "zeal without knowledge." False zeal is seen in king Saul (1 Sam. 14:38ff), and Judas Iscariot, (John 12:4-6). There is a zeal for evil, (Isa. 5:18), opposed to a zeal for good. There can also be a zeal that makes men like a kind of wild fire. It sends them into a frenzy without restraint or guidance; zeal without knowledge. There are the people Paul was speaking about in Romans 14, "Who art thou that judgest? who art thou that condemnest thy brother?" A zeal without knowledge is *ruinous* to the church.

How do you exercise godly zeal? Does this rebuke by Christ not reprove you who are lazy Christians? Does he reprove you? Are you in some measure infected by the virus of the Laodicean Christians? Are there some things that you are zealous in and other things that you are not? William Fenner said, "To be zealous against one sin, and lukewarm against another, this is not zeal."[5] Does God work in halves? Is partial reformation not a full offense to God, or does he require you to be zealous and repent? It is, in this passage of Revelation 3 a time of occasional repentance. A time when Christ says, *be zealous.*

You must examine yourself in this, doing all things zealously for King Jesus. Not only are you looking to see whether you are zealous or not, but even in your examination you can discern whether such is a zealous examination for Christ in the Spirit, or not. What might you find in it?

Examine your own life to determine whether you have a heart enflamed with zeal for God, true zeal, true biblical heat and spiritual fervor to follow God in all his prescriptions. If your outward performance of true religion stems from the inward change made by the Holy Spirit, then such zealous action on behalf of Christ is heartily commendable. As a Christian you take heaven by storm, violently seizing the Kingdom of God by force, and press into the Kingdom with all your might. If you are zealous, you will zealously affect the church; do you? How useful are you to Christ in his body? What good does the Spirit of God use you for?

If you are zealous, you will rejoice in Christ no matter the affliction. That is a difficult one for many. Such a zeal will make you fearless in your duty, no matter what opposition you may face in this life. External religious acts do not argue zeal in accordance with knowledge. Is this

---

[5] Fenner, William, *A Treatise of the Affections*, (London: A.M., 1650), 147.

you? What is this mixing of the world in God's worship? Were not the Laodiceans deluded in their walk with God? Were they not spiritual fornicators, in open idolatry? Was this not what the church did with the Moabites, where they were plagued, until Phinehas' zeal interceded for them?

Unbelievers are very easily persuaded off the path of righteousness to mix the world with the church and call it religion – it attracts so many people in their flesh. Has the church done this today? Those who have are spiritual adulterers joined with idolatrous practices. David Dickson said, "Idolatry is a breach of wed-lock with God, and an adulterous joining of a man's soul to an idol; they joined themselves to Baal-Peor. Communion with idolaters in worship, ... proves the communicants to be guilty of idolatry. ... Men's devices in religion, and God's acceptable ordinances stand in opposition to one another. For men's inventions cannot please God. For in this way they provoked him with their inventions. And so nothing draws on more sudden and sore judgement, then change of the true worship of God with men's inventions. They provoked him to anger, with their inventions: and the plague broke in upon them."[6] And what is happening today that the plague has broke out, well, everywhere?

Those who are living under the eminent means of grace but possess a superficial affection to the things of God are called Gospel hypocrites, and their zeal is false. They introduce a form of godliness but deny the power of God, because God is only in those things that he

---

[6] Dickson, David, *A Brief Explication of the Last Fifty Psalms*, (London: T.R. and E.M., 1654), 69–71.

prescribes, otherwise he stands outside, at the door, and knocks looking to be let back in. Does not, in the last, the Apostle Paul say, "from such turn away?" (2 Tim. 3:5).

Christ desires, even amidst rebuke and chastening, your zealous work in a heated zeal that you might be transformed by the power of the Holy Spirit, not joined to any idolatry, doing all things zealously for King Jesus. How shall your church ever see any revival without the Spirit working in the midst of the people, and their hearty zealous repentance from waywardness back to God? We will never see a revival of religion without zeal, and religion will never become our full business without it. Today, we ought to be zealous to find this basic Christian characteristic in ourselves, in our families, in our churches, in our communities and in our nation; especially now in our elders in the church. It is the command of Jesus Christ for every Christian church member to be zealous and repent.

Your zeal must be guided by the word of God, doing all things zealously for King Jesus. Without the word, without the Spirit working in the word, there will be no biblical zeal, for it will be a zeal without knowledge, which is condemned. True zeal begins where the word begins (Romans 14:23), and ends where the word ends, for whatsoever is not of faith is sin.

True zeal makes us willing to be admonished by Christ. Christian churches that reject Christ's rebuke, that do not want to change, that are not willing to change and repent, will never stop the plague; and they will have their candlestick removed, for the Savior will leave off knocking, and they will be blotted out of his book.

True zeal which has as its object the glory of God loves him with a fervent heat. True zeal hates sin, and it is true, godly zeal is most grieved at the sins of the church, because their sins are more grievous then the sins of unbelievers, for they sin against their Lord. Will they, will you, enact repentance, and see by the Spirit's power, revival?

It is your Christian duty to glorify Christ by godly zeal, doing all things zealously for King Jesus. God is to be given all our affections and desires zealously. Do you ever come to pray and feel *blah?* Ever come to study and you're tired? Ever walk into the foyer of the church and think, let's just get through this? Ever sing in worship with hesitation? Ever think on Saturday, tomorrow, I have to put down all those things I love to do for the Lord's Day? Ever been asked to help in a ministry of the church and be put off? Whenever we pray, we are to pray to him zealously. Whenever we praise him, to praise him zealously. Whenever we rejoice to rejoice zealously in his mercies. Whenever we adore him to do so admiring all his goodness and character and love. Again, William Fenner said, "Whenever we enter his courts, to enter with zeal, reverencing his footstool, trembling at his Word; in all our ways seeking how we may be most zealous of his glory: for if God demands the zeal of our affections, there is no keeping anything back."[7] What do you keep back where God requires you to be zealous?

What if we do not give God zeal in all our exercised duties? If God requires zeal and we do not give him zeal, then we ought to examine whether we can give it to him?

---

[7] Ibid.

It is really a question of conversion; converted people can, unconverted people cannot. If God requires zeal upon pain of death, or be spewed out of the mouth of Christ, if we have no zeal in godliness for anything that God requires, we are in a lost state. Are unrepentant people saved? Can they be? Those who do not repent, or cannot repent, are lost. Remember, repentance has a few parts to it. Repentance is breaking the heart before God, and turning from sin. Can this be done as lukewarm? Can it be done partially? Can it be done only a little? Is it not a humbling of the soul in confession, now in light of this Revelation 3 passage, with zeal? If there is no zeal, there is no repentance, no humility, no salvation.

Can such be *called* "believers in Jesus Christ" who have no zeal for his honor and his laws? If a man isn't in Christ by faith, he cannot be saved. You must take time to think this through, and examine your life in light of it. "Can I be in love with Christ who is in love with his church, and not be zealous for him? Do I count everything else as a loss for Christ? Am I like the Psalmist, do I hunger after him? Do I pant like the deer after the waterbooks for him? Am I like the Shulamite, who was sick with love to him? Can I count the loss, pant like the deer, swoon like the bride and not be zealous for Christ?" It is impossible not to be if we are converted. Phinehas was zealous for God's name and sake; zealous and faithful for both. The Psalmist in Psalm 106 expounds it, that was counted to him for righteousness. "And that was counted unto him for righteousness unto all generations for evermore," (Psa. 106:31). Nothing can be counted to a man for righteousness, but by faith alone, and in this text, in this commentary, it is speaking about Phinehas' faith because he demonstrated the outward fruit of the Spirit's zeal in him. If you have true faith, you will be zealous for God, intense for God, on fire for God. Otherwise, your faith is either like a smoking flax or a bruised reed and needs help, or you do not have faith. And if you have no faith, you cannot be humble, cannot confess and pray in the Spirit, are *not* saved. Such are in a state of damnation that do not love the Lord Jesus Christ zealously; could that not be said, sincerely? What does that say about the church today? What does that say about the chastening of the Lord on the church today and its continuation for months now? What does that say about God's use of layering other difficulties on top of the plague?

Zeal should be the fire of your Christian soul. It doesn't take very long to look at your life and consider what you are most interested in and what or who you love. What are you most on fire for? What do you enjoy most? What does the church today want most? Do they want to be sanctified? Or do they merely want the plague stopped? Would they be ok with the continuation of the plague to be more sanctified if God's wills that they drink that bitter cup? Do they pray as Christ prayed, "Thy will be done," in light of such a cup?

Everyone is either set on fire of Christ, or of the devil. Either the Father in heaven sets the heart ablaze, or it is the fire of the devil and hell that sets a man ablaze. Men are either lost or saved; there is no in between. You can't be cold. Jesus won't allow that in his church. Neither can you be luke-warm. And "a knock" by Christ at the door of the church is a last plea, a last attempt. What will the church do? Do you hold a Scriptural javelin in your hand, or a righteous whip of cords for King Jesus? Are you zealous of God's glory? Is your church on fire for God's glory, or on fire for the world? We shall see ... won't we?

Will the plague be stopped this week? Will repentance be sought this week? Will the church rewrite their books of church order, will they hold steadfast to the highway of holiness that their forefathers sought out, will they go back to the church's sound confessions, will they uphold the word of God upon pain of death? Or will they give themselves over to the world more fully, will they compromise? How will they live after the plague has ended? Will they be better? Or worse? Will they be zealous for King Jesus still, or more negligent in their walk? What do people generally do after affliction is over? Are they the better for it, or worse? Because if they are not zealous for God, if they do not hold the javelin in their hand, if they are not ready to thrust it through whatever sins are causing Christ to chasten his church with all manner of affliction in this day, then they demonstrate themselves to be merely a show, like the Pharisees. They are not zealous for God, but content with the world; I am wealthy, rich, needing nothing. But, do they make, "haste, and delayed not to keep his commandments," (Psa. 119:60). What will a billion mediocre prayers accomplish today? What will a billion half-hearted attempts to repentance accomplish? What will the false worship of hundreds of thousands of churches accomplish? What will the continued rejection of Christ's will and laws accomplish? They are boosting up the sound systems readying themselves for the party, and cannot hear Christ knocking at their sanctuary doors.

There is great grace in what Christ said, where his love constrains his people to be zealous. Do you think that what Christ did for you in dying was done in zeal? To say it was a terrible ordeal is to infinitely underrate it. He went to the cross in joy? In purpose? In obedience? In holiness? In righteousness? All that you do for King Jesus and on behalf of Christ if you are converted, is covered by that zealous blood he shed. It is a covering for all your well-intended attempts at exercising zeal towards his cause and purposes for you, his prescriptions, regardless of how poor they are performed, in the ultimate sense of the word. His zeal in that way covers your lack of it; his zeal is given to you as if you were that zealous in God's sight. You might think, "I thought all this plague stuff was just about judgment and such." No, it is judgment and correction and chastening and rebuke but from a loving Savior to his people that they might be made more like him, to be zealous as he was. "I thought it was about repenting and getting right with God, so all of this affliction just stops." There is a hope that it stops, certainly, but that our perspective must be realigned. It is to see the love of the Savior more clearly, even when he casts a rebuke or sends an affliction to us; it is a most extravagant love in this way. It surpasses and ascends the most wise and knowledgeable Christian, and it is too deep for any to fully fathom. Do you know this love, and is it your all-consuming desire to grow by it and in it? Are you zealous to reap the most you can for it and from it? Be zealous and repent.

"As death and the grave devours all, so love and jealousy, zeal, consumes and lifts up, not sparing;

for the love of Christ constrains, (2 Cor. 5:14), and the zeal for his glory, eats up the godly, (Psa. 69:9), for divine love is as restless and as hard to be pleased, as that greedy appetite and womb of death, (Prov. 30:16), so that the soul can never be quiet, but consumes itself, (Psa. 69:9; 119:139) until the soul is filled with [Christ] himself."[8]

Are you zealous in that way to see your soul filled up in the service of King Jesus even amidst this time of occasional repentance? *Be zealous, therefore, and repent.*

In the next chapter, we take all these and roll them into one and set them under the banner of being comforted in it all by the Savior, who is the eternal Word of God.

---

[8] Wilson, Thomas, *A Complete Christian Dictionary,* (London: E. Cotes, 1661), 132.

Chapter 6:
Afflicting Providences

"He hath filled me with bitterness, he hath made me drunken with wormwood," (Lam. 3:15).

Before dealing with Lamentations, a notation needs to be made. When dealing with any of the larger Biblical plagues God brings on a people, there is an atonement made of some kind, an intervention, and the *plague stops.* "And Aaron took as Moses commanded, and ran into the midst of the congregation; and, behold, the plague was begun among the people: and he put on incense, and made an atonement for the people. And he stood between the dead and the living; and the plague was stayed," (Num. 16:47-48). "And he went after the man of Israel into the tent, and thrust both of them through, the man of Israel, and the woman through her belly. So the plague was stayed from the children of Israel," (Num. 25:8). "And David built there an altar unto the LORD, and offered burnt offerings and peace offerings. So the LORD was intreated for the land, and the plague was stayed from Israel," (2 Sam. 24:25). Even the Philistines, when they captured the ark, and had a plague among them, when they returned the ark, the plague stopped. It was a relatively short time. If it was not leprosy, or a sickness (as in an individual difficulty of affliction brought to a single person), but if it was a plague brought to a people, it was, biblically speaking, stopped in a short time by repentance. There are instructions given for how the plague is stopped. Moses gave instructions, Solomon did as well in his prayer.

Speedy repentance in humility, confession, prayer, and zeal were the remedy. Social distancing, or other temporal measures, will *not stop the plague.* God's purpose will not be halted because people stay at home. Neither is it helpful to say "let the plague run its course, and it will stop on its own." Either way, those are ungodly ideas because the answer to any plague, which is never an accident and not part of the normal course of human existence, but is brought on by God against his covenant-breaking church, is to repent.

The plague today is not stopped; 10,000+ died in the last week, that's 2,000 a day. It is two months now for the US, and four months for the world. It continues, with further difficulties now attached to it because of the way it was handled across the globe. What then, knowing that God has brought this to his people, shall we think about its continuation and its affects, whether God-made or manmade? It's really overwhelming in many ways if one thinks about it.

Here we turn to the prophet drunk with bitterness during the destruction and fall of Jerusalem. This was a terrible time. Israel was sent into captivity previous for sin and spiritual adultery. Judah did not learn, they did not take heed; they did not repent even seeing what God would do to his church, so God brings catastrophe on them. Lamentation 2:5, "The Lord was as an enemy: he hath swallowed up Israel, he hath swallowed up all her palaces: he hath destroyed his strong holds, and hath increased in the daughter of Judah mourning and lamentation." When God swallows up whole cities, whole countries, the whole planet, what is the church to do if it

151

is a continual time of suffering? What do righteous people feel? What had Jeremiah done to feel embittered in this way? Jeremiah 1:6, "Then said I: "Ah, Lord GOD! Behold, I cannot speak, for I am a youth. I am the man that hath seen affliction by the rod of his wrath," (Lam. 3:1). "He hath led me, and brought me into darkness," (Lam. 3:2). This is a *very* solemn time for the prophet. All the difficulties of the church are laid on his shoulders and he feels the weight of God's rod against his people.

The structure of the book gives a hint to what this verse in 3:15 emphasizes about being drunk with bitterness. In chapter 3 it is set up in an acrostic, where the Hebrew alphabet is used to pinpoint emphasis intentionally as a literary device. Three times in chapter 3 for emphasis this is found and the anticlimax to the book, is found in 3:15, the heart of the chapter; the exclamation point if you will. The exclamation point is, "He hath filled me with bitterness, he hath made me drunken with wormwood," (Lam. 3:15). This is a synonymous parallelism – the same thing twice said for emphasis in different ways. He hath filled me with bitterness... ...he hath made me drunken with wormwood. "Filled," where the causative word is used by Jeremiah being over satisfied by it. "Maror" with *bitter things or bitternesses* – which is a plural word. There is not one thing, but many things. Jeremiah is on the brink of being overwhelmed entirely.

God has done this, and he has "ravah," *saturated* the prophet with these things, caused him to drink them to the excess, in fact, to be drunk with bitterness. The Hebrew "la`anah" *wormwood* is a metaphor for bitterness. It is a singular word, a descriptive word, of the affects of the affliction on the prophet. The two half-lines of verse 15 are fully parallel in their meaning. The Hebrew word for "the bitterness" with which Jeremiah is filled is the same used of "bitter herbs" in Exodus 12:8, "And they shall eat the flesh in that night, roast with fire, and unleavened bread; and with bitter herbs they shall eat it." Voluntary bitterness was to be contemplated in the Passover. This extends to the Lord's Supper, but it is not bitter that we taste, but bitter that we *contemplate* what Christ tasted. Similarly, wormwood is medicinal, a plant that is bitter-tasting but ultimately helpful. The idea behind the phrase is not that Jeremiah is bitter, as if he is *angrily bitter* at God for all that is occurring. It is not the idea when someone says "That person is very bitter with a root of bitterness." That is not what Lamentations is saying here. Although, it is certainly true that people can become negatively bitter in that way if they sin. It is not, here, bitterness like *anger* and *disappointment* at being treated unfairly; having some form of *resentment*. That kind of bitterness is sin against God. That would be a most heinous charge against God. Certainly, in afflicting times God may be charged by people in a wicked state of mind who blame God for something they think is unfair. This is not the case with Jeremiah. He is experiencing what is fair and knows it. But really, this bitter idea follows this impression, "he has caused me to suffer greatly, even to the extent that I feel like I am suffering more than I am able to endure." He is set under a bitter taste in this way, a hard taste of life. It is more akin to saying, *God has providentially made me suffer like one who is forced to swallow the most bitter medicine.*

Jeremiah was forced by God to be drunk with bitterness as a result of God's heavy providence; on the brink of being overwhelmed with such providence. Is the feeling of being overwhelmed to a degree something that can be tasted in a bitter affliction? Seeing those who are drunk with alcohol and inebriated show them to be overwhelmed and to lose their sense, to become numbed to what is going on around them. Recovering alcoholics see drunkenness as abhorrent in this way – they do not like being numbed to the world once they begin the road to recovery.

Was Jeremiah out of his mind? No. But it is a double bitterness – one where the right mind is intact, but the circumstances satiate the soul with difficult lamentation. He cannot escape God's just judgments on the church. There is no escape, "My flesh and my skin hath he made old; he hath broken my bones," (Lam. 3:4). No audience to be had in the midst of it, "Also when I cry and shout, he shutteth out my prayer," (Lam. 3:8). No defense, "He was unto me as a bear lying in wait, and as a lion in secret places," (Lam. 3:10). What could he do against God? No relief, "He hath bent his bow, and set me as a mark for the arrow. He hath caused the arrows of his quiver to enter into my reins," (Lam. 3:12-13). The word "reins" is literally the "internal organs where the seat of emotion lies" deep within; striking at the utter depths of his soul. Lamentations 3:15, *bitter, i.e.* lamenting. Not annoyed, or bored, not thinking that the captivity of the people and the destruction of the temple were things ridiculous. Synonyms for this word are things like distressful, heartbreaking, sorrowful, woeful, and truly lamentable.

These are not "perspective" facts. This wasn't just the possible interpretation of the prophet in the midst of afflictions. God had done this to him. As if to say to him, "Jeremiah stop looking from the wrong perspective? Consider my sovereignty and providence over my people in this judgment, for judgment begins at the house of God." God had affected the very depth of his emotional being to excess in that he felt drunk with being overwhelmed with the bitter taste of affliction. What will his response be to this? Jeremiah must say, he has brought me low, but not to hell. He has made life very difficult, but not so far as hell. He has brought judgment, but the not the ultimate judgment of hell. He has brought affliction, but not the ultimate judgment of affliction and torment in hell. He is at the brink of temporal affliction and being overwhelmed where he has been made to taste the bitterness of judgment in this.

It is not wrong or sinful to express this kind of bitterness, and travail of soul, in difficult situations, so long as one has a sound perspective in understanding God's providence and sovereignty. This is not to say that Jeremiah simply thought, "I don't like this providence, and I am mad that God has brought it to me." That is not what Jeremiah is saying. Life may become difficult, and the judgment of God may be seen all around, but the prophet keeps a holy perspective on it, though he feels overwhelmed in a godly way. The Holy Spirit inspired a book of the Bible *solely given* to the topic of lamenting. Other examples abound – Job lamented, David lamented, Naomi lamented (changing her name to Mara - *bitterness*).

Even Jesus lamented, "My God, my God, why hast thou forsaken me?"

The DOCTRINE: that God's afflicting providences are especially sharp to Christians while they live in the world.

The drunken Christian, the overwhelmed Christian, the Christian who lives in the world of wormwood in bitterness is not discontent with life; he is stunned with the heaviness of the affliction as to resign his strength into the hands of God alone. His bitter trial forces him into the hands of God. Such hearty afflictions are often overwhelming, difficult. God chooses what calamities and what afflictions he pleases in order to exercise his people in godliness. As many as the Physician loves he chastens and rebukes. This can be positive and negative. It is positive in that they are sanctified by his work on converted souls. It is negative in that it may be a chastening and rebuke, and those are never happy circumstances. Yet sometimes, it so far reaches that it may cover a whole church, or a whole city, or a whole country, or a whole world, where things look grim and life becomes very difficult in various ways; that there is a new normal, as there was for those going into exile in Jeremiah's time. "For the time is come that judgment must begin at the house of God: and if it first begin at us, what shall the end be of them that obey not the Gospel of God?" (1 Peter 4:17). How hard is it for those people?

How or in what sense the godly are drunk with bitterness, overwhelmed in a calamity, feeling despair and distress? Isaiah 54:6, "For a small moment have I forsaken thee." Sometimes God's providence renders the emotional affect in a person as one of *desertion*. This is by personal perception. But it is never totally: Isaiah 54:6, "For a small moment have I forsaken thee; but with great mercies will I gather thee." Desertions and judgments in this way are not the interruptions of God's love for his people, but the acts of his love, as they are with all his chastenings and rebukes. His affection is the same to his church, but the expression is varied because of hindrances to their relationship that have emerged. God has the love of intention and the love of execution. Love of intention is to save his people, his elect: eternal, immutable, infinite, and unchangeable in Christ. Love of execution, that is a different case altogether: the expression of his love towards his people may be suspended and restrained for a time. He may in fact send them a sword, or famine, or a plague that swallows up the world. He may close the doors to the church. He may make their means of grace to be placed at a distance for a long time. God cannot ever stop loving his people, although, for whatever reason, his people may not see the full expression of his love always. This causes them to be embittered, overwhelmed, numbed, drunk with wormwood; where they can turn nowhere else but to God alone. Especially when the spiritual layer is exasperated by the physical layer. The work of the Spirit is vexed and the sweet comfort feels far away, and on top of that, the plague roams the earth. Though wormwood is medicinal, it is still bitter.

In calamities like any sword, famine or plague, the Christian may be embittered by the event. I am not speaking about *discontentment*. This is not a passage that applies to personal discontentment in sinning against God because one does not like things happening around them so they bark at God and others. What disposition does a child take when his security blanket is ripped from his arms? The child has no idea it's going into the wash to be made clean. But until the child receives the blanket back, it cries bitterly. No amount of comfort will do until that security blanket is returned to his grasp. They are overwhelmed with sorrow. (Christians, though, must guard against immoderate sorrow.)

Christians are embittered by the withdrawing influence of grace to them. God is not stingy with his grace, or one that takes it back. He does not come to Jeremiah or any Christian and remove grace that he has given to them in covenant. Rather, he simply does not pour it into them as abundantly as they would like. The sailboat may be fit with a sail and rudder, but what will it do without the wind?

They may be embittered by the withdrawing comfort from them which comes from the ministry of the Spirit. Comfort is from a word which imports strength into a person. Discomfort is the weakening of the soul in that it falls and faints without admonition. Even if there is just the *thought* of God bringing in some great calamity for the Christian for a time, and then realizing the reality of its possibility where they become overwhelmed, it will feel as though God is shooting arrows at them. The soul may be numbed in its perspective and it may faint! Psalm 42:5, "Why are you cast down, O my soul? And why are you disquieted within me?" What reasons could such a person be in such a state?

There are five reasons for having the sharp feeling of being overwhelmed in affliction. First, consider, God will bring great bitterness of soul to the Christian for his glory. Everything God does is always for his glory first. From the throne of God is found his incomprehensible nature; here he displays his sovereignty and power. Who said, "Is it not from the mouth of the Most High that woe and well-being proceed?" Jeremiah did in Lamentations 3:26. Psalm 18:11 says, "He made darkness his secret place; his pavilion round about him were dark waters and thick clouds of the skies." Isa. 45:3 says, "I form the light, and create darkness: I make peace, and create evil: I the LORD do all these things." All men can do is bow before his incomprehensible and sovereign throne and the works of his hands. Isaiah 43:7, "Everyone who is called by My name, Whom I have created for My glory; I have formed him, yes, I have made him." Everything exists for him and to him. John 2:11, "This beginning of miracles did Jesus in Cana of Galilee, and manifested forth his glory; and his disciples believed on him." It is the manifestation and realization of that glory that he is always after. To show how glorious he is in all things. And he will always do this with the best ends in mind. He accomplishes his own ends and purposes in the lives of men. 1 Sam. 2:7, "He brings low and lifts up." If he desires to bless Solomon with kingdoms and wealth, or desires to create bitterness in the weeping prophet Jeremiah, or the embittered Christian, he shall do it to bring himself glory. If governing circumstances in a particular way to make people drink wormwood is the best course of action for his glory, this God will do. He is the King, of glory in all his works. Psalm 24:9, the *King of glory.*

Second, God will bring great bitterness of soul to the Christian church in sword, famine and plague to cause them to know their sinfulness. Deut. 8:15-16, "Who led you through that great and terrible wilderness, in which were fiery serpents and scorpions and thirsty land where there was no water; who brought water for you out of the flinty rock; who fed you in the wilderness with manna, which your fathers did not know, that He might humble you." What will he press Job to do? Job 42:6, "Therefore I abhor myself, and repent in dust and ashes." Who is Job before the Holy God of the universe? He will bring his people low that they may know who they are and who He is, more clearly. Was Job not embittered, overwhelmed, in his speeches? And who said (Lamentations 3:39-40), "Wherefore doth a living man complain, a man for the punishment of his sins? Let us search and try our ways, and turn again to the LORD." Jeremiah knew that even amidst the bitterness of God's chastening on his people, even though he had rebuked them, even though he sent them into a miserable physical time of sword, plague and famine, it is set on the church to try their ways and turn again to the Lord. Comparatively speaking, does God delight in pressing his church into the winepress? Or bestowing great blessings on them? It is found and seen in the comparison to heaven, and in a comparison to the travail and tribulation of life. Comparatively speaking, it is much better to receive only blessings and benefits in the positive sense, than to be made bitter, overwhelmed by God, in sharp afflictions.

Third, God will bring great bitterness of soul to the Christian: to appraise the work of all his graces in believers. There is no such thing as a Christian who is not tried of God in this life; if Christ was tried and he is the master, what of the Christian? You always hear many say that Christians should cling to the promises of God – true. This is a promise: Acts 14:22, "We must through many tribulations enter the kingdom of God," (Mark 8:31), "And He began to teach them that the Son of Man must suffer many things, and be rejected by the elders and chief priests and scribes, and be killed." Those who believe they will not suffer in this life as Christians, are not thinking according to the bible. Those who do not suffer are not Christians. The promise is made to them, and it is true. Job 23:10, "But he knoweth the way that I take: when he hath tried me, I shall come forth as gold." 2 Tim. 3:12, "Yea, and all that will live godly in Christ Jesus shall suffer persecution." Promise! There is no escaping this promise. The question becomes how much of the promise will be realized? What level of the promise will be realized in the Christian's life? What level of the promise is being made to the Christian church even now? How will overwhelmed Christians deal with such things? 1 Peter 1:6-7, "In this you greatly rejoice, though now for a little while, if need be, you have been grieved by various trials, that the genuineness of your faith, being much more precious than gold that perishes, though it is tested by fire, may be found to praise, honor, and glory at the revelation of Jesus Christ." What is then, in such calamity, the "genuineness of your faith"? Is it a genuine faith, or a counterfeit one? Is it a murmuring one, a complaining one, or one that trusts in God though overwhelmed in lamentation?

Fourth, God will bring great bitterness of soul to the Christian: to necessitate trust. Job 13:15, "Though he slay me, yet will I trust Him." Job was a good theologian in this respect. Though bitterness and travail entered the marrow of his bones, he trusted God. When his wife pressed him to curse God and die for the affliction, being angry in her sinful bitterness, Job trusted God and though, with heavy affliction, on the brink of an overwhelming affliction, continued to trust God. Shall we expect only good from God and not evil? What is trust but a sure hope in God and his promises? Hope, not hoping something will happen: maybe something will happen. Hope, that it will happen because God has said it would happen, and so in eager expectation it is desired quickly.

Fifth, God will bring great bitterness of soul to the Christian: to chasten them for their sins. What would be a more fitting text than the weeping prophet and Lamentations? Judah's sin brought lamentations to bear. Jeremiah 2:19, "Your own wickedness will correct you, and your backslidings will rebuke you. Know therefore and see that it is an evil and bitter thing that you have forsaken the LORD your God, and the fear of Me is not in you," Says the Lord GOD of hosts.'" Does this sound even faintly applicable to the church today with a plague all around them, and layer upon layer of difficulty now emerging. What do the worldly say to it? "Well get through this. We always do." But what is the church's reaction to it?

Afflictions are any trouble, grief or evil no matter what it is, that happens either to soul or body, name, goods, or property, for correction of sin, or for trial, as it applies to the godly. What a blessing it is that it is not for

162

punishment and vengeance as it is to the wicked. What will the church find in going through and acknowledging such afflictions? Will they be so overwhelmed to lose trust and abandon their convictions further? Will they see the message of the chastening Lord and his rebuke to them to find solace through his ministry to them that even in making things bitter for them, he is doing them good?

Consider then that Christ ministers to the afflicted as one who was afflicted. Christ was afflicted more than all others as the sin bearer. Christ's soul was afflicted and tormented with sorrow and pain the entire time of his passion. This is why John places a great portion of his Gospel on the last week of Jesus' life. It was a week of bitter affliction. Christ is said to have experienced it "with strong crying and tears," (Heb. 5:7) that is a godly bitter taste. There is the degree to which the Savior was afflicted, which is a greater degree than by Jeremiah, or by Job or by any Christian. He was so afflicted that he cried out with great cryings and tears. His soul was embittered, in fact, the Gospels mention that he was greatly afraid, concurrently overwhelmed, even fainting in great anguish of mind. He was berated with full contemplative sorrows as the hour approached. His Father's wrath was kindled and the heat was getting closer and closer, hotter and hotter. God's wrath was going to be against him, and count him as an enemy as the sin-bearer. The heavy hand of God's wrath was coming in the most grievous manner any man would ever know. Did Christ not say in crying words, "My God, my God why hast thou forsaken me?" *Desertion.* Was he not overwhelmed with wormwood at such a time? Yes, more than any other. He was covered with the shadow of death and walked deep within its valley. What grief could possibly be compared to this? He bore condemnation even though he was innocent, and yet, did so willingly. He was the brightness of the Father's glory, and yet, he would travail under the sorrows of bitterness in being overwhelmed with tears and anguish. It was all sorrow above sorrow. Was Jeremiah this embittered? Not remotely as much as the Christ, though he tasted it. Who has ever been so filled with bitterness of this sort, vanquished by God's providence, as the Christ had? Who has ever been brought so low and so despised and so forsaken as the Christ? And yet, in the anguish and the bitter cup, did he lose trust? "...the cup which my Father hath given me, shall I not drink it?" (John 18:11).

As Christ was heartily afflicted and in great anguish and bitterness of soul, flooded with sorrowfulness, he knows how to minister to those who are in anguish of soul. Remember that even though the physical pain and misery of the curse of death was apparent, and crucifixion would be a horrible death, the spiritual side of the curse was far worse. What of the way, then, Christ ministers to Christians? They are in anguish at times, and most of the time it being physical. Do people anguish and become overwhelmingly sorrowful under the heavy hand of God's providence spiritually? They certainly do not anguish as Christ did. They cannot. It is impossible. Christians have really little to complain about in light of the sufferings of Christ. Once they contemplate Christ's cryings and tears, and the reason of that spiritual transaction on the cross for sin, as the sin-bearer hung cursed, they would never think that whatever is happening to them in God's providence was anything likened to what Christ experienced. So, Christ ministers to them by their contemplation of his bitterness and anguish which is found in the word. They recollect what he has done, and they cannot but see their sorrows and their bitternesses as far less than Christ's. They would see being more overwhelmed as impossible. So, they look to his ministry to them to help them in their time of affliction, even if he is the Great Physician to bring such an affliction and to bring the cure. They are near to Christ's heart because Christ died for them on the cross and took their punishment, and they know it. What providences are causing them exhausting sorrow can be seen through the glasses of that work of Jesus. By application of this, let's look at some remedies he brings in this way.

There are *remedies* for feeling overwhelmed with the difficulty of God's providence, for being embittered for you. When you are embittered and drunk with wormwood, when calamity ensues and you feel overwhelmed, there are remedies which Lord Jesus has given his people that they may be lifted up; things that he ministers to them.

Remedy 1: Repentance and Reformation of Life. Any inward affliction or sorrow or bitterness of a person, is part of the case of God's desertion of them for a time. It is what is called a *spiritual desertion*. This is what Christ agonized over; forsaken. To be separated in his humanity from all the experimental blessings. When the Lord, for whatever providential reason should be pleased to give you that "feeling" that you are missing his presence, and that he leaves you in a kind of darkness of spirit, even though

165

you are a believer, and you have a great interest in the Lord Jesus, yet for a time, you may be left alone in such a providence for a God-ordained reason. When this occurs, your spirit will be afflicted with sorrow, fear, maybe even a sense of dread and trouble, because of a perceived absence of his help. As Christ knew, there is no affliction like this affliction, there is no bitterness of soul like this bitterness of soul. Christians are frail humans, fallen and tainted with sin. To be left to their own devices for a time, to be called by God back from whatever dark vale they are in, is a most difficult journey. Sinners who are unsaved, those who are not spiritually minded, see these events and things in their life as only a kind of unhappiness. Things they would rather like to have or do or be or experience, they do not do them, or cannot do them, and as a result, they are saddened. They bite their upper lip, and press through, "they'll get through it," they think. But the Bible shows you that afflictions where God is separated by his moderation of love to you and the church are the most real afflictions in the world. They seem so deep and wide to you as a believer. If God is not pouring his Spirit into you in great measure, that which you long for, all seems so difficult, and overwhelming. Again, such desertions are not the interruptions of God's love for you, but the acts of his love; even if you do not *feel* as though that's true. This is not the same for sinners who die impenitent in their sins. They experience God's full desertion of both his love of intention and execution. He does neither for them. And hell is the reality that they then serve in an angered bitterness where there is weeping *and* gnashing of teeth, *not just weeping.* Jeremiah was weeping; but weeping without gnashing. For the lost, this is not so. They are embittered to become *angrily bitter* and strike out back at God for such things they hate and do not want to yield to.

How do *you* act in such things? Are you thinking, "He's brought me low, but not to hell." For you, these spiritual desertions are when God withdraws himself for a time, from a perceived presence with you. What will you do when you feel overwhelmed with the bitterness of sorrow and lamentation? Jeremiah was overwhelmed. The church was being struck heavily. And it continued for a good long while. How long and how many layers will this coronavirus continue? What sorrow is being brought forth on God's people right now? Will you cry "day and night before thee," (Psa. 98:3) when outward afflictions are joined with spiritual desertion, this is the greatest affliction you can experience in this life. There is nothing greater for the believer. Verse 15, "I am afflicted and ready to die ... while I suffer your terrors I am distracted," (Psa. 88:15). Are such verses sin? No. Such verses are hearty instruction to the overwhelming nature of sharp affliction to Christians who live in the world.

There are remedies for you when you are afflicted in soul, and overwhelmed in this kind of bitterness and sorrow. Look to Jesus Christ. Jesus Christ is the great deliverer, the sin-bearer and he has born all your punishment if you are a believer. What part of the curse is left for you to bear? *None at all.* Though you experience temporary difficulties, you have the Christ who knows their depth, to cling to and run to. You have been delivered by his anguish, by his embittered soul, his overwhelming sorrow, so that you might hope and look to him; and not have a sorrow that crushes you. Though you might be going through something hard, consider that you really do not understand the depth of what Christ accomplished for you. You must exercise faith in him; for he knows your need. Exercise it in this way:

> "I know that you, Lord, were afflicted. A man of sorrow, acquainted with grief. You were deserted in the worst way. Your soul was heavy to the very point of death, and you gave yourself up to the will of God in death, and you took all God's wrath for me. You engaged in that combat which I could not. You sweat drops of blood in anguish, you poured out your blood on the cross in being forsaken of the Father in utter darkness, that I might not go to utter darkness. I know that by your work you will not withdraw your love for me, yet, I long to experience your grace to me that I might again taste of your sweetness and beauty. You were forsaken so that I might be sanctified by your holy work, and not forsaken to the pit. You were really and truly forsaken for me, that I might not be eternally forsaken by you."

Christ was forsaken for your sake, that your heart might run to Christ, that you might look to him. Isn't he full of grace and goodness? Will you petition him for this grace and goodness? Will times of rebuke and chastening that bring you and the church into a bitterness beyond any other you may have ever experienced, bring you to the throne of God and closer to the Lord? He will send you his

Advocate in great measure. Who is this? Jer. 50:34, "Their Redeemer is strong, the Lord of Hosts is his name, he shall thoroughly plead their cause, that he may give rest ..." All your trials and tribulations, all your overwhelming experiences of bitterness of soul are encountered as you live here in the world. Jesus said, "be of good cheer; I have overcome the world," (John 16:33). You are not as the world that merely pushes through it. You want the benefits of his work on your soul. You will drink a cup that is prolonged if he so desires because you know it is for your good, though it is bitter to the taste in any sharp affliction. He is able, he is worthy, he is at the exalted right hand of the Father, and can send you his Spirit in great measure. He is the one to look to in all affliction, in all bitterness. Even though you feel sharp pains under the weight of your trial or your overwhelming affliction, consider, that in Jesus Christ you have been delivered. He has delivered you. You might not experience the fullness of that immediately when in a tribulation and anguish of soul, but there is a way to cultivate that.

Consider this, look to Christ as you did when you were first saved. Do you remember that? How did you go to Christ when you were first saved? Consider, when you first went to Christ then, you were an enemy. But not now; now you are friend. How does God deal with his friends? How did you feel when you sought him to be a friend to you? Consider, the work of grace was new to you at that time, never having experienced it before. But not now; now you have experienced a good many providences of his grace. Consider, you trusted the Lord implicitly with little to no knowledge then, maybe having heard only a single sermon, and there you were converted. But you have so much more knowledge now. Consider, you were delivered from the fires of hell at conversion. But you are far from those flames now justified in Christ, and having walked the sanctifying road of salvation for a good time now. You look around at all the things happening to you this day, in this plague, and you might be overwhelmed, embittered in your soul, overcome, crushed in many ways, swamped and inundated with worldly thoughts. You lack the evidences of grace that you would like to see right now, and even in your superficial search, you cannot find them. So then, go back, and recall what Christ did for you at the beginning. Remember those things afresh.

Look only to Christ and do not rest in anything else of the world. There is nothing that will help you more than sound thoughts of Jesus. It does not matter how much comfort you lack right now, know the truth of the word and what it says about Jesus Christ. There is comfort in Christ. There is deliverance in Christ. There is hope in Christ. There is grace in Christ. There is power in Christ. There is love in Christ. There is help in Christ. Whether you are a Jeremiah, or a Job, there is help. For if you do not find rest in Jesus Christ, if you are not cured in your melancholy by him and his Spirit of grace, if you do not find any solace in the word of God, or the ministry of the ordinances of God, then you will never find a remedy in any other thing in the world. This is a great temptation that Satan brings in. He says to you, "Oh, so you feel overwhelmed, your soul is in agony, and you say Christ has deserted you now when you need him most? Go find a remedy then somewhere else. These sermons cannot help you. The bible cannot help you. Prayers bouncing off the ceiling will not help you. God is not so near as you thought, so try the things of the world. See if they are a comfort or remedy for you." Be very watchful against such temptations. There is enough in Jesus Christ and all his ordinances to help you in any providence where your soul is overwhelmed.

Remedy 2: Confession. The Christian ought to search out and confess to his heavenly Father those iniquities which have provoked God to hide his face or bring his deadly arrows against them. Do this in humble, speedy, and earnest prayer. Since sin is generally the culprit of a dark providence, confession to Christ may very well be the first remedy. The unbelieving do not flee to God with their bitterness, they nourish it. They do not unburden their souls into the heart of God. Lament turns to self-pity. Self-pity is really a devious kind of pride. The Christian prays; and you must pray; you are commanded to pray, and that even daily, to be delivered. "If my people humble themselves and pray..."

Remedy 3: Hope. You should cast yourself on the love, mercy and grace of Christ, and the hope of his faithfulness to restore you to joy. God is in the business of taking those overwhelmed with wormwood and causing them to rejoice in his work in their life. Lamentations 3:21-24, "This I recall to my mind, Therefore I have hope. Through the LORD's mercies we are not consumed, Because His compassions fail not. They are new every morning; Great is Your faithfulness." Is this not in the Lamentations of Jeremiah? Are they not in the very chapter? "The LORD is my portion," says my soul,

"Therefore I hope in Him!" Jesus Christ stands ready to pour into his vessels of mercy, the grace and mercy they need to endure anything; even if they feel deserted. Sorrow draws out the compassion of God to his people. His compassions are renewed every morning. What is the cause of your bitterness? Work, home, relatives, dark providences, sin, calamity in the world like the virus? It may be that God has brought you to Lamentation 3:15, but no further; yet. Jesus' name is "Faithful and True" and he is the AMEN, and he is the one who brings providences in and out. 2 Cor. 7:6, "God...comforts those that are cast down." You *must* believe this.

Remedy 4: Christ's Goodness. You must remember that the rod of God, and the bitter wormwood which flows from it, is for your good. Only the people of God can say this – wormwood is a bitter but helpful herb, it has medicinal properties to it. It casts down, but heals. Romans 8:28, "all things for good." You may call on Christ, and you may in bitter lamentation pray, but you may never murmur or complain. This is not what the passage is teaching. It is not what the bible teaches. God brings such lament to you, to make your deliverance sweeter. Isaiah 49:13, "Sing, O heavens; and be joyful, O earth; and break forth into singing, O mountains: for the LORD hath comforted his people, and will have mercy upon his afflicted." He will have mercy on you even when life is hard and seems overwhelming.

Remedy 5: Meditation. You must meditate on the fact that the bitterness of your present dark providence is nothing compared to the glory which awaits you in heaven. Romans 8:18, "For I consider that the sufferings of this present time are not worthy to be compared with the glory which shall be revealed in us." Is there suffering now? Is there difficulty now? It's global and affecting all peoples in all places. Meditate on all the providences brought to you and correct your perspective so that it does not turn into an angry bitterness, where next you gnash your teeth at God, but bring all your difficulties to Christ, cast your cares on him for he cares for you, and will deliver you. It may not be in the way you see. It may not be in the way you would like. But it will be according to God's purpose and good for you. It will certainly be for your good.

There are two warnings in this. Warning 1: You must be careful not to cross the line from lament and the feeling of being overwhelmed, to a bitter anger. God will, as a righteous Father, chastise you in a greater degree if you do not learn your lessons in Christ's school of affliction speedily. Look at the church today. The plague is here to stay now. Where is church reformation? Still, it will be for your good, but it will be a difficult good; a new normal.

Warning 2 is to the Lost. Unless the Gospel of Jesus plows up the fallow ground of your heart, until it melts your heart, and draws you into the grace of Jesus Christ and his work, merit and mercy, all the sorrow you experience in this life, is never quenched, but aggravated until hell swallows you up, where it is multiplied to a greater degree than you can possibly imagine. To remain at a distance from God is the beginnings of the sighs of hell. Do not cultivate this. Cast your heart on him, and look to him, for there is no tragedy that is greater than Christ is a Savior. He knows all things, and will save you not merely from temporary difficulty, but from eternal condemnation.

Learn how to remove this ungodly kind of angry bitterness and contempt against God through Christ alone. Have an interest in it. William Gouge said, "This must be done by taking bitter pills, which are the pills of a contrite heart, Matthew 26:75; 2 Cor. 7:10. This is manifested by spiritual grief for offending God, and for the danger we bring to the soul, Psalm 51:4, 12. They who thoroughly feel the bitterness of sin will willingly take these pills," (2 Chron. 33:12; Luke 7:38 and 18:13. Acts 2:37; 2 Cor. 7:11).[1] He is the physician who dispenses grace in *spiritual pills*. They are bitter to the taste, but satisfying to the soul.

The next chapter will now take us to the comfort we can have in times of great afflictions.

---

[1] Gouge, William, *A Learned and Very Useful Commentary on the Whole Epistle to the Hebrews*, (London: A.M., T.W. and S.G. for Joshua Kirton, 1655), 319.

Chapter 7:
Comfort Through the Word

"This is my comfort in my affliction: for thy word hath quickened me," (Psa. 119:50).

The Psalms are a treasury of blessings for the people of God. The Hebrew title of the book, תהלים, "praises," or, to give a form-critical rendering, is the Hebrew idea of "hymns", translated as tehillim (תהלים), or sepher tehillim (ספר תהלים). The whole book has a borrowed title from such psalms as Psalm 145, where the inscription is "David's Psalm of Praise." Song, or Praise, hymn or song, song or hymn; all of them are grouped as the same thing. This is why the Apostle Paul says that the church should sing *psalms, hymns and songs*, and where James says if anyone is joyful to *sing a psalm;* they are all the same thing. Song, or praise, hymn or song, song or hymn; all of them are grouped as the *psalms.*

The book of psalms is divided into five smaller books, like the Pentateuch but is written in Hebrew poetry, with various authors. David is a key author, having written most of these psalms, hymns or songs, and then Asaph, the Korahites, Heman, Moses, Solomon, and fifty of them are anonymous. Psalm 119 is the longest psalm, as an acrostic, most likely written by David and it focuses on the superlative nature of the word of God. It combines the hymn, prayer and aspects of the word of God (the law) together, and quite extensively intertwines them.

In Psalm 119:49, the psalmist is found looking to the word for hope. "Remember the word unto thy servant, upon which thou hast caused me to hope." He asks God to call to mind what he has said to him. Such a word of hope has been in some kind of delay, which the psalmist would like to see brought forth quickly. Whatever God has said is where his hope lies. It is not a generic promise, but a word to the servant of God. Those who serve God can find hope in his word, for they are promises to them from their King. It is a promise that the psalmist can hope in. As the psalmist looked to stir up God to remember what he has said on his behalf, equally, in parallel, he is stirred up to remember what the word says so that he can hope in it. "Caused me to hope" is "remember" and "hope."

Then in verse 50 he says, "This is my comfort in my affliction: for thy word hath quickened me." "This" which is the word of God. It "is my comfort." He is moved with consolation. The comfort received by the psalmist (or the church) after a loss or disappointment, is what is meant. This is the same word as, "Comfort ye, comfort ye my people, saith your God. Speak ye comfortably," (Isa. 40:1-2).

Where is this comfort, but "in my affliction." The comfort is set in the *context* of affliction. Why would one need to be comforted unless they were afflicted? The word can be translated both as affliction *or* misery. The psalmist has his afflictions. Take very careful note, that may even be disappointing to most, the psalmist is not released from troubles, but comforted *in* his affliction. Hold that thought for a time.

"For your word..." The promise of the word of God is his support. The word of God is very powerful to affect a great many things for him as a believer. One of these benefits is the comfort the psalmist gains in the midst of misery and afflictions. What does this comforting word do?

It "...has sustained me." It has quickened him, sustained him. It is the life of God in the soul of men, through the word. It is directly related to the word of God which God has spoken. This is a very important but simple point to make. The comfort that this psalmist hopes in and gains, which is a quickening comfort, a soul-hoping comfort is through the word of God which God has spoken. Not speaking, not going to speak, not going at some future time to bring; he has no idea what that might be or when. God *has spoken* to his servant up to this point, and his word *sustains*. It is not alluded to be found in any other place. This is part of the heart of this psalm. The psalmist is saying that in the most difficult of circumstances, comfort to the miserable soul, to the embittered soul, comes by the word of God alone. This is what God has said, in his law, and commandments.

DOCTRINE: In times of affliction, the church finds full comfort through the Word of God.

The comfort that the Christian receives is divine comfort. "In the multitude of my thoughts within me thy comforts delight my soul," (Psa. 94:19). Thomas Manton "To prize and esteem the scriptures, and consult with them often: there you have the knowledge of God, who is best worth our knowing; and the way how we may come to enjoy him, wherein our happiness lieth."[1]

Where is this comfort – "*thy* comforts", comforts that come from God. Jesus said, John 15:11, "These things have I spoken, that my joy might remain in you, and that your joy might be full." Things spoken by God bring in joy, which is the source of all comfort. It comes from God, from the word of God. Many Christians encumber themselves with trying to find comfort in worldly things. These are things that take up their time, but offer no comfort. These are things that keep them busy so they forget the difficulties that they are afflicted by. Some resolve to being busy in and of itself in a hobby or such (which are not sinful, but can be very deterring if not used lawfully). Some even take on other sins, like gluttony, or drinking, and any addictive behavior. But true comfort is only found from God's rich mercy with whom is plentiful redemption. In this there is a great concern to understand the covenant of God, and to understand the covenant of God is to understand what God *has said* about it. It is important for a man to understand what covenant he is under, for from that there is either terror or comfort. Is he in Adam? Is he in Christ? Does he know it, and what does the word say to him about it?

God's covenant is the place where God deals with all men. Without understanding this, men cannot understand where they will find comfort in affliction. Without a proper knowledge of the nature of the Covenant that men have before God, they can never

---

[1] Manton, Thomas, *The Complete Works of Thomas Manton*, Volume 7, (London: James Nisbet & Co., 1872), 32–38.

understand what sin is, how they break the law, how they transgress the covenant, how God has a quarrel with covenant breakers, especially in light of the plague, and how they might be redeemed from it and ultimately, from hell. They can never understand whether God is showering down mercies or afflictions in his love or displeasure if they don't know what covenant they are in. How will the riches of God's grace even be known among them if they do not know what God is doing, or what God said he would do in such things? Terror under God's covenant, or comfort under God's covenant, comes from a true knowledge of the covenant men are under.

God's people are under the covenant of Christ's grace as stated by the word of God. If men are under the first Adam, they are in the covenant of works, and under condemnation. There is no comfort to be found there, only death. God's words to them are a terror, and there is no comfort in terror. If men are under the second Adam, Jesus Christ, they may find a great deal of comfort given to them by the word of God. "In his days Judah shall be saved, and Israel shall dwell safely: and this is his name whereby he shall be called, THE LORD OUR RIGHTEOUSNESS," (Jer. 23:6). Sin will not have dominion over them. "Let not sin therefore reign in your mortal body, that ye should obey it in the lusts thereof," (Rom. 6:12). The Law will be indelibly written on their mind and heart, as it is with all who are born again. "Which shew the work of the law written in their hearts, their conscience also bearing witness," (Rom. 2:15). They have Christ as their Mediator, in full. The Christ, Testator of the New Covenant, who was afflicted and killed, yet rose again by the power of God, and ascended into heaven and now sits at the right hand of the Father to dispense the Spirit in great measure, extent and fullness to them. He sends great comfort to them, by the Spirit, in the Word which tells of his work and his will for them. And when they are afflicted by the temporal afflictions of the world, in whatever form they come, even in a physical plague, or famine, or sword, they look to the spiritual word, which is divine, and raises them to great heights of understanding and comfort. This is my comfort in my affliction, your word has sustained and quickened me.

This comfort is all-embracing and inclusive of all Christ's benefits. What affliction could ever be given, or experience ever experienced that the word of God is silent on? There is wisdom to be find in it for life and godliness of all kinds. There is no affliction which the word of God does not give the church appropriate consolation. What affliction can anyone name that cannot be comforted by the word of God? How extensive are the promises of God to hope in? Can the psalmist, can the Christian, hope in the word that quickens and sustains? What promises are inadequate in the word? What part of the word will fail a believer? Infallible, unable to fail the Christian. This is housed in the nature of God, "he cannot lie," it is impossible for him to deny his Word. If God has said it, it necessarily comes to pass and he will make good on it. Are there afflictions of health that are not covered in the word? Are there afflictions in plague, famine or sword? Are there times of prosperity that have no blessings promised to them, where Christ does not minister by his Spirit to them? Are there times and seasons that the Scriptures do not adequately and divinely apply in or to? What need is there that a Christian might have where they do not have an adequate promise to sustain them? Is there not a promise for every situation for them? One might say, "There is a plague today, the coronavirus, and so what might comfort us for that which is not spoken of in the bible? The word of God assures God's people of his gracious presence regardless of what befalls them. Is that adequate? The word of God assures God's people of power to stop the plague if his people are zealous and repent, confess their sins, humbly come before him? Is that not adequate? The Bible does not need to *name* every virus or every event, just like it does not need to make a running list of eternal life promised to all believers, where it cites them by name, one after the other. All their names are not in the book. It does not matter what happens to the afflicted church by God's appointment, but they are able to rely on his promises and his power and his word to sustain and quicken them, that they may be comforted and have hope in him through it. It is divine, exhaustive in its application in that light, and it quickens the Christian.

This word *quickens*, or is life giving. Reviving and mortifying is key here. It revives the soul. It gives life, and that more abundantly. The word cultivates that life on a spiritual level. Is this not what Christ said, that he came to give life and that *more abundantly?* It causes the soul to be lifted up. Your word has *quickened* me. The word is the sword that kills sin. There is no zapping away sin; the Spirit does not merely look at a Christian and pick a sin and zap it away some night while they are sleeping. The Spirit uses the spiritual power of persuasion and causes

181

the Christian to receive a great comfort in the truth of the word, which in fact they believe, and so, such belief overcomes sin, and mortifies sin in the strength of the Spirit. This is done *through* the Spirit, but only if they take hold of the promises and *rest* on them. It stirs good affections, to be appreciated always that they might be quickened by the word daily. The importance of being in the word all the time is a great benefit to killing sin, and reviving the soul. It will yield in this way, a great comfort in affliction. Christians are then subject to the Spirit of God in which they cultivate that spiritual persuasion to understand the word, and its comfort to them. Carnal men can never be comforted by the word; they have no light but a notional knowledge. Only those possessing the Spirit of God can be comforted by the divine consolation that comes by it, because the Spirit of God dwells in them and testifies to it experientially. They rely on this divine word, which brings divine consolation, a word they believe, and are able, by the Spirit's power to rely on his promises, his word to sustain and quicken them, that they may be comforted and have hope in Christ through it. One might hope one day to meet the President of the United States, but actually meeting the president is much different than thinking about that meeting. One is real, the other imagined.

It is God's Fatherly care of his people that he gives them this word; he sustains them by it. God's Fatherly care over his people includes giving them the inscripturated word. He could have spoken from heaven once, and required all people to heed it. He did not do that. He writes down his will for them to know, and this will, this word, persuades them to trust in God, rather than look to the difficulties of that which is swirling around them. This is very gracious. To have a bible is very gracious.

When God takes them into his family, all his works with them are Fatherly, and this provision is a Fatherly provision. He has sent them messages through the word of God, which, in any affliction, they may be comforted. Their Father works on their behalf in a most gracious manner, and has given them a word that they might trust in what God says he will do. Where is the trust? Matt. 6:32, "Your heavenly Father knoweth that ye hath need of all these things." The key here, is that they believe what he says. It is true, that all those whom God loves, he corrects. This is especially true in a time of occasional repentance, when a plague is still flowing across the face of the earth, and other difficulties are being layered one upon another. Where is the Christian's hope? In the news? In the CDC? In data? Aside from any constituted means that they may use as wise Christians, comfort is in the word which God gives them. There he promises much comfort no matter what is going on. This is my comfort in my affliction: for thy word hath quickened me. This is a very great comfort indeed. What does he promise them that would be comforting?

All comfort is set in his promises, in the Word of God. Forgiveness of sin is a promise. Promise of eternal life in Jesus Christ is a promise. The promise of power worked in them by the power of the Spirit, adopted as sons and daughters is a promise. The promise of tribulation is a promise. The promise of God's Fatherly care in tribulation. This can only be applicable to the Christian who is already assured of God's favor, and knows he shall have abundant happiness when he dies and goes to heaven. Such promises help a Christian in instructing him how they may support his heart with sufficient contentment against all the miseries that can assault him from the time of his conversion, until his death. He will not escape affliction, but will rest in God while they occur. He looks to the word in his affliction, for there he has hope and comfort. Though he has received the forgiveness of Jesus Christ, still, he is directed by the word that many things will still oppose his comfort. Christians in this way will meet with temptations and afflictions of all kinds. They will have reproaches, and adversaries. They will have trouble in their spirit, and plagues to deal with; they will have financial issues, health issues, family issues, work issues, and even many hard providences. But, no matter the issue at hand, there is no affliction that the Word of God will not give a divine and complete consolation to them. Such a word from God will sustain them abundantly in Jesus Christ, by the Spirit's power.

Such promises of God in the word of God are called the, "unsearchable riches of Christ," (Ephesians 3:6, 9). These promises assure God's children that each child brought into the fold of God's house, where his banner over them is love, they are indeed very rich men and women. They have, as the Apostle Peter says, "great and precious promises," (2 Peter 1:3). Promises that are hidden away in the heart, are far more precious than costly jewels that hang around the neck, more valuable than the *Hope diamond.* They are useful to the Christian for their entire life; not part of it or a portion of it or certain aspects of it. The word of God will drive away grief, discouragement, fears, any affliction, and sweeten them all in Jesus Christ, who is the YES and AMEN of the word. These promises build up and confirm faith. "His word is true, and righteous altogether," (Psalm 19:8). These Christians have the very blood of Christ, the death of the Testator, to confirm all the promises contained in the Bible. This is why he is called the YES and AMEN. "For all the promises of God in him are yea, and in him Amen," (2 Cor. 1:20). For, "him hath God the Father sealed," (John 6:27). God made everything infallibly sure when he sent out his Christ. He sealed his commission in all things that concerned the happiness of his people, and established the covenant of peace with his people through this Mediator.

Comfort is found in the Word of God preached which quickens them by exercising faith in it. The people of God no doubt receive more profit and comfort by the Word preached, then by the Word read. How well do they hear the voice of God in the preacher? How well, then, does the preacher preach? "Faith comes by hearing" the Apostle says, Rom. 10:17, and in 1 Cor. 1:21, "it hath pleased God by the foolishness of preaching to save such as do believe." Gods words are very mighty when they are preached in the Spirit to comfort the soul. He attends that preaching in a very special manner. When Paul says that the Gospel is the power of God unto salvation, what does he mean here but the preaching of the Word of God? And such comfort comes by way of application; to have the word applied to the soul.

The comfort received by the word of God in times of affliction, that which will sustain the soul, is because the Christian does not rest solely in the universal promises of

God. He knows that they cannot minister any true comfort and consolation to the soul except there is a *particular application* of this to himself, worked by the Holy Spirit. This is the importance of godly meditation on such things, as the sermon, as on preaching. Meditation chews the word and applies it to the soul. Without it, what comfort will ever come? Jesus says that men who come to him he will never cast away, and they will find rest, and so the soul must ask, "Can I come to him?" If that isn't applied in the right way, the soul *never* comes to him. What will it gain for a general truth knowing that he can come, but doesn't know if he can come? It must be particular to them. And the divine consolation that comes from the word is particular, though it may even be generally stated.

This is why preaching is so important in this light of consolation to the Christian. The preacher is to apply it. The preacher should be able to do so. Samuel Hieron a puritan divine said, "Those who fear God, and tremble at his words, and in humility desire to know the secrets of the Lord's covenant, find that when they increase in the knowledge of the truth, which is according to godliness, and in power of godliness, do find their judgements better strengthened, their faith more confirmed, their consciences more worked on, and their affections more quickened by the word when it is effectually preached and applied, then when it is but only read to them."[2] Yet they must exercise faith in it, but especially when it is preached with a purpose.

To be comforted by the word is in the context of affliction. The scripture shows us the true doctrine about

---

[2] Hieron, Samuel, *The Preachers Plea*, (London: R. Field, 1604), 122.

afflictions, and shows to us the author, cause, and end of all our afflictions. The author is God, the cause is sin, the end is to humble, mortify, and correct his children, that they may be more capable to take in heaven and God's glory. It is God visiting his people. The plague is hard, people are dying, but God is visiting his people as the *Author* of affliction. It is not by chance the plague came about, (for chance is really nothing as a first cause). God does all things with the most exact wisdom for his people, and with love, and with tender mercy. And as afflictions continue, as the plague continues, the end is the Christian's spiritual good, for Christ says that those he loves he chastens. His chastisements are a kind of medicine, brought by the Great Physician, prescribed that they would be humble, repentant, confessional, and with much zeal. They will cure them, all those who take the prescription rightly, of some spiritual disease. But they must have some comfort, and not all affliction. Or rather, comfort of the Savior in affliction. What do they hope in? They *hope* to be delivered. This is not what the psalmist concentrates on. What do they look to? They look to the word of God which sustains them. They look to it, because they love it. They look to Christ to transform them further, not merely to take away that which is difficult. They are happy to go through whatever Christ sends them, for even in affliction, they are quickened by his word. The love of the word is a help to comfort in affliction, and may quicken a Christian's heart, in them that are saved. "This is my comfort in my affliction: for thy word hath quickened me," (Psa. 119:50). How will a Christian fulfill his obligations to God, even just in being content, in the midst of occasional repentance, without knowledge to know what he is to do or how he ought to feel? Why talk about the plague, humility, confession, repentance, prayer and fasting, zeal and lamentation, without being able to know how those things all apply in the promises of God in which the Christian loves to follow God? These people love to follow God not on mere feelings, but in informed feelings. Yes, the Christian is an emotional being. Whatever afflictions are swirling about him, whatever difficulties are there, he will in some way become emotional about them. The word of God, though, informs their mind, so that they may be able to inform their heart as to how those emotions should react. But the text gives the Christian an assurance that through the word of God, if they understand it, if they hear it rightly, if it is ministered to their soul, they can be comforted by it. The Spirit will do great things in this as a result. He will spiritually persuade them of all that Christ's benefits can do, and they will take hold of it by faith. But if they do not love the word, if they do not turn to the word, how will they be comforted? If they do not take time to think about it?

Comfort in the word of God, is comfort in the Logos of God. Anytime the bible says anything about *anything* is a communication of the divine word of God to the believer. If there is a written word, it is the Logos of God, the word of God, the Son of God, communicating. It doesn't matter what is being said, in some context, in some manner, in some way, the Logos of God is being poured forth. The Logos of God, the Christ of God, the Word of God are all one. To be comforted by the word of God which quickens, is to be comforted with the Word himself, who sends his Spirit in operation to quicken and give comfort through his power, which is of his essence, the word of God.

The Logos was the Logos before all worlds were created. He did not cease to be the Word of God when he assumed the human nature of the Christ. He was always the second person of the Triune Godhead. Christ, as the Logos, is the active Word of God, the origin and instrument of all things, even in framing the world. The Logos is the one who appeared to Adam and walked in the cool of the day with him. This Logos is the same who appeared in Genesis 17. It is said in verse 22 of that chapter, "That God went up from Abraham." Of the appearance of three in human shape to Abraham, that the person to whom Abraham particularly addresses himself, calling him his Lord, was the Son of God, attended then only but with two visible angels. The Logos was that Angel of God who wrestled with, and blessed Jacob. The Angel whose protection Jacob prayed, and saw in a vision as they ascended and descended on the Logos, the ladder which reached to heaven and touched the earth. He is mentioned so often as the Word of the Father. It is by this Logos that the Lord gave all physical laws to nature, and also gave the moral Law to Israel. It was the Logos who appeared to the people from the mountain and spoke, in the wilderness in fire, and smoke and glory. Between the cherubim, and on the cover of the Ark the Logos appeared yet shrouded with thick clouds at the sacrifice. He appeared in the appearance of brightness, where the glory of God was said to have appeared in or at the Tabernacle. The ark itself being called the mercy seat, and the glory of God in beautiful luster. Even David said he saw the glory or radiant presence of God in the sanctuary. It was the glory of the Word, the Logos of God, whose glory shone on the Ark, by many places in Scripture which speak of the Ark as a type of the Son incarnate. The High-Priest, with Moses and Aaron, was, a type of the Logos. The Logos spoke out of the glory cloud above the ark to the priest, above the Cherubim, the High-Priest, then being the mouth of God to the people, a Logos of the Logos so to speak; to speak to the people. The Logos is the one Isaiah saw seated high and lofty. This is the same Logos as in Ezekiel's chariot of majesty, his chariot throne by the River Chebar, the Divine Logos in shekinah glory commanding wheels inside wheels seated on the throne. God spoke formerly by his Son as his Logos or Ministering Word, and in the latter times by his Son incarnate, or as begotten by the Holy Spirit of the substance of the Virgin.

Hebrews says that the throne of Christ, as God's Logos, was from everlasting, but that in the incarnation the Logos took on flesh. This Word both spoke by the Prophets things to come, and also by himself, being made subject to the same infirmities of the flesh with his people.

In surveying Paul's writings, when one compares the Angel of the Lord in the Old Testament being used by the Divine Logos as the immediate minister of himself to the people, and then Christ speaking with his own mouth under the Gospel as the God-man incarnate, and looking at the great mystery of the Gospel consisting in the manifestation of God in the flesh, Paul had very good reason to prefer the Gospel before the Law in this way because it housed more light. Though, in the beginning

190

was the Logos, and the Logos was with God and was God, he then, as John depicts, is God with his people. Immanuel. This one John saw in a vision, in which the Logos , God Omnipotent (Rev. 19), the King of Kings, and Lord of Lords, or Lamb, God-man, appeared on his throne, crowned, and with eyes like flames of fire, upon his head were many crowns, and there was a name written on his that no one knows but himself. He is the AMEN, the FAITHFUL and TRUE witness. Witness to what? To the truth and Word of God and to himself and his character.

When the Christian looks for comfort in the Word, he looks for comfort in the Christ, in the Logos of God; the *logic* of God. The word of God is the medium of comfort, "in my affliction," the word is the comfort, because the word is the person of the eternal WORD. Christ draws close to his people through the word, through himself. Christ sends suffering and then uses the word to those who will exercise faith in what he says, to comfort the afflicted. Christ looks to crush his people in order for them to be useful to his kingdom. Crushed? Disciples are like wheat, and wheat, to be useful, must be made into bread. They are plucked, crushed, milled, mixed, beaten, molded and placed in the fire. The plague, here today, is a fire. The massive change in the world structure of interaction, is a fire. But in all the crushing, there is consolation. Christ endured being roasted as with the fire of God's wrath, with much suffering. An end of this work, the Logos was to be a comfort to his people. How could he be the Consolation of Israel to anyone without having gone through suffering himself? Hebrews 2:18, "For in that He Himself has suffered, being tempted, He is able to aid those who are tempted." How does he bring aid? Does he step down out of heaven off a cloud and make house calls in his person? He does in a loving sense, send the plague to his people. And then he expects them to look to his word. It is there he not only makes house calls, but is in every heart that believes on and in him. But in such a difficulty, he sends his Spirit in conjunction with the word to the hearts of his people to comfort them – to give them a word of comfort and consolation; to believe what he says which is in fact believing him. If the Christian is going to be inwardly comforted in their soul, he must hunger after the Logos, and be satisfied with the bread of heaven found in the word.

How do *we* gain this comfort in any affliction especially in times of occasional repentance? When we come to God's promises, we must abandon all our own merits, and recognize that all the grace we find in the promises, is in and through Jesus Christ, the eternal Word. All the promises are yes and amen through him, and only him. There is nothing we bring to the table in that regard.

Second, when we have the promises opened to us, we must believe them ourselves and apply them or they will do us no good. You must take time to think about them. You might say, "That's takes so much work and time." Every relationship that is worth anything takes work and time. What kind of relationship do you desire with God?

Third, we must be careful to, "hide them in our hearts," as this psalmist said, that we may think about them and meditate on them. It will do us no good at all if they merely sit on the pages of the bible. They must be engraved on our hearts, and thought about in our mind. That is why godly meditation is both so neglected, because it is hard, but so necessary because it makes the promises of God applicable to us.

Fourth, when any affliction comes to us, we must go to the Logos, to the Word, and look to him for strength, and plead those promises that the Spirit would work in us consolation. It is a trusting on the word already spoken and written down. Christians are not to have their bible on their lap, and look up to heaven, hoping the Spirit will zap them with a word from the Father about what Christ will do for them. They must open its pages and read it.

Fifth, you must not rest on the world, or the love of the world, or the help of the world; there is no comfort there. If you desire that God would have access to your heart, you must cast off the world, so that you will rest on the word. You can't ever have a sweet taste of God's book if the world tastes sweet to you. Until the goods and pleasures of the world are disgusting, and unpleasant to you, God's word will remain difficult, and tedious and unpleasant. It is impossible to have one eye looking up to heaven and one eye looking down to earth. How will one receive consolation from heaven if he is divided? Can one serve two masters? If your affections are fixed toward earthly things, you cannot enjoy the comforts of looking up to Christ, the eternal word. Earthly things quench the comfort you would gain by the word if you look to them for comfort.

You might ask, why must we go through these afflictions at all? Well, we must suffer afflictions because by them we are conformed to Christ Jesus. God orders them for our good. They are those messages and rebukes and chastisements of our heavenly Father which proceed from his love to his church. He provides the cause and also provides the remedy. He provides the plague, and provides the word. Is he not gracious to provide that which will cause you to be drawn closer to him at times? They are, in fact, sovereignly given to his people, and eased by his mercy through the word. They are sweetened, with many comforts from Christ. They are medicinal to your soul. Such afflictions will bring you to a great sense of your sins, and should, through the affliction, sorrow for them. But, as we considered, they will quicken our zeal and devotion to God because we are prone to desire to be freed from them. Daniel Featly said of this, "Afflictions preserve and free us from everlasting torments. If we patiently endure them, our reward shall be plentiful in heaven. They teach us to be compassionate to our brethren, and comfort them in their adversities."[3] But where do we learn such things?

We learn Christ's love both in the affliction, and yet, as we turn to the word while in affliction. Here we see and experience the heart comforted from Christ. Life is filled with promised misery. *The 1647 Westminster Shorter Catechism* asks in question 23, "Into what estate did the fall bring mankind?" Answer, "The fall brought mankind into an estate of sin and misery. What is misery? Unhappiness, distress, suffering, anguish, anxiety, angst, torment, pain, grief, heartache, heartbreak, despair, despondency, dejection, depression, desolation, gloom, melancholy, woe, sadness, sorrow. "He has filled me with

---

[3] Featley, Daniel, *Ancilla Pietatis,* (At London: Printed for Nicholas Bourne, 1626), 283.

bitterness, He has made me drink wormwood. He has also broken my teeth with gravel, and covered me with ashes," (Lam. 3:15-16). There is a lamentation of a godly soul in bitter affliction.

Which one of you does not need to be comforted in affliction? Did you think that being a Christian, suddenly, life is a bed of roses? What...do you think once you were converted you would no longer feel the effects of sin in your life? Have you been so delivered by Christ that you experience no turmoil, no difficulties, and that your life is a walk in the park? To be a Christian is to suffer. "In the world you will have tribulation." Yet he gives his disciples a word of comfort, "but be of good cheer, I have overcome the world," (John 16:33). Why did Jesus use the word "I?" He used it because he is the eternal Logos, the eternal Word, that you constantly need. And the smallest amount of joy reaped from God's word in Christ's comfort is greater than the heaviest affliction or suffering, even a plague, or sword, or famine. A drop of Christ's comfort alleviates a mountain of affliction. The only discernable difference is that the greater the affliction is, the greater the comfort. Affliction can never quench the comfort God gives through the word; unless you ignore it. "This is my comfort in my affliction: for thy word hath quickened me," (Psa. 119:50).

Affliction and comfort are always the same in Christ, in that they are through the Spirit of Grace, but, they are of varying degrees. Some are heavy, and some are light. But affliction is still difficulty at any level. God is infinitely loving, tender, and compassionate towards his people in all their afflictions; big or small. He orders all your afflictions and waits to give you consolation through the word which will quicken you and sustain you; will you look there?

God is a loving God who loves you as his people. "But as for you, you meant evil against me; but God meant it for good, in order to bring it about as it is this day, to save many people alive," (Gen. 50:20). Was God "with" Joseph? Was he with him only as chief steward over all Egypt, or was he with him even when he was thrown into the pit, or sold as a slave, or thrown into prison? Was God with him in all those circumstances?

God orders everything. He is sovereign over all suffering of every kind. He sees you, cares for you, afflicts you, and rescues you. He knows how to comfort you because his affliction is a refiner's fire. "Then shall the virgin rejoice in the dance, And the young men and the old, together; For I will turn their mourning into joy, and will comfort them, And make them rejoice from their sorrow," (Jer. 31:13). "Let my teaching drop as the rain, My speech distill as the dew, As raindrops on the tender herb, And as showers on the grass. For I proclaim the name of the LORD: Ascribe greatness to our God. He is the Rock, His work is perfect; For all His ways are justice, A God of truth and without injustice; Righteous and upright is He," (Deut. 32:2-4). Drops of the bible, biblical consolation here and there makes all the afflictions lighten up. So, the smallest amount of comfort bestowed is able to alleviate such seemingly difficult providences.

You must not forget that affliction and word-based comfort are glorious messengers from Jesus Christ. It is not enough to simply say that God ordains trials and afflictions for your good, and stop there. This is true, but it has been said so much that it becomes cliché with many. This is where the misery of the situation overrides your informed mind. You begin to believe it is cliché. You toss this into the box of, "God ordains everything. So, this is just how it is." That is not how God desires his people to deal with afflictions. There they lie on the bed of affliction waiting for the waters to be stirred and day after day they in great difficulty looking for respite, of even the least kind, looking for that small drop. They, many times, miss the whole sanctifying idea of affliction. This is so true of the plague now among us.

Affliction is a messenger of love from Christ to the you. "All the paths of the LORD are mercy," (Psa. 25:10). What about afflictions, is that mercy too for you? Comfort far outweighs the suffering, and it will be a delight to your soul when God brings it in due time. Think on it, is there any suffering and trial greater than the cross of Christ for you? His suffering was so great, that before the actual time of his curse and death, the very thought of the curse and death caused the Christ to sweat great drops of blood in intense agony in the garden. He sweat blood. It is unfathomable to the finite mind to understand how the Christ endured such suffering and torment; willingly. Incomprehensible was the prospect of undergoing infinite wrath, not for his own deeds (which were perfect and without blemish) but for the deeds of others – for Adam's curse and your personal sins. "For the joy that was set before him endured the cross, despising the shame," and what was the comfort? "and has sat down at the right hand of the throne of God," (Heb. 12:2). Christ was exalted in due time, with an exaltation as remarkable as the cross was horrific. Comfort through the word, in this way, is a sweet messenger from Christ.

This comfort is delivered by means of the word of God. The word is used by the Holy Spirit in you to supernaturally deliver comfort. This is gained when you believe the word by faith when it is heard or read. You are refreshed and comforted with particular favors God has assured you of in his word. He will not deal with us after our sins, "nor reward us after our iniquities," (Psalm 103). It is great comfort. He will, "spare us, as a man spareth his son that serveth him." No father can show compassion like God is bound to show to his children, (Malachi 3:17). It is great comfort. In all times you have, "access to the throne of grace," to go boldly to ask, "in the name of Christ, and it shall be given," (Hebrews 4:16). It is great comfort. "In all their affliction He was afflicted, And the Angel of His Presence saved them; in His love and in His pity He redeemed them; And He bore them and carried them All the days of old," (Isa. 63:9). What great comfort is this? "He giveth power to the faint, and to them that have no might, he increases strength. They that wait on the Lord shall renew their strength," (Isaiah 40:29, 31). It is great comfort from great promises. How do you know this? *This is my comfort in my affliction: for thy word hath quickened me.*

Next, we will deal with the hammer of Christ's judgment at his second coming, in which all the difficulties in this life are mere birth pangs.

Chapter 8:
Tokens of Eternal Displeasure

"All these are the beginning of sorrows," (Matt. 24:8).

There are certain events which must occur before the return of the Lord's final coming. What are they? What might they look like? Before the final appearance of the Christ to usher in the full Kingdom of God, there are certain signs and events which must come before the final judgment. Scripture says Christ will return in "a very little while," (Heb. 10:37), or, "quickly," (Rev. 22:7). There are a variety of encouragements to watch for his coming, (Matt. 24:42; 25:13; Rev. 16:15). Yet, in the parable of the talents he teaches that the Lord of the servants came to reckon with them "after a long time," (Matt. 25:19). "And as they heard these things, he added and spake a parable, because he was nigh to Jerusalem, and because they thought that the kingdom of God should immediately appear," (Luke 19:11). In the parable of the ten virgins the bridegroom is "tarrying," (Matt. 25:5). Paul says in 2 Thess. 2:2, "That ye be not soon shaken in mind, or be troubled, neither by spirit, nor by word, nor by letter as from us, as that the day of Christ is at hand," (2 Thess. 2:2). 2 Peter 3:3-9, "Knowing this first, that there shall come in the last days scoffers, walking after their own lusts, And saying, Where is the promise of his coming?" (2 Peter 3:3-4). "But, beloved, be not ignorant of this one thing, that one day is with the Lord as a thousand years, and a thousand years as one day," (2 Peter 3:8).

In this passage of Matthew 24 Jesus teaches to watch for his coming through *signs*. "And Jesus went out, and departed from the temple: and his disciples came to him for to shew him the buildings of the temple." "Look at the magnificence of the temple, Lord," the disciples pointed out. Look at the great stones. Now keep in mind this was the second temple, where the grandeur of the first was gone, but in restoration God built a smaller one, for the good of his church up to this point. Verse 2, "And Jesus said unto them, See ye not all these things? verily I say unto you, There shall not be left here one stone upon another, that shall not be thrown down." Not only is the temple going to be destroyed, but it will be utterly deserted by God. Such a prediction is fulfilled in AD 70 at the destruction of the temple. But keep in mind that the manner in which Jesus speaks in this passage is to be very discerning in speaking about both things temporal, as well as things that concern the final coming of the kingdom. Some things concern temporary judgment, and other things the final judgment, even through Matthew chapter 25. This is not the place to deal with all of those. But only to say that Christ intertwines both temporary judgment and the final judgment in his discourse, two different ideas for two different times. It is *not* chronological in his speech. He moves in-between the two ideas throughout. Knowing this helps the student of this passage not to become confused by his weaving and intertwining of thoughts.

Verse 3, "And as he sat upon the mount of Olives, the disciples came unto him privately, saying, Tell us, when shall these things be? and what shall be the sign of thy coming, and of the end of the world?" Who is not interested eschatologically about the end of things, whether temporal or eternal? The disciples were. "Tell us, when shall these things be? and what shall be the sign of thy coming, and of the end of the world?" When shall these things be? Their rightful assumption is that Christ is coming to do this. And, ... tell us about the end of all things, since temporary judgments are a sign of eternal judgments. Even the disciples knew this. Jerusalem's fall in the temple's destruction, the house of prayer, the place of the church's sacrifice and meeting, would mean the end of the world, so to speak; at least a picture of it. But again, Jesus separates the temporary from the eternal. He explains both, but at different times. One soon, and one final. Verse 4, "And Jesus answered and said unto them, Take heed that no man deceive you." Not everything that you think is a sign, is a sign of the end of the world. There are general signs which point in that direction, and you must be discerning about them. Verse 5, "For many shall come in my name, saying, I am Christ; and shall deceive many." False deceivers are sign posts to judgment, but they are not the end. False deceivers will come in Christ's name, they will deceive many, but they are only a precursor. Verse 6, "And ye shall hear of wars and rumours of wars: see that ye be not troubled: for all these things must come to pass, but the end is not yet." Wars and rumors of wars are precursors, but the end is not yet. Verse 7, "For nation shall rise against nation, and kingdom against kingdom: and there shall be famines, and pestilences, and earthquakes, in diverse places." These are also precursors to the end in that they are a "not yet" of what the final "yet" will be to a

201

greater affect; let me give some examples. Shaanxi earthquake January 23, 1556, China, 820,000–830,000 dead. On Nov. 1, 1755, 60,000 people perished at Lisbon, Portugal in an earthquake. Russia, 1952: 9.0, more than 2,300 people were killed when this earthquake hit Siberia's Kamchatka Peninsula, causing a tsunami felt as far as Chile and Peru. Haiti, 2010: more than 200,000 killed, in a 7.0-earthquake. What terrible earthquakes, but, *the end is not yet.* Famines - 800–1000AD Severe drought killed millions of Mayan people due to famine that destroyed their entire civilization, Mayan areas of Mesoamerica 1,000,000+. In 1230–1231, there was the Kanki famine, possibly the worst famine in Japan's history, 2,000,000 died. 1769–1773 Great Bengal famine of 1770, 10 million dead (one third of population). In India, in the city of Bangladesh (present day) 10,000,000 died. Famine, but ... *the end is not yet.* And what of plagues? The plague of Justinian arrived in Constantinople, the capital of the Byzantine Empire, in 541 AD. Plague-ridden fleas hitched a ride on the black rats that snacked on the grain. The plague decimated Constantinople and spread across Europe, Asia, North Africa and Arabia killing 50 million people, at the time, perhaps even half of the world's population. The Black Death, Europe 1347, claimed 200 million lives in just four years. London was struck by this after, again, as the plague resurfaced roughly every 20 years from 1348 to 1665: 40 outbreaks in 300 years. And with each new plague epidemic, 20 percent of the men, women and children living in the British capital were killed. Coronavirus, 2019, claimed so far, 600,000+ in just 4 months. But, *the end is not yet.* Earthquakes, famine, pestilence, wars, and false teachers are signs, *but the end is not yet.* Jesus says, verse 8, "All these are the *beginning* of sorrows," (Matt. 24:8). Not the end of sorrows; not the final time when these things are seen, *yet.* Only the beginning of the end. Certain things happen, verse 12, and then the end. The Gospel must be preached to the ends of the earth, verse 14, to all nations. Then in the ensuing verses he continues to go back and forth between the destruction of Jerusalem and the temple, and the end of the world, as differing events, but things temporary are the beginning of sorrows.

The remaining discourse of Christ on these beginnings of sorrows, and the subsequent end of the world, things both temporary and things eternal, are set in the context of his coming judgment and reign and the need to be watchful for the Christ who returns in glory. "And then shall appear the sign of the Son of man in heaven: and then shall all the tribes of the earth mourn, and they shall see the Son of man coming in the clouds of heaven with power and great glory," (Matt. 24:30). It is not known when it shall be. People will be going about their business and the end will come swiftly, and it will be without mistake; everyone will know it. It will be like the flood of Noah. It will come while people are feasting in their house. It will come when people are doing their daily chores. It will come when people are at work. "Watch therefore..." (Matt. 24:42). For the kingdom is likened to wise and foolish virgins, some who had oil and others not. Some who slept unawares, who were not ready. Some who were ready. And in the end, in the final end, when judgment shall ensure, "When the Son of man shall come in his glory, and all the holy angels with him, then shall he sit upon the throne of his glory: And before him shall be gathered all nations: and he shall separate them one from another, as a shepherd divideth his sheep from the goats. And he shall set the sheep on his right hand, but the goats on the left," (Matt. 25:31-33). "And these shall go away into everlasting punishment: but the righteous into life eternal," (Matt. 25:46). The beginning of sorrows is not the end. Temporal rebukes and temporal chastisements on the church are a token or precursor to the coming of final judgment of the Son of Man.

DOCTRINE: All sufferings experienced in this world by sinners are the mere beginnings of sorrows.

I want to divide the saint from the sinner, biblically but briefly. I have spoken at great length to the church about her covenant breaking sins. But, amidst such, God uses these times of pestilence to send sinners signposts of his judgment to come. "But the men of Sodom were wicked and sinners before the LORD exceedingly," (Gen. 13:13), these sinners are unconverted, lost, unsaved, goats, *i.e.* sinners. "Blessed is the man that walketh not in the counsel of the ungodly, nor standeth in the way of sinners, nor sitteth in the seat of the scornful," (Psa. 1:1). "Then will I teach transgressors thy ways; and sinners shall be converted unto thee," (Psa. 51:13). Not converted people to be converted, but sinners to be converted. "Let not thine heart envy sinners: but be thou in the fear of the LORD all the day long," (Prov. 23:17). Do not envy people outside the covenant. "The sinners in Zion are afraid; fearfulness hath surprised the hypocrites," (Isa. 33:14). There are hypocrites in the church. "For I am not come to call the righteous, but sinners to repentance," (Matt. 9:13). Conversion towards godly repentance is done by sinners. "Now we know that God heareth not sinners: but if any man be a worshipper of God, and doeth his will, him he heareth," (John 9:31). The wicked's prayers are an abomination, *wicked sinners.* "But God commendeth his love toward us, in that, while we were yet sinners, Christ died for us," (Rom. 5:8). They are sinners, then they are converted. "For as by one man's disobedience many were made sinners, so by the obedience of one shall many be made righteous," (Rom. 5:19). In Adam, and in Christ, there are those who are represented. There are sinners in Adam, and there are *converted sinners,* made saints, made righteous, in Jesus Christ. "To execute judgment upon all, and to convince all that are ungodly among them of all their ungodly deeds which they have ungodly committed, and of all their hard speeches which ungodly sinners have spoken against him," (Jude 1:15). Overwhelmingly, throughout Scripture, *sinners are lost* and can be saved, and when they are saved, they are then called other things, such as: elect, saints, beloved, new men, followers of the way, Christians, believers, good servants, fruitful trees, sheep, righteous in contrast to the wicked because of the work of Christ on their soul. That does not mean they do not sin. "My little children, these things write I unto you, that ye sin not. And if any man sin, we have an advocate with the Father, Jesus Christ the righteous," (1 John 2:1). Or, "Let us lay aside every weight, and the sin which doth so easily beset us," (Heb. 12:1). There is a division though, to sufferings, which are still for the believer and are tokens of final judgment, but work in a far different way than they do to the wicked. This will be considered for the saint in the next chapter. But know at this point, all suffering, all misery, all of it is due to the fall, to sin, and they are all shadows of hell for sinners, for the lost, for the wicked, for the goats. Some overcome by the blood of Christ that are then saved, and some are crushed beneath these sorrows, for all things turn to sorrow for the sinner.

[1] All suffering experienced in this world is due to sin. This has been proved in other chapters. Pestilence, sword or famine exists because of sin and the fall. Why is the plague here across this planet right now; why have there been plagues, why will there be more plagues? The pestilence is here because of the real pandemic which is sin, "as by one man sin entered into the world, and death by sin," (Rom. 5:12). The reason that plagues exist is a result of the curse of God in the fall against Adam; as said before, sin is the real pandemic. Death is a result of the fall. Sickness is a result of the fall. Pestilence is an infection, a deadly disease, sent of God upon men for their sins; it is part of the misery of this life. "The LORD shall make the pestilence cleave unto thee," (Deut. 28:21). The fall and sin are the reasons there is pestilence. If Adam had not fell, there would be no plagues, no sickness, no disease, no sleeping, no tiredness, and no death. By way of reminder, *The 1647 Westminster Larger Catechism,* question 28 asks, "What are the punishments of sin in this world? A28: The punishments of sin in this world are either inward, as blindness of mind, a reprobate sense, strong delusions, hardness of heart, horror of conscience, and vile affections; or outward, as the curse of God upon the creatures for our sakes, and all other evils that befall us in our bodies, names,

estates, relations, and employments; together with death itself." All of this is due to sin.

[2] All suffering experienced in this world due to sin are tokens of future misery for sinners. They are the "beginnings of sorrows," *travail,* (taken from childbearing in pain as part of the curse.) These are dire calamites that precede the coming of the Messiah as sorrows for the wicked. They are vouchers, receipts, rainchecks, and promises. Of what? ... of the future calamity that will befall them into eternity after they are separated at the judgment seat of Jesus Christ from the righteous. Sorrows are a deep distress, they are sadnesses; they are a regret for losing something they loved where now there is a resultant unhappy or unpleasant state. And if a sinner is unhappy or unpleasant now, what will they be like under the full and terrible future sorrow after they are judged according to their deeds in the flesh? Pestilence is so dreadful now. What will the final death be for them at that time? This is a mere beginning of sorrows, before future sorrows which run into eternity and hold the weight of infinite full and terrible judgment by the Christ. Future sorrows begin at the judgment of Christ, and extend into forever for all unrepentant sinners.

[3] All suffering experienced in this world due to sin are tokens of the misery declared by Christ against the wicked at the last judgment, by Christ, the glorious Son of Man. Oftentimes people think because God does not act immediately, that he will not act at all; men sin, and they wait for the lightening from heaven, and none comes. But, this idea is contrary to God's purpose in Scripture, knowing that God long suffers for a time, in order to allow

sinners to fill up the exact measure of their sin, for the exact time of judgment by God's Christ. It is true, this means that he puts up with sinners in order to damn them further under his just judgment as a result of both their fallenness in Adam and in the further damnation of their wicked deeds. The longer one sins the more wrath they treasure up, and the greater God's vengeance will be at last. As sin increases, so will the wrath of God's vengeance in the end. "For the iniquity of the Amorites is not yet complete," (Gen. 15:16). "...always to fill up the measure of their sins; but wrath has come upon them to the uttermost," (1 Thess. 2:16). Jesus Christ will appear to judge the world. Should this not, then, press sinners to repent with humility and godly sorrow now? Revelation 1:7 says, "Behold He comes with clouds, and every eye shall see him, and they that pierced him shall see him, and all the kindreds of the earth shall wail because of Him, even so, amen." Acts 17:30-31, that, "the times of ignorance God winked at, but now He commands all men everywhere to repent." Why? "Because God hath appointed a day in which He will judge the world by that man, Christ Jesus." Every man should repent because God has appointed a day where Christ will judge them to the exact measure of every sin. There is a day where Christ will judge the world; therefore repent. Such a day will be of God's vengeance. It will be unalterable. It is accomplished by the God-man, the holy and righteous Son of Man. Face to face with the divine Son from heaven. In the future time of sorrows, at the judgement, all men will see Christ, the Son of Man, in immediate judgment. All are appointed once to die then judgment. From here men go into Christ's courtroom where the Son of Man opens the books of their life, and they are judged for every thought, every action, every word, every idle moment, every wicked sin, every wandering eye, every vain thought, everything. 600,000 people have done this in the last four months having gone from the beginning of sorrows to the final sorrow of their judgment if they died unrepentant, hard hearted sinners.

Christ does this at the last judgment. God is holy, and he is just. The justice of God is an essential attribute of God. Romans 2:5 says, "But in accordance with your hardness and your impenitent heart you are treasuring up for yourself wrath in the day of wrath and revelation of the righteous judgment of God." God's justice *demands* sin is punished with death. Romans 1:32, "who, knowing the righteous judgment of God, that those who practice such things are deserving of death, not only do the same but also approve of those who practice them." It must be done for God to stay consistent with his character. A righteous judge would be seen as crooked and wicked if he suddenly allowed a murderer off the hook though the murder was guilty. God cannot allow men to continue to defy his character and break the law without punitive justice. The penal sanction of death is based upon the just nature of God. Everything associated with justice derives from God's nature. Eternal death is not simply an arbitrary sanction that God "came up with." It depends on the holy nature of God. Job 33:12–13, "For God is greater than man. Why do you contend with Him?" It is a just act based on holiness and Law. The reason it is a just act to damn those who sin unrepentantly is that sin is infinite in relation to its attack upon God who is infinite, therefore punishment must be infinite as well. It is committed against an infinite God, so sin must be of infinite duration in this respect against him. Sin can only be removed by Christ's blood, or else it stands forever and must be punished for an infinite duration by God's holiness. The place where this judgment occurs by the Christ, God's man, is at the last judgment.

At the soul's final judgment, the destiny of sinners shall be unalterably determined by the Christ. Against the wicked, God's judgments in this life, are the *beginnings* of future judgment. In Deut. 32:42, "I will make my arrows drunk with blood (and my sword shall devour flesh) and that with the blood of the slain, and of the captives, from the beginning of revenge upon the enemy." All this is but the beginning of God's vengeance on sinners. People, now three or four months or so into this pandemic, are ready to think that enough is enough. Let's get back to life as we had it before. Such a plague is but the beginning of sorrows, life will never be the same because there are eternal consequences to the *signpost* of the pandemic. Though the Lord many times has made pestilence lace the earth with the blood of its victims, yet it proves only to be but the beginning of sorrows. What would the 600,000 people say if they were allowed for moment to return from the dead and speak to the world on the news? Even if one were brought back from the dead sinners *still would not listen.* Let us eat, drink and be merry for tomorrow we die! And since such temporary judgments have been brought on the earth in these past months, how scarcely has the church turned to God, how scarcely have wicked people turned? Is the gate of the Kingdom of Heaven further away than it was before to sinners? Has it been brought closer that men would repent and turn from their sinful ways? These beginnings of sorrows point to a future sorrow for sinners.

The future abode of the unrighteous is a place of future punishment. The wicked shall go away into everlasting punishment, as Christ said. The Bible teaches that the unrighteous suffer from the loss of all earthly goods, from exclusion from the gracious presence and favor of God, from utter reprobation (the final withdrawal from them of the Holy Spirit's gracious influence), from the consequent unrestrained dominion of sin and sinful passions, from the operations of an evil conscience, from utter despair, from the company of evil associates including demons and the devil, and the never ending torment of God's wrath on their soul and body. The design of eternal punishment is set in the conscious existence of the soul after the death of the body. It is unending physical, emotional and spiritual torture where there is no escape, repentance or reformation; future sorrow. It is the judgment of the Christ on sinners forever for their rebellion. Those who depart this life unreconciled to God remain forever in this state of alienation and are therefore forever sinful and miserable under the full torment of Christ's hell. The prophet Daniel in 12:2 says of the wicked, that they "shall awake...to shame and everlasting contempt." In Luke 3:17 it is said that Christ shall "gather the wheat into his garner; but the chaff He will burn with fire unquenchable." In Mark 9:42-48 our Lord says that it is better "to enter into life maimed, than, having two hands, to go into hell, into the fire that never shall be quenched: where their worm dieth not, and the fire is not

211

quenched." Christ will say to the wicked on the last day, "Depart from me, ye cursed, into everlasting fire." "And these shall go away into everlasting punishment." Jude says that for such apostates (verses 12-13) there is reserved for them "the blackness of darkness forever." In Revelation 21:8 is found a short list of the sins of men who shall ultimately reside in hell, "But the fearful, and unbelieving, and the abominable, and murderers, and whoremongers, and sorcerers, and idolaters, and all liars, shall have their part in the lake which burneth with fire and brimstone: which is the second death." They are self-willed in that they continue in unbelief, though God has furnished them with a remedy in Christ now; and he throws them signposts to direct them in their course to consider the signs of the times; but they do not consider.

[4] Lost men often think better of their situation in afflictions, thinking that things will become better even during a time of sorrow. They declare this in opposition to the word of God. In today's pandemic, they say "we will get through this." To get through, to muster through, to move past it, hoping to get rid of it. But it is the beginning of sorrows, in which points to a continuance of sorrow; and they are missing the message. They will not be able to move through it, to overcome it, to get passed it. It is a pointer, a road sign to other things; eternal unavoidable truths and realities. Sinners make anything to be their comfort other than Jesus Christ when sorrows occur. Good ministers of God threaten God's judgments in temporary occurrences. God has a quarrel against his church, and there is seen, now in this very day, some tokens of God's wrath on the earth. The church's sins have

brought on these signs of judgment even on sinners too. This is what Jesus said when he references the house of prayer, yet spoke to his disciples about both the temple (covenant believers) and sinners. Men think, well, let the worst come, we will press through it. They say, "the worst is over." Whatever men think they can do, they cannot. Men's thoughts will move here and there and try to find some temporal means to placate them only to result in an epic fail for them. They are worldly men who think in a worldly way, and all worldliness is *vain*. God says, "You think to outsmart my beginnings of sorrows that you now see in this place, on this earth, you will be greatly disappointed. For my wrath and displeasure shall pursue you in every way, in every place. For it is a very vain thing to cast off temporary sorrows and not see them as my token of displeasure towards future sorrow. You are missing my message and will be further judged for doing so by my Christ." It is a very great affliction and misery to be forced to stay indoors, to stop working, to lose businesses, to starve, to have commerce interrupted, to have hundreds of thousands of people meet their end in a short time period as this has been. It is a great sorrow for the people of God, even for sinners, to have the church close its doors and have no place to hear the preaching of the word that converts sinners to saints. What shall they think as they cannot have the freedom of God's worship in their churches that are closed? They are not giving it two seconds thought.

All these are merely the beginnings of sorrows. If men cannot bear the beginnings of sorrows, how shall they bear the inevitability of those things that will come in their fullness at the last day? If there is some peace they look for or try to find at present, what will they do when the flood comes and the hammer drops? They often think things are far better, for they suppress the truth in unrighteousness and misuse the very providence that is warning them of the impending judgment to come, whether in their death, or at the return of the Lord of Glory.

[5] All these tokens are shadows of hell. If these are the beginnings, what will follow for sinners? What must follow if these are merely birth pangs? All suffering experienced in this world due to sin are tokens of the full and terrible misery declared by Christ against the wicked at the last judgment. Though it is sent to Christ's church, it is quite applicable to sinners secondarily.

They are going to be *full and terrible*. As overwhelming as temporary miseries are now, they are nothing in comparison of the fullness of the wrath of God at the final judgment. Fullness of wrath against sin. Fullness of wrath by the Almighty Christ. No one can fill up a proportion of a full and necessary punishment of such a wickedness of evil, except for God himself. "Who can stand before his indignation? and who can abide in the fierceness of his anger? his fury is poured out like fire," (Nah. 1:6). No one can. Hell is "the spiritual and material furnace of fire where its damned victims, in their minds, bodies, and souls, are eternally tormented to the full degree and capacity of their beings by God, the devil and his demons, damned human beings, and themselves, through their memories and consciences, without any possibility of relief by mercy nor pity from Christ." Hell is just a word. It does not capture enough of the word *terrible*. Men must flee from the wrath to come, (Mark 3:7). It is the greatest evil that can befall a soul. And this is that which above all things, a man should flee from. There is no sorrow likened to that of the wrath to come. What is a respiratory disease to hell? Hell is the most dreadful and terrible existence that can befall a soul, with no possibility to escape it once there. Consider that after this life men shall have to deal with God immediately and in hell forever. They fall into the hands of the living God immediately. It is not by a phone call, or by some intermediary manner. He has in times past used plagues, like the coronavirus, a virus to torment and plague men which are "go betweens." And if God can show forth such misery by a virus, how much more by his own immediate hand? The virus is a mere shadow of hell. Christ accomplishes this by way of revenge, and most dreadfully. "Vengeance is mine, and I will repay," (Deut. 32:35). There shall be a just recompense of reward to every sinner, (Heb. 2:1-3). The wrath of God is dreadful, for it must be a just revenge, a full recompense. If it is such a beginning of sorrow now, where God lets out a little of his wrath on the earth, what will it be like when he stirs up all his wrath, and deals with men by fury poured out. There is nothing but the wrath of God that can make a man fully and perfectly miserable in hell. It shall be pure wrath, judgment without mercy, (Job 2:13). "They shall drink of the wine of the wrath of God without mixture," (Rev. 14:10). As much as any present calamity might be terrible now, they are mere tokens, and do not compare to the coming calamity of the final judgment on sinners.

Eternity is forever always beginning. Hell is set in that context for sinners. The Bible uses a variety of names and designations for hell. Hell is designated as a dwelling of fire. As "burning flames", it is described in a number of different ways in relation to "fire". Imagine a place that, no matter where you went, you could not escape being burned by the fire. With a burning building, you could escape the flames if you were to run out of the firetrap onto the street. But in hell there is no escape from the fire. Wherever you turn, wherever you run, wherever you look, there is unquenchable fire. It is called "everlasting burnings" in Isaiah 33:14b, "...who among us shall dwell with the devouring fire? Who among us shall dwell with everlasting burnings?" It is deemed "fire unquenchable" in Luke 3:17, "Whose fan is in His hand, and He will thoroughly purge His floor, and will gather the wheat into His garner; but the chaff He will burn with fire unquenchable." It is a "lake of fire" as stated in Revelation 19:20b, "...these both were cast alive into a lake of fire burning with brimstone." And its most graphic picture is as a "furnace of fire" as Jesus describes it in Matthew 13:42, "And shall cast them into a furnace of fire: there shall be wailing and gnashing of teeth." It is a real and literal fire. It is a fire that is kept burning forever; it never goes out, and there is no relief from it. Imagine the pain associated with a third degree, chemical burn on someone's arm. With such a burn there is medical treatment, although having your arm chemically cooked and burned in that manner is more painful than most will experience in this life, and most would undeniably opt out of ever experiencing it voluntarily. In hell the pain is equally present on every part of the body, and the degree of pain is far worse than from a chemical burn. It is a torment that cannot be placed into words and cannot hardly be imagined. It is an all-encompassing, torturous experience that never ends for you as an unrepentant sinner.

Though the Scriptures describe hell as a place of fire, this concept is not completely definable by us. We cannot fully comprehend this kind of fire. Why is this so? Is fire something too difficult to understand? Though hell is a place of fire, it is also a place of darkness. If it is a place of darkness, it must be a special kind of fire, indeed, that gives way to an eternal darkness. Jesus describes hell as "outer darkness" in Matthew 22:13, "Then said the king to the servants, Bind him hand and foot, and take him away, and cast him into outer darkness; there shall be weeping and gnashing of teeth." It is called "blackness darkness" in verse 13 of Jude, "...to whom is reserved the blackness of darkness for ever." And it is referred to as "chains of darkness" in 2 Peter 2:4, "...God spared not the angels that sinned, but cast them down to hell, and delivered them into chains of darkness, to be reserved unto judgment." Darkness is not something people enjoy except when they are sleeping—and, when they are asleep, they do not know it is even dark. Every horror movie encompasses some kind of terror with the *dark*. People are most vulnerable in the dark. They cannot see what is coming next or what unleashed horror may abduct them, wound them, or even kill them. In hell people will never sleep, but they will experience the horror of darkness. Little children often keep their closet doors closed tight and desire a night-light because it is out of the darkness that come the "bumps in the night." When someone visits an amusement park attraction, like a "haunted house," the main element that makes the journey frightening is the lack of light. It is pitch-black. Out of the blackness come the frightening aspects and jolts of the performers, or mechanical devices, whose job it is to scare you while you wonder what will emerge from the darkness next? They jump out of the darkness with just the right sampling of light to fully scare you. (And people enjoy this?) Darkness plays a huge role in causing people to be frightened. The infinite God of the universe decided to make hell dark, with a special kind of fire that caters to that darkness. We know, based on Lazarus and Abraham being able to see the rich man in hell, that there is some sort of light. But we also know from Scripture that there is a heavy darkness suited to that place. Such a setting of fire and darkness make hell all the more intolerable and horrible. Hell is the ultimate, interactive unending horror show.

Though hell is a place of fire and of darkness, it is also categorized in Scripture as a place of the worst, unimaginable torment. Literally, Jesus refers to it as a "place of torment." From the lips of the rich man in hell, in Luke 16:28, "For I have five brethren; that he may testify unto them, lest they also come into this place of torment." Over every part of the constitution of the rich man's soul, he was being tortured, *but*, not tortured to death. There is no end to the pain. It is ever constant and never weakening. This torment is so horrible that it is referred to as a "second death" in Revelation 2:11, "He that hath an ear, let him hear what the Spirit saith unto the churches; He that overcometh shall not be hurt of the second death." Death is frightening for the world. The thought of dying in a difficult manner is frightening. A slow death is regarded as the worst kind of death. That is why inhumane torture, as described in graphic books or films about what Hitler and Stalin did, make people cringe; yet these are only the beginning of sorrows. That is why people hate to think of dying slowly in a hospital bed over a period of five days or a week by the coronavirus. It is a terrible plight, especially when you know someone who is going through it, or if you are going through it yourself. A slow death of any kind is a horrible thought, and this is how God has so ordered hell, that those there would describe it as a living death where one never dies.

When people are cast into the blackest of darkness and the fiery rage of hell, they enter the second death by which they can never escape. It is a living hell. They are alive, but experiencing the pains of the eternal "death" of God's wrath. This death is described as a dreadful "destruction" in Matthew 7:13, "Enter ye in at the strait gate: for wide is the gate, and broad is the way, that leadeth to destruction, and many there be which go in thereat." It is described as "everlasting punishment" in Matthew 25:46, "And these shall go away into everlasting punishment."

But the worst title of all, in the New Testament, is "the wrath," as found in 1 Thessalonians 1:10 when it speaks of "the wrath to come." The beginnings of sorrows now in comparison with the wrath that will be heightens the torment to inexpressible degrees. They live out more than their worst possible nightmares under the wrath of God's judgment—the living death they are consigned to for eternity.

Sorrowing now in comparison to then ... the beginning of sorrows versus the finality of eternal sorrows, who can imagine? Sinners, are you sorrowful? Or are you obstinate? How would you know sorrow now in comparison to the eternal sorrow that will be then? Godly sorrow must be worked by God's means. Acts 2:37, "When they heard Peter say that, they were pricked in heart." The preached word pricked their heart. They mustered up nothing themselves. It is God's rod in wrath.

Godly sorrow comes from God and leads to Christ. Hosea 5:15, "Surely in their afflictions they will seek me diligently." Sorrow that is worldly drives men from God; blocks them from Christ. The coronavirus will elicit many people to be sorrowful at the death occurring, but these will look to other people and their courage and bravery to make them feel better about what is happening; they will not look to God. Any sorrow for sin that causes people to neglect God, to discount the spiritual nature of the plague, is of the devil. Thomas Taylor said, "Godly sorrow keeps God in sight still."[1] He says of this kind of godly sorrow that if it exceeds a time and is immoderate, or if it takes away joy from a Christian, it is not godly sorrow, for all godly sorrow ends in Jesus Christ. Godly sorrow does not go away, but rejoices in God's love and favor.

What will the wicked man's sorrow be like? It is helpless. It is comfortless, and the beginning of everlasting sorrows. It does not remedy their sin through Christ. It is an external show of religion, like Esau or Judas. Such a sorrow disparages affliction as absolutely evil. Has the

---

[1] Taylor, Thomas, *David's Learning, or The Way to True Happiness*, (London: William Stansby, 1617), 84–104.

virus not been called this on TV time and time again? *Evil.* True afflictions are in their nature evil, but not absolutely evil because they are only the beginning of sorrows. There is some respect of good in them for they lead a person to consider God's message of wrath in temporary times as this. Seeing that will not save them. But it will direct them to certain ends. Such scornfully beginnings are ruled by God's wisdom and power, so, also, if used rightly, profitable to the soul. But what will sinners do? Will they acknowledge every affliction to be God's work in our midst? You always hear them talk of blessings, and give God some lip service to that end; "I'm so blessed," they say. But, blessing only comes through Christ. When adversity comes, *when tokens of wrath come*, do they thank God? No, they run after worldly things, and when the hammer drops on them at the final judgment of the Christ, it will be an eternal future of misery.

Smaller troubles, such as the virus, point as tokens to the final judgment. And the greater the affliction is, the stronger the sign. God afflicts the body to press the soul to respond in such things, to consider the eternal realities that await. Where are the preachers and preaching of those kinds of messages in this time? What will sinners do with tokens of God's judgment? All sufferings experienced in this world by sinners are the mere beginnings of sorrows; and this is why they need the Christ, the saving Christ, who can deliver them from the wrath to come.

In the next chapter we will talk about the final judgment of Christ in light *of the saint.*

Chapter 9:
Tokens of Displeasure
Turned to Joy

"All these are the beginning of sorrows," (Matt. 24:8).

There are certain events which must occur before the return of the Lord's final coming. In this passage of Matthew 24 Jesus teaches to watch for his coming through signs. "And Jesus went out, and departed from the temple: and his disciples came to him for to shew him the buildings of the temple." Look at its greatness! Verse 2 "And Jesus said unto them, See ye not all these things? verily I say unto you, There shall not be left here one stone upon another, that shall not be thrown down." This temple will be utterly destroyed. Such a prediction was fulfilled in AD 70 at the destruction of the temple. Verse 3, "And as he sat upon the mount of Olives, the disciples came unto him privately, saying, Tell us, when shall these things be? and what shall be the sign of thy coming, and of the end of the world?" *When shall these things be?* The Christ comes as judge, both temporary and eternal. And, ... tell us about the end of all things, since *temporary* judgments are a sign of *eternal* judgments. Jerusalem's fall in the temple's destruction, the house of prayer, the place of the church's sacrifice and meeting, would mean the end of the world. Jesus explains this in separating the temporary from the eternal. He explains both in the same discourse, but shows one is soon, and one will be final. Verse 4, "And Jesus answered and said unto them, Take heed that no man deceive you." There are general signs which point in that direction, and you must be discerning about them; discerning the signs of the times. Verse 5, "For many shall come in my name, saying, I am Christ; and shall deceive many." False deceivers are tokens of judgment, but they are not the end. False deceivers will come in Christ's name, they will deceive many, but they are only a precursor. Verse 6, "And ye shall hear of wars and rumours of wars: see that ye be not troubled: for all these things must come to pass, but the end is not yet." Wars and rumors of wars are precursors, but the end is not yet. Verse 7, "For nation shall rise against nation, and kingdom against kingdom: and there shall be famines, and pestilences, and earthquakes, in divers places." These are also precursors to the end in that they are a "not yet" of what the final "yet" will be to a greater affect. But ... *the end is not yet*. Earthquakes, famine, pestilence, wars, and false teachers are signs, but the end is not yet. Jesus says, verse 8, "All these are the beginning of sorrows," (Matt. 24:8). Not the end; not the final time when these things are seen, yet. Only the beginning of the end. In the following verses he continues to go back and forth between the destruction of Jerusalem and the temple, and the end of the world, as differing events, but things temporary are the beginning of sorrows.

The remaining discourse of Christ on these beginnings of sorrows, and the subsequent end of the world, things both temporary and things eternal, are set in the context of his coming judgment and reign and the need to be watchful for the Christ who returns in glory. "And then shall appear the sign of the Son of man in heaven: and then shall all the tribes of the earth mourn, and they shall see the Son of man coming in the clouds of heaven with power and great glory," (Matt. 24:30).

It is not known when this coming shall be. People will be going about their business and the end will come swiftly, and they will not miss it; everyone will know it. It will be like the great flood of Noah. It will come while people are feasting in their house. It will come when people are doing their daily chores. It will come when people are at work. "Watch therefore..." (Matt. 24:42) And in the final end, when judgment shall ensure, "When the Son of man shall come in his glory, and all the holy angels with him, then shall he sit upon the throne of his glory: And before him shall be gathered all nations: and he shall separate them one from another, as a shepherd divideth his sheep from the goats: And he shall set the sheep on his right hand, but the goats on the left," (Matt. 25:31-33). "And these shall go away into everlasting punishment: but the righteous into life eternal," (Matt. 25:46).

The beginning of sorrows is not the end. Temporal rebukes and temporal chastisements on the church are a token or precursor to the coming of the final judgment of the Son of Man. To those who can watch for this, they are instructed to do so. "Watch therefore, for ye know neither the day nor the hour wherein the Son of man cometh," (Matt. 25:13). Those who are saved enter into the joy of the Lord "enter thou into the joy of thy lord," (Matt. 25:21). Those who have shall be given more "For unto every one that hath shall be given, and he shall have abundance," (Matt. 25:29). These alone enter into eternal life "And these shall go away into everlasting punishment: but the righteous into life eternal," (Matt. 25:46).

DOCTRINE: All the beginning of sorrows for the saint, are turned to everlasting joy at the final judgment of the Son of Man; turned into comfort at his coming.

Recall from the last chapter about dividing the saint from the sinner. Unconverted, lost, unsaved, goats, *i.e.* sinners, differ from converted sinners who are now made saints by Christ. Elect, beloved, new men, followers of the way, Christians, believers, good servants, fruitful trees, sheep, righteous in contrast to the wicked. This is because of the work of Christ on their soul, and the power of the indwelling Spirit that Christ has sent to them. "For who maketh thee to differ from another? and what hast thou that thou didst not receive?" (1 Cor. 4:7). That's easy, *Jesus makes one to differ.* All his work in and for their soul makes the difference. And so, there is a division to sufferings and afflictions which are still ordained for the believer as tokens of final judgment, still surround sin, still surround the fall, but work in a far different way than they do to the wicked. All suffering, all misery for the sinner is due to the fall, to sin, and they are all shadows of hell for sinners, for the lost, for the wicked, for the goats. The coronavirus is a shadow of hell for the sinner. Converted people, overcoming the world by the everlasting blood of the covenant of Jesus Christ, that are saved, still experience sorrow in this life, like the virus, but that sorrow has an end, and it will not continue. Sin certainly makes all sorrows the beginning of sorrows, because it changes the very nature of death, by making something which seems to be the end of suffering, to be the very beginning of eternal torments for the wicked. But not so for the righteous. The wicked begin to feel the continuance

225

of sorrow when they are at death's door. The curse of sorrows is that when they come into the world as ordained of God, because of the fall, they are tokens of the miseries of hell itself for sinners. The *least* sorrow of any sinner in the world will be exceedingly terrible to them, because the *least sorrow* they ever feel here will, into eternity, be terrible to them. Those sorrows now are precursors to the worst of sorrows. They feel pain, loss, affliction of all kinds, yet, Christ says this is the beginning of sorrows for them – hell is their final sorrow. But ... what of the saints?

[1] Sorrows are sorrows for both sinner and saint. But the saint has them turned into joy at Christ's coming. Saints know that all sorrows in this life are from God's hand purposing and ordaining them. Are they not to be (Rom. 8:29) conformed into the likeness of the suffering Servant?, Are they not to be predestinated to be like the image of Christ? ... conformed into *his* likeness? All such suffering is appointed to that end for them to the glory of God. Saints know that all sorrows are from God's hand executing them and for their good. What of Joseph,[1] Gen. 45:8, where he said to his brothers, "God sent me before you." The brothers plotted and schemed, but yet, *God* sent Joseph. And did not Job himself say, 1:21, "The Lord hath given, and the Lord hath taken away." Saints know that afflictions are from God's hand ordering and disposing them in their causes, circumstances, kinds, manner, measure, and time even when they begin and when they end. Does not God say in this light, Isaiah 45:7, "I make peace, and create evil, I the Lord do all these things." Peace

---

[1] See my extensive work, *Joseph's Resolve and the Unreasonableness of Sinning Against God.*

of mind, or the calamity of affliction and sorrow are all ordained of God. Saints know that in all that befalls them in this life, any sorrows that they encounter, are, first and foremost, for the glory of the Christ; so they know all things tend to their good. Such things manifest Christ's glory in manifesting his mercy, justice, wisdom, power, sovereignty, providence, to them personally. They know that Christ is personally interested in his people, his flock, his bride, his church. And they know, the glory of their Christ in his coming is all glorious in such a way as to be a benefit for them in turning all their sorrows to joy, and so the saints long for it. This glory we will consider in a moment. But, in and during sorrowful times and events, the saints are comforted by Scripture and know that in the coming of the Son of Man from heaven in his final judgment and the end of all things, all such sorrows lead to their everlasting salvation and eternal joy. This is true for them whether Christ returns, or they die and go to be with the Lord. So, they know, even temporary sorrows, as hard as they might be, are of a conforming nature for their good, for they make them more like Jesus Christ.

[2] How are such sorrows turned to comfort at the glorious appearing of the Christ in his second coming? The coming of Christ is not a sorrow for the saint, but a comfort. For the wicked, the judgment of Christ is a continuance and eternal derivation of sorrow. They are unable at the end to escape its affects because of sin; their sorrow turns into hell. But for the saint, all sorrows in this life are set at an end. When Christ comes in his glory it is called the Day of Redemption. Sorrows press the saint to pray "come Lord Jesus, quickly." They are not like the

wicked who do not desire the coming of the Christ. They are not like the demons who wondered if the Christ came to torment them before their time. Even they knew torment is coming. But for the saint, Titus 1:13 says, "Looking for that blessed hope and the glorious appearing of the great God, and our Savior Jesus Christ." Is this not what the Christian looks for? We have looked at this Scripture in the past, 2 Tim 4:8, "Henceforth there is laid up for me a crown of righteousness, which the Lord the righteous judge shall give me at that day, and not to me only, but unto them all that love his appearing." Remember, three crowns for the Christian, life, righteousness and glory, looking for the appearing of the Christ to bestow rewards on them and cause all sorrow to cease and every tear wiped from their eye. It is a time of full and glorious comfort. The wicked have a full and terrible judgment by the Christ. The righteous have a full and glorious comfort in the judgment Christ. This is the time of their full and complete glorification. They know Christ will come to judge all things correctly, and to make right those wrongs that have befallen them and his church. Jude 1:5, "To execute judgment upon all, and to convince all that are ungodly among them, of all their ungodly deeds, which they have ungodly committed; and of all their hard speeches, which ungodly sinners have spoken against him." 2 Thess. 1:6-7, "Seeing it is a righteous thing with God to recompense tribulation to them that trouble you: And to you who are troubled, rest with us, when the Lord Jesus shall be revealed from heaven, with his mighty angels." They know that all the troubles of the devil will be put to an end. Romans 16, he shall tread Satan under your feet shortly. All sin shall be put to an end. "But now being made free from sin, and become servants to God, ye have your fruit unto holiness, and the end everlasting life," (Rom. 6:22). The saints shall see the glory of their Christ for eternal joy and comfort. Heaven itself is called the joy of the Lord further in this discourse in Matthew 25:21, "Enter into the joy of your Lord." What would it be like to constantly live in a state of perfect joy forever? Can it be imagined, a place where one would never lose an ounce of joy, but would always gain more and more as eternity progressed? To think in this way is unimaginable while living amidst such a transient world of fading beauty and of plague and pestilence.

There will be nothing to create any kind of sorrow in the joy of the Lord. Nothing but joy. Thomas Watson said, "Here on earth, joy enters into us; there we enter into joy."[2] The joys that saints shall have with Christ, are without measure and without worldly mixture. "In your presence is fullness of joy," (Psalm 16:11); full joy and comfort. The saint's heart shall be filled with the joy of Christ. All their senses will be filled with joy. They shall see with their eye, and hear with their ear, and smell the fragrance of the sweetness of Jesus Christ. There is nothing but Christ that fills heaven with joy, and so the saints will be satisfied in him forever. There will be nothing in the joy of the Lord but what shall add eternally to their divine happiness. The beginning of sorrows, shall end, and forever begins where the elect rejoice in Christ and his

---

[2] Watson, Thomas, *The Believer's Privileges in the Covenant of Grace*, (Crossville, TN: Puritan Publications, 2017) Chapter 8, the third royal privilege, electronic version.

work in them forever. In this, the Christian has a great hope even amidst sorrow now; what is the travail in comparison to the reward? One day he will have every tear wiped from his eyes and every pain removed by the hand of Christ's healing power. He will live in God's joy in a state of perfection for all eternity, fully enraptured in the joy of the Lord that will become sweeter with each passing moment. For them, the joy of eternity is forever always beginning.

[3] It is everlasting joy. Everlasting God will set up a kingdom which is to be universal and everlasting. In this kingdom the Messiah is to be the head (*cf.* Gen. 49:10; Num. 24:17; 2 Sam. 7:16; Isa. 9:6-7; Micah 4; Psalms 2, 45 and 110). When Christ comes again, those who are then alive will be changed, their corruptible shall put on incorruption, and their mortal shall put on immortality, and they will forever live with the Lord in the new heavens and new earth. It will be a place of incomprehensible blessedness through the unhindered beatific vision of God. It is a place filled with the fullness of God in the face of Jesus Christ.

Everlasting ... *joy.* It is hard to imagine everlasting joy in comparison to the beginnings of sorrows in this life. What would it be like to be wrapped in a blanket of joy? This is not *mere* happiness. People can experience happiness by buying a new pair of socks, or remodeling their home. I'm not talking about being merely pleased with something in a temporal sense. Generally speaking, the word *happy* is something "common" in the English language. The word "happy" is defined as being "pleased or glad over a particular thing." For example, I'm happy you are reading this book. That type of happiness can be applied to anything and everything. What I am talking about is unbounded everlasting joy. Joy is connected with the idea of *satisfaction*. Defining joy is a bit trickier since it rests in this idea of being *completely satisfied*. Joy is the emotion evoked by well-being. One is only well if one is in Christ. There is no wellness apart from him. He is the fountain and full of all joy. He says, "enter thou into the joy of thy lord," (Matt. 25:21). Not one's own joy, but God's joy. God's covenant joy. God's joy of salvation in Christ. It is possessing what one desires, and then delighting in it. The Christian desires to delight fully in Jesus Christ; they shall possess him fully. This joy is possessing that delight, and reveling in it. Everyone wants to be a little happy, but what would it be like to be wrapped up in a blanket of unbounded joy? To define it, *joy* is the sweet motion of the soul, in regard of some present, or hoped for good bestowed by Jesus Christ. This joy is eminently spiritual and heavenly. Rom. 5:3, "We rejoice in tribulation." John 15:11, "That your joy may be full." Such spiritual joy is the direct work of Christ on the soul, and the fruit of the Spirit of God. Gal. 5:22, "The fruit of the Spirit is joy, peace," etc. Such a work gives the saint, a joyful speech, or a joyful song of thanksgiving and praise. Psalm 126:2 says that "our tongue" is to praise God "with joy." All their praise comes from joy, as joy comes from the good things of Jesus Christ.

Joy is the opposite of sorrow. Though sorrow may ensue for a time now, still, that sorrow for the saint still turns *to joy*, even if they are downtrodden for a time. Why? It manifests the glory of Christ in them, and reminds them of their future fullness of joy. It is a sure hope in him.

The manifestation of Christ's glory and the fullness of joy to come is eagerly hoped for. The end of God's appointing this judgment day, is for the manifestation of the glory of his mercy in the eternal salvation of the elect; "... For then shall the righteous go into everlasting life, and receive that fulness of joy and refreshing which shall come from the presence of the Lord," (1647 Westminster Confession of Faith, Chapter 33).

Christ's coming to judgment will be glorious to the saints. His very coming is a great manifestation of this glory which will turn their sorrow to joy. Daniel 7:10, "A fiery stream issued, and came forth from before him, thousand thousands ministered unto him; and ten thousand times ten thousand stood before him, the judgement was set, and the books where opened." The coming of the Son of Man is glorious apart from the saints. But glorious to them and for them. Jude 1:14, "And Enoch also the seventh from Adam, prophesied of these, saying, Behold, the Lord cometh with ten thousand of his saints." And in 2 Thess. 1:7, "And to you who are troubled, rest with us, when the Lord Jesus shall be revealed from heaven, with his mighty angels." Matt. 16:27, "For the Son of Man shall come in the glory of his Father with his angels." The saints know that this Christ, this glorious God arrives in the highest most glorious manner to render all judgment even to the saints.

What shall come of the saints in this glorious arrival of the Christ, where sorrows are turned into everlasting joy, if no one can stand before him? Is he not gloriously terrible in his judgment? "But who may abide the day of his coming? and who shall stand when he

232

appeareth? for he is like a refiner's fire, and like fullers' soap," (Mal. 3:2). Matt. 24:30 says, "And they shall see the Son of man coming in the clouds of heaven, with power and great glory." What will saint's do? Christ will require an account of all things done during his absence from the earth by his servants. They shall be called to account for their works. Whatever his servants have done in the body, and done with their talents, Matt. 25. He will judge all things; what have they done? Have they lived well, or have they beaten their fellow-servants? Have they become the drunkard or the adulterer? Have they challenged God's worship in the church? He will take a tally of all things done, and those things which are not becoming of the Christian ... are burned up. But *they* will not be burned up. The hall of faith in Hebrews 11 shows that no sins are mentioned by any of the faithful, only the works of the Spirit worked through them are mentioned. Great faith.

The saints are covered by the everlasting blood of the covenant of Jesus Christ. There is great safety in appearing at the final judgment in the covering provided by the Christ; he is their mercy seat. When Christ first came, he came as the suffering servant. Phil. 2:7, "But made himself of no reputation, and took upon him the form of a servant, and was made in the likeness of men." Christ came for his elect to render the sorrow of sin mute; to redeem them fully. He did this by becoming the sin offering for them; by becoming sin for them. Martin Luther said, Christ was the greatest sinner in the world, not by way of inherence but by way of imputation. Luther called him *Peccator maximus*, the greatest sinner in this way. All the sins of all the saints rested on his shoulders at the crucifixion and the Christ became a thing so heinous that God forsook him in that offering for a time of darkness, and an experience of utter sorrow, to be acquainted with grief. Christ in coming into the world had all the sins of the elect of God imputed to him. In this he rendered the affect of the fall and sin mute in his work for those saints to be. He took their sin, and gave them the righteousness of the everlasting blood of the covenant. His blood now applied to them saves them from the wrath to come. The Righteousness of Christ is the righteousness that the Law of God required of all men and his work, his merit answered the demand of God's character, and so when they have this covering, and the mercy seat covers them, they are safe to appear before the judgment seat of God. His work ends all sorrow for them. His work is transforming, even to the fact that sorrow turns to joy. At the coming of Christ, and the saint's account of their life before Christ's judgment seat, there, all things are wondrously altered. They are flooded by hope, by joy, by comfort. All things become theirs by way of inheritance. They know as saints that even now, in the midst of sorrow, all things are for their advantage, all things are for their benefit and all things will prove to be for their comfort at the Lord's coming. They long for this. They pray daily for it, "thy kingdom come." They know that every sorrow for sin, every sorrow in the world, in whatever size, shape or providence, will never remedy sin. There is nothing that is in the world that can fix sin. Sorrow merely enlarges sorrow if not dealt with through the covenant work and blood of Jesus Christ. The Lord Jesus and his work makes appearing at the judgment seat not only tolerable for the saint, but glorious for them. Such a faith set on the Christ concerning the second coming, is sufficient to support their souls, and to give them comfort in all difficulties, trials and afflictions. They live in a longing and eager expectation of the bridegroom's coming.

But one might ask, "Shall Christians go through the judgment?" There is a difference for the Christian between going to the judgment, and being *condemned* in the judgment. Those who believe in the Lord Jesus, who are ingrafted into Christ by a true and living faith, those that are indwelt by the Spirit, shall not come into condemnation in the judgment. "Verily, verily, I say unto you, He that heareth my word, and believeth on him that sent me, hath everlasting life, and shall not come into condemnation; but is passed from death unto life," (John 5:24), that is, of condemnation in judgement. The saint will not be condemned or overthrown by their sin; Christ has taken it away in his death and resurrection. He comes into the *judicium absolutionis,* the judgment of absolution. In judgement the saint shall stand out with Christ having been given a new name, and having on the white robe of Christ's merit and righteousness, being covered with the wedding garment of being born again. All will be brought into judgement. No one should ever think that they escape the bar of God's justice, but the saints arrive there in the safety of Christ's blood. They will be judged by the Red Hand of Christ. His red hand, pouring out blood, covers all their deeds in the book of his remembrance, and God sees nothing but Christ's blood. The saints are not charged with what is cancelled or blotted out of God's book. Isa. 38:17, "Thou hast cast my sins behind thy back, as men cast

235

behind them such things as they list not to look on" Micah 7:19, "Thou wilt cast our sins into the depth of the sea." If it is cast into the sea it is utterly gone and lost. Such sin shall not be brought into the judgment against the pardoned sinner. They will find there is "no condemnation for those in Christ Jesus."

One might say, "This all sounds so nice and helpful, but how can I be sure of it?" You can be *eminently* sure in Christ, certainly more sure than anything else. People cannot be sure of the world or things in the world. It's vain and transient and passing; fleeting. To know the truth is to exercise the mind, not the body. To know anything, is first to know one's own spirit. Otherwise nothing can ever be known from that which is tangible; it is not the disembodied brain that knows, but the spirit of a man exercising the mind, and the consciousness that knows. A man must know his own spirit before he can know anything else. He can be more sure of *his spirit*, then he can of the world he lives in. But the saints have this heightened by the illumination of the Spirit of God. So, the saints know they have their names inscribed by an immutable pen of iron in God's book of salvation if Christ has saved them. "Rejoice that your names are written in God's book of life," Christ tells his disciples. God has chosen his saints for salvation, elected them to glory, even before the foundations of the world in Jesus Christ. God has promised them eternal happiness in the Son; joy. It is a promise of eternal life, ever sure. This, they know. They know the truth of the word, and the Spirit of God testifies to their spirits that they are sons and daughters of the most high. If God has promised everlasting joy, will he not be faithful to bring it to pass for the saint's eternal pleasure? Has not the Lord Jesus Christ purchased this joy for his people? Is he not the covenant Mediator? Does he not bring joy, "I bring you good tidings of great joy," (Luke 2:10) the angel said of the coming of the Christ. "These things have I spoken unto you, that my joy might remain in you, and that your joy might be full," (John 15:11). It is so sure what Christ accomplishes that it is even called a "purchased possession," (Eph. 1:14). And as certain as it is from God's promise to the saint's ear, so is the possession itself. The Holy Spirit given to them as a deposit of that which is to come. Christ is in heaven for them right now preparing a place for them. Christ even prayed, while he was here in the travail of sorrows before his crucifixion, that his saints would have a mind enraptured with this joy while they too travail in sorrow here on the earth. John 17:24, "Father I will that those which thou hast given me be with me where I am, that they may behold the glory which thou hast given me." That they too would come to heaven, into the joy of the Lord.

Surety, in this way, comes from a lively faith. Belief in the truth of this doctrine is to know it. All the beginning of sorrows for the saint, these are turned to everlasting joy at the final judgment of the Son of Man, turned into comfort at his coming, as they are translated into heavenly bliss.

Do you find comfort from Christ's coming to judgment at last? From the time of Christ's ascension into heaven to the second coming of Christ (whenever that will occur) are the last days. We are *between* his two comings. But we are in eager expectation awaiting the full coming of the kingdom. We all long for that joy with all the saints. How shall we live in this light?

There are so many exhortations in Matthew 24-25 and various illustrations that lead to practical considerations in such things in waiting for the coming of the Lord. What do I mean by this? Jesus in his discourse to the disciples about sorrows now and then likens his people to a number of practical kinds or types: such as: People who are persecuted for the Gospel and those that are not. Which are you? Those who endure to the end, and those who do not. Which are you? Elect or carnal? Which are you? A fruitful part of the fig tree or a dead branch? Which are you? Mindful of eternal things, or mindful of worldly things? Which are you? Taken up with the vanities of this life, or a mind set on Christ above? Which are you? One who watches, or one who busies themselves with the world? Which are you? Ready for the Lord's Coming or ill-prepared? Which are you? A wise virgin with oil or a foolish virgin without? Which are you? The faithful servant who uses their talents to gain more, or one who is idle and unprofitable to the kingdom? Which are you? A sheep or a goat? Which are you? One who ministers to the brethren, or one who neglects them? Which are you? Wicked or Righteous, sinner or saint? Which are you? Can you look only for Christ's benefits, in that you look for his second coming, all his glorious benefits to you as a professing saint, but do not faithfully uphold Christ in the way you would like in your daily walk and life? What characterizes your walk? There goes a saint filled with the joy of the Lord! How different the church would look if all the saints were described in such a way. Do you desire his coming to have your joy made full, or simply to be relieved of the burden of life? The wicked think that death relieves them of the burden of life, but this is only the beginning of sorrows for them. "A woman that never cares to hear from her husband cannot be said to desire his coming; so if Christ has often knocked at the door of our hearts, and we will not give him entrance, how can we be said to look for his appearing?"[3]

Christ's coming again is full of comfort and joy for you if you are a saint. But, knowing he is coming presses you to consider certain things while you travail here in sorrow under various tokens of God's displeasure on his church. The coronavirus as a temporary sorrow, is ordained of God. It could have been avoided, or even stopped if the church took its position seriously. It is true, sorrows are temporary, and sin is displeasing to God. And sorrows, well, who would ever say that are a "good time?" James says that we must *consider* them joy. But, does he not teach you the duty of patience and contentment under all your sorrows in the world now while you wait for his return or your ushering into the kingdom? James 5:8 says, "Be ye all patient, stablish your hearts, for the coming of the Lord draweth nigh."

The doctrine of joy in Christ's coming again in judgment to turn all your sorrows to joy in him, should cause you to be better Christians now. Not only should it cause you to deal with the beginnings of sorrows now, but that in them you improve your life in godliness each day

---

[3] Manton, Thomas, *The Complete Works of Thomas Manton*, Volume 16, 218.

knowing that sorrow *may be sorrows*, but *are* useful, and good will come out of them.

Is it not your daily prayer that Christ exhorts us "thy will be done on earth as it is in heaven?" 1 Cor. 1:7 says, "So that ye come behind in no gifts, waiting for the coming of our Lord Jesus Christ." This is where the doctrine of "holy improvement" comes into play. Jesus even spoke about this in our text with the parable of the talents. *Holy improvement:* to be greater in religion each day while we wait for Christ's coming, even amidst sorrows all through the earth, knowing that Christ's coming will be glorious, satisfying, delightful and will fill you with unspeakable joy.

It should cause you to be watchful over your life. Jesus is watching; the Judge watches, to judge rightly. Jesus is going to bring you to judgment, but not to condemnation if you love him at his coming. Will he expose all your sins to all men? No, he has taken all your sins from you. His judgment will be of pardon. There is no condemnation for you any longer. Your sins still make you sad before him now, but this is a means of sanctification for you. He has delivered you from them all. They are born on his shoulders on the cross. There is nothing but the red hand for you at the judgment as a saint. And his blood alone can cover all your sins; even those you think are the worst; but are your sins greater than Christ is a Savior? Certainly not, therefore, rejoice that your joy may be made full in him. Such a thought ought to be a provocation to you to keep a good conscience towards Christ, while you live here in this world; shall we go on sinning that grace may abound? No. At the second coming, 2 Peter 3:11 says,

"Seeing then that all these things shall be dissolved, what manner of persons ought ye to be in all holy conversation and godliness?" It could be that there is very little time between you and that blessed state in heaven, second coming or death; who knows their day? You do not know when you will be called to bow the knee to Christ at the judgment. As a saint, you will enter into the joy of your Lord, and such an entrance shall be ministered unto you into the everlasting kingdom of Christ, so that the very foundation of your existence upon entering that celestial city will be nothing else but delight and satisfaction in him; you will be then as a shining one. The opposite of sorrow; all sorrows turned into joy. The fullness of a glorious body. The fullness of a glorious soul. Habitations for you that are mansions. The company of other glorious saints. Gospel Treasures beyond your wildest aspirations. Dignity and honor alongside of Christ to judge the world with him. Peace and rest forever with the fullness of joy with eternal satisfaction in the presence of the Christ. What is, then, the beginning of sorrows here for the saint but tokens of future joy in the Christ?

The next chapter will revisit for the last time Lev. 26:27-28, where we will look at what it means to be a continued rebel daring God to do his worst.

Chapter 10:
Daring Christ to Do His Worst

"And if ye will not for all this hearken unto me, but walk contrary unto me; Then I will walk contrary unto you also in fury; and I, even I, will chastise you seven times for your sins," (Lev. 26:27-28).

As we began, so now we end, with this chapter on God's covenant. The church is to be a holy people because God is holy and he has commanded them certain duties that they must fulfill in his covenant as he prescribes if they are to be his people. What was the reason for this? "I am the Lord, your God." Because God says. Because this is what God prescribes. Because this is what the church does to show they are the church. All of Leviticus is set in the context of God's gracious covenant of grace. Blessings and curses are joined with an evangelical grace, and it houses instructions on restoration if the people break God's covenant.

More particularly Lev. 26:14–39 is a curse to the covenant breaker, or those disobedient. "If ye will not hearken unto me," proportionately, to the privileges of the covenant will be the criminality and the severity of judgment on them; even up to 7 times, meaning, as many times as it takes. In 26:15, "If ye despise my commandments..." Despising or abhorring God's commands or judgments is doing anything not commanded, or not doing anything that he has commanded.

In verse 16 "I will even appoint over you terror," where this terror is famine, sword and pestilence, where pestilence is a plague.

In verse 17, God's blessing is no longer on them, his "face" is removed; pestilence may be defined as a turning of God's face away from his people. How shall one live in light of God's face if his face has turned?

In verse 18, "if ye will not yet for all this hearken to me, then I will punish you seven times more." He will bring more calamity, calamity upon calamity; calamity will build; famine, wars, injustices, riots in the streets.

In verse 19 their might is broken; their high view of themselves, their privileged view, God will crush.

In verse 22, "your highways shall be desolate" where commerce will be interrupted; freedoms will be restricted.

In verse 31, "I will make your cities waste." Flourishing cities will not look the same. And, meeting places, places of safety, God will "bring your sanctuaries unto desolation, and I will not smell the savour of your sweet odours." Worship will be abhorred by God and he will close them down. The references to sanctuaries refers to the various departments of the tabernacle and worship.

In verse 33, "I will scatter you among the heathen." The church will be mixed where they will not stand out as they ought; they go to take refuge in their cites, and God brings in calamity whether by sword, famine or pestilence.

And yet, even in the midst of the pestilence, verse 40, "If they shall confess their iniquity," The passage still sets down the gracious promise of divine forgiveness and favor if they will repent. Who? Egyptians? The Philistines? No, the church.

There must be humility and repentance from his covenant breaking people enacted speedily. He will curse them for breaking his gracious covenant with them. "And if ye will not be reformed by me by these things, but will walk contrary unto me; then will I also walk contrary unto you, and will punish you yet seven times for your sins." But, if you don't want to be reformed, so I will make no distinction between you and the heathen and I will walk contrary to you in fury. I will chastise you, discipline you, instruct you, admonish you, seven times for your sins, (Lev. 26:23-28) if needs be; and it will be calamitous. If you dare me to do it by continuing in your sin. If you will "not be reformed by me by these things" (Lev. 26:23). If they continue in their sin, it is as if they are daring God to do his worst. So God tells them that if they will not amend their life, if they will not follow his word, if they will institute things God has not commanded, if they will disparage his commands, and his laws and his statues, and walk contrary to him, he will act in a hostile manner towards them, and they will know it when the pestilence comes. He will be the cause of bringing in misery against them to correct them, even to wrestle against them, as the Hebrew intimates.

And note here in Leviticus that God has given them specific commands and laws which shadow the coming of the Christ, that they were to uphold these shadows and rites and ceremonies in such a way as to be precise, not for salvation, for that is gracious in Christ, but for sanctification and blessings. If they continued in sin, they would show a dislike of God's leading and instruction. Not hearing, not walking, walking in fact contrary to God. Such a walking is against God's justice to demonstrate their rebellion against him, and a dare to God to do his worst according to his word to them. They despise what God's provision for reformation is, and instead would do what they want to do. In doing that they dare God. God knew that if they rejected his commands, that it would not be beyond a doubt that soon, they would reject him outright. In fact, rejecting his word is rejecting him. But would they then be corrected by God? Would they strive for reformation? Here it is seen that to continue to sin is to dare God to do his worst. It is a very rebellious place to be.

DOCTRINE: The church's obstinance in continuing in covenant breaking sins dares God to do his worst against them.

Any continued obstinance against God is sin. Any obstinance and rebellion against God's word is sin. To continue in it is a sign of apostasy. It is the duty of the covenanted Christian to hate all sin as sin. There must be a love for what God loves, and a hatred for that which God hates. All sin must be hated with a righteous hatred by all pardoned souls. "You who love the LORD, hate evil! He preserves the souls of His saints; He delivers them out of the hand of the wicked," (Psa. 97:10). The Psalmist does not say do what you want, do what you like, or even, put up with sin, but to hate sin. Wicked people bear with sin. They never really hate it. Covenant breaking sins relate directly to God. To break covenant with God, to sin, to continue in it, is to be rebellious. This is a very dangerous place to be since God does not equate this unbiblical idea of backsliding, with the opposite of righteousness. In other words, God does not see Christians in a state of carnality or backsliding by degree. There are two kinds of people. Sheep and goats, righteous and wicked, covenant keepers and covenant breakers. Backsliders are not people falling into sin, or falling through sin, they are in it, continue in it, and are to be deemed by God and his church as apostate. Continued covenant breaking sins, are opposite to the new life that God has given his people in Jesus Christ, through the transforming power of the Spirit of God. Covenant keepers are pleasing to Christ. They abhor that which is evil and cling to that which is good. Whatever God hates, they hate. And to hate what God hates necessarily means they love what God loves. But will the church continue in sin? Will they be reformed? Will they continue in their obstinate rebellion against him? Hatred for sin is in the whole inner man and it is motioned and stirred by the righteous production of holiness in the Spirit. "to be strengthened with might by his Spirit in the inner man;" (Eph. 3:16). It is a permanent fixture in the heart of a covenant keeper to hate all sin.

This continued obstinance is a covenant breaking sin. Edmund Calamy said, "Covenant breaking is an act of the highest sacrilege that can be committed."[1] The absence of following the Law of God was the enactment of covenant breaking and sin. Sin is any want of conformity to or transgression of the Law of God, as the confession says. These people are covenanted with God together as

---

[1] McMahon, C. Matthew, Editor, *Light from Old Paths: An Anthology of Puritan Quotations*, Volume 1, (Coconut Creek, FL: Puritan Publications, 2014) Obedience.

one body; vowed to uphold what God desires. What does it mean to covenant with one another in a visible church? These are very evil days, and perilous times. There are many sins that attribute themselves to making the times very evil and very perilous. Sins of perilous and evil times are the following: being, "filled with all unrighteousness, sexual immorality, wickedness, covetousness, maliciousness, full of envy, murder, strife, deceit, evil-mindedness, whisperers, backbiters, haters of God, violent, proud, boasters, inventors of evil things, disobedient to parents, undiscerning, untrustworthy, unloving, truce-breakers, unmerciful..." (Rom. 1:29-32). In 2 Timothy 3:3 Paul uses a term "truce-breakers" there as well. "Without natural affection, trucebreakers, false accusers, incontinent, fierce, despisers of those that are good," (2 Tim. 3:3). Other translations outside of the Greek and the KJV use an aberrant word such as *unforgiving*, which is an extremely poor way to convey the idea. The Greek literary renders "one who will not be persuaded to enter into a covenant." Paul marks this sin among 19 sins in this section of 2 Timothy as sins of perilous times, and 23 sins of Romans 1 of the evil day where God gives people over to a reprobate mind. Those who refuse to enter into a covenant together with a church, to join it, specifically under the context of the worker who works among the people of God in 2 Timothy, and in perilous times where sin abounds, is a covenant breaker – a truce-breaker – or ... those who sin against God in covenant with him, called covenant breakers. In Romans 1:31 Paul lists this same covenant breaking sin in line with giving people over to a reprobate mind; part of God's judgment. "Without understanding, covenant breakers, without natural affection, etc." (Rom. 1:31). It is a very serious sin. It is a sin of those who willfully reject God's authority, and his imposed authority in the church. It is a sin of pride. It is the description of a sin of people who do not want to uphold their promises made to God, or to make promises to him.

This continued obstinance is a covenant breaking sin against God. "And now we call the proud happy; yea, they that work wickedness are set up; yea, they that tempt God are even delivered," (Mal. 3:15). It is against God, against his Christ, the Mediator of the covenant. Satan rebelled against God and was thrown from heaven. Adam rebelled and was expelled from the garden. Wicked men rebelled against God and God destroyed the earth by flood, Sodom and Gomorrah by fire, and such things. The church acts like the devil, acts like the wicked, acts like rebellious Adam, when they continue in their obstinance and break God's covenant. Some people are very confused at this idea, thinking that Christians are somehow not obligated to keep covenant, or not obligated to uphold the righteous character of the law of God. They believe they are under grace, at the expense of the law so the law of God has no relation to them, they think. They are sorely mistaken in this. They will be judged accordingly at the coming of the Son of Man by the law of God. Not the ceremonial law with its rites, but the moral law to which all things are attached. Now, Christ delivers his people that they may not be condemned by the law, but then leads them back to the law in order to keep its moral nature for their sanctification through the power of the Holy Spirit. They cannot be justified by the law, for Christ has saved them by his work and merit and the Father has declared them just on that account. But they can be sanctified by it. Don't lie, don't steal, don't kill, worship God according to his prescriptions, etc. have very sanctifying affects for the Christian who is indwelt by the Spirit. And this is the very quarrel that God has with his church in Leviticus 26. Why do you want to walk contrary to what I have laid down in my word? Why will you break covenant with me by doing what you will instead of my will? Have I so given you a license to sin? As Paul said in Romans, God forbid. And if it is against God's will, it is against God's character, for his law is a demonstration of his holy character.

This continued obstinance is a covenant breaking sin against God's provision in Christ. The obstinacy and rebellion of the church against God in sin reaches its epitome in sinning against God's Christ. This does not matter if one sins against the Christ to come, as the Old Testament saints did, or sins against the Christ who came, as the church does today. The Christian will be very careful to take care and make a conscience effort of walking worthy of his interest in Jesus Christ; to not sin against him and his provision for salvation. All those riches and Gospel treasures given to the saint by God through Christ and deposited in them by the Spirit, God has given, and so now it is their responsibility to make a holy improvement on their sanctification day by day. Do they have a suitable progress in religion in this way, truly, really, purely, as much as they have received the Christ and his saving work? Do they live godly in the Mediator, or do they become rebellious and obstinate in some continued sin against him which casts doubt on their profession? Was this not God's quarrel with his church in Leviticus 26? Will they be careful of walking worthy of God's interest as he so promises this Christ, this Mediator, in all the shadows and types of the Old Testament? To walk in the right way is to walk according to the pattern of the Mediator. Or will they walk contrary to him? In the church today, what is their interest in him? Is it only for his benefits? As many as have Christ, they have put on Christ, they must leave off their old ways and conversations, their rebellions and obstinacies and now labor to walk after a more holy, and blameless, and innocent life, or God will walk contrary to them. How will they know if they are walking rightly or if they are walking obstinately as a church? They will find plagues, and wars, and earthquakes, and famines, and such things as precursors and tokens of God's displeasure against them if they are rebellious. Will they then amend their ways and doings? Do they so prize Christ that they would do all they can to look on him as the most desirable good in the whole world? Or will they continue to walk contrary to him? How will one know or see what is occurring in this? All they need to do is look to the plague – is it stopped, or does it continue?

God has provided a means of grace and his church rejects this as something not desirable. Is this even fathomable? Christ offers himself as their Savior, his blood for them as a satisfaction to God; prescribes for them his holy worship, and godly conversation, and they exchange the truth for a lie to have a party in their churches instead of worship. And this Savior they reject, trample, and go another way, so they think, to gain favor with God with things they enjoy. They will fight vehemently for things *they* favor. They are free in Christ to do whatsoever they want, so they think. And so they rebel against him and he sends them a plague. And they do not repent. And the plague continues. In this continued rebellion they dare God to do his worst. They do not really believe him, and they challenge him. Ezekiel Hopkins said, "It is an injury done to the tenderest of God's attributes, his mercy," for, "it is an affront upon his dearest Son, the Lord Jesus Christ, and, therefore, shall be revenged with a most aggravated condemnation."[2]

This continued obstinance is a covenant breaking sin against God's provision in Christ to dare God to do his worst. This is what the bible calls living in a way of provoking God to jealousy. What does it mean to dare God to do his worst? The church must seriously consider how their strength matches up to God's strength. What man, what group of men, what whole church, what group of churches, even if it is the whole professing church in the world, is their strength sufficient to oppose or resist the strength of God? What is the church thinking in opposing God in this way? It is to dare him to do his worst against them. Have they not read their bible where it teaches that God is the enemy of everyone who provokes him to jealousy? Does he not in this very passage say that if they continue in their obstinacy and rebellion and will not amend their ways that he will visit them seven times for their sin? Will he not walk contrary to them? What strength will they muster up against the Lord's Christ? He

---

[2] Hopkins, Ezekiel, *The Works of Ezekiel Hopkins*, Volume 3, (Philadelphia, PA: The Protestant Episcopal Book Society, 1874) 308.

will be as an enemy to all those that continue in this way and will execute his wrath on them with his great power if they do not repent. The church, today, does not act very concerned on these matters. They continue to add to their sin more sin. They go on provoking him more and more every day, and, to dare God to do his worst against them. "Woe unto them that draw iniquity with cords of vanity, and sin as it were with a cart rope," (Isa. 5:18). Have they given a moment's thought to the power of God? How much power is there in God's ability to bring in earthquakes, wars, famine, even the pestilence that is all over the earth right now with 600,000 people dead? Did he not stretch out the universe and create the whole earth? Did he not set the stars in heaven? What strength does the church have apart from God? How proudly are they acting? How are they lifting their own heads above Christ's prescriptions for holiness in that they would challenge God's will and worship? Do they not dare God to do his worst in temporary judgments even now? Man is a worm, Job 25:6, "Man that is a worm and the son of man that is but a worm." And what are all the rebellions of the church against this God even brought together in one blow against him, they are but a collection of worms. What can they do against God? They mimic in this way the wicked who rebel against God, the devil who rebels against God.

What does it mean to dare God? To challenge God, to confront him with boldness. An audacious presumption in sinning. Presumption joined with boldness to walk contrary to God no matter what he has said. Who would do such a thing? Sadly, Christians do this every day in every sin that they sin against Christ. They love the benefits of the Lord Jesus, and think it is far easier to ask forgiveness for their sins than to strive against them. It is a devilish infection in their thoughts, that causes them to sin against God as an atheist would. "The fool hath said in his heart there is no God," (Psa. 14:1). When the Christian sins they sin atheistically. It is a disrespecting and disregarding of God's will, which defends sin. Calling evil good, and good evil, light darkness, and darkness light, sweet bitter, and bitter sweet, as the Prophet says in Isa. 5:20. Such a person fights against God hand to hand. What strength will such a Christian have in doing this? What will he gain in victory over God? What will a covenant breaking church do? This is to provoke "the Holy One of Israel to anger" as Isaiah speaks in (Isa. 1:4). Such a presumption is in their language, in the way they talk, and in their actions in the way they walk. They dishonor God where God ought to be worshiped in the beauty of his holiness. It is to abuse him face to face in his own house. "And they consider not in their hearts that I remember all their wickedness: now their own doings have beset them about; they are before my face," (Hos. 7:2). When the church willfully dishonors God in a time where they should be humble, especially in a time of occasional repentance as when a plague is rampart through the earth, if they continue in their obstinacy, they rebel against him. They are running into sin, they are missing the signs of the times, they are warned by the tokens of providence, yet they continue against his word and will. This is when they quench the Spirit and despise preaching (1 Thess. 5:19, 20), to resist the Holy Spirit (Acts 7:51, 1 Thess. 4:8) and his instruments. Oftentimes, like Pharaoh, men who rebel against God, the more they are struck by famine, plagues and such, they are further hardened in that providence. Like Pharaoh, whose heart was more hardened, the greater the plagues which God inflicted on him. This can certainly happen to the church. One might say, "May it never be." One might answer, Laodicea, Thyatira, Philadelphia, and such; where are they. "They that despise me shall be lightly esteemed," God says (1 Sam. 2:30). If they think so little of God and his law, God will think little of them. One might say, "I surely hope the church never comes to be obstinate and rebellious in this way of provoking God." Yet, every presumptuous sin against God hands his people over to such provocation. "Woe to him, that striveth with his Maker!" (Isa. 45:9). "It is hard for thee to kick against the pricks," says our Savior to Saul (Acts 9:5). If you "will walk contrary unto me," says God, "Then will I also walk contrary unto you," (Lev. 26:23-24). O! then let that of David be the church's prayer, "Keep back thy servant from presumptuous sins; let them not have dominion over me: then shall I be upright, and I shall be innocent from the great transgression," (Psa. 19:13). What is the church praying today?

To dare God is to engage in the most extreme levels of unbelief. As if the church would say, we do not believe you will do your worst, Lord; we challenge you in this. You will not walk contrary to us, we are under grace! And all those who are guilty of commission or omission of God's law, more openly dare God, more directly act contrary to the light of Scripture. On this ground Christians may complain as the prophet did, Jer. 23:10, "The land is full of adultery; because of swearing the land mourneth." What is this but to dare God to judge his people? "And if ye will not for all this hearken unto me, but walk contrary unto me; Then I will walk contrary unto you also in fury; and I, even I, will chastise you seven times for your sins," (Lev. 26:27-28).

When the church is past their shame for sin, they bring on themselves a reality that they desire to be past hope. They dare God to punish them; to chastise them, to rebuke them; what fool would desire that at God's hand? They call God to witness their serious intentions to perform them as covenant keepers, and instead, over time, like the frog in the pot that slowly boils, unaware that he is being boiled to death, they call God to be a witness to their lie simply because they dawn the title Professing Christian. They started out well, and with good intentions, and would have never thought that they call God to witness against them. Many have heard it said, it is not how one begins but how one ends. It is always a striving, pressing violence into the kingdom that the Christian engages in. One does not stop short before he wins the prize in a race. When they covenant with God, entering into an oath with him, will they then go and break it for the sake of expediency or for some bosom sin? Take for example, the church has taken all kinds of liberties with God's worship in the past 100 years. How long will God long suffer with them? Not long it seems. When the church rejects its allegiance to God and sins willfully, they do, as it were, dare God to do his worst. Do they wish a strong war? Do they desire a hard affliction in famine? Do they desire economic tragedy? Do they want a plague that covers the face of the earth? Do they wish some heavy affliction to fall on them if they do not fulfil the duty of their oath to King Jesus to whom they have sworn allegiance? Doesn't the apostle say that he that eats and drinks the body and blood of Christ unworthily, he is guilty of damnation, guilty of the Lord's blood? Why? Thomas Manton said, "because these solemn rites do not only confirm the promises (Christians love the promises), but confirm the threatening; and there is implied not only an invocation of blessing, but an imprecation upon ourselves; that is, if you do not fulfil the duty of the covenant, you offer yourselves as it were to God's curse."[3] Is this not the very words of the text of Leviticus 26? Is this not the very thing among the church today? They are disparaging God's Christ and his work, and God will not tolerate that for long. They do not regard him as they ought. They do not regard his word as they ought. They do not regard his worship as they ought. They dare him to do his worst against them. And what is the worst of the Christ? Is he not the Sovereign Judge of the universe? What is an Almighty worst? What is an infinite worst? What is a just worst? What is a wrathful worst? Lam. 3:1, "I have seen Affliction by the Rod of Gods wrath." Will the church see nothing but wrath and curse, and fiery vengeance dispensed to them in their bitter things?

Why is the plague still among us? It is unfathomable to dare God to do his worst if this is contemplated. But it is also a great wakeup call as well to us all. What sins do you harbor? What sins do you hide deep in your heart? What is buried there so deep that you

---

[3] Manton, Thomas, *The Complete Works of Thomas Manton*, Volume 8, (London: James Nisbet & Co., 1872), 93.

hardly even think about them? What causes you to stray from the road of salvation? For, to sin, to hold a heart-sin, a bosom sin, and continue in it, is to dare God upon it every time you commit it. Instead, take it to heart yourselves that God will not be dared, and will act, and that ... with great power. Think about all the warning passages and judgments against the church in Scripture to be possibilities to you personally; they are written for you. They are warnings to you as a Christian in a church. Who do you think they were written for? If it were not for the grace of God and his word, where would you be? What would you be doing? Where would you be worshipping Christ even now? How might you guard yourselves against declension in your worship? How might you guard against idolatry and service to God that is accomplished with reverence and godly fear?

By your own voluntary sins, you dare God to his face. You think to yourself, "my O my, there are a great many heinous churches all over the world that are covenant breaking with God, have despised his worship, have not served him as he has prescribed which result is this plague among us." Who has brought the plague to the earth? You think, "they have. They are idolaters. They are those in doctrinal error. They are those that have exchanged the worship of God for something else." Are your actions, and thoughts, and deeds, and works all perfect? Are your righteousnesses not as filthy rags?

By all your presumptuous and secret sins, you dare God to prove that he is an all-seeing and all-powerful God. You wonder by action whether God will really discover your hypocrisy in your sins. You point the finger to other churches, to others who do not really know the word as much as you do, and so blame them for all that is befalling the world. But are your sins exempt from bringing in the plague? Why is the plague here? Why is famine ensuing? Why economic disaster?

You tempt God by your unbelief. When you sin you do not believe that God cares what should be done by you. It is a mistrust of Christ's word. You do something you love more than you love God at the time, and you engage in some path of your making, some sin, and tempt God to do his worst against you by its very action. And this, every time you sin, you enter into this. How many sins did Korah commit? How many sins did Achan commit? Was it not but one? Is God not very, very, very gracious to you in Christ for not making the ground swallow you up? What happens when the church sins as a collective body? And that for a long time? Wars, and famine, and pestilence, and earthquakes and such are sent as tokens of the final judgment of the Christ. Has this been so dismissed? Will you not believe God's providence even today? Is God but a liar because he sent a plague and he really doesn't mean what he says in this passage to his people? It doesn't have anything to do with us ...

If the church of Christ in the earth does not repent, will you? The entire passage is about the sin of the church, and whether the church continues obstinately in sin enough for God to plague them, to bring war and famine, or ... if they will repent and reform he will bless them. This is a word to his church. Did they reform? Will you reform? Is your life categorized as a continued reformation? Do you make God wait a long time for your reformation? Are you so very serious about it, or lukewarm, or cold? Will you be like the Samaritans who feared God, but worshipped their own gods? Your reformation will be little better than theirs if you do not follow God's prescription of his holy will. And you cannot be fully satisfied in your reformation. To be such is to be at an end of it. That you have reformed. Who has done this? What church is not in need of further instruction, or refinement or encouragement? Who does not need more of the blood of Jesus Christ? Who does not need more covering from the Mercy seat?

The problem with today's church is the problem with todays' Christian – that they have rebellion set in the context of their reformation. So, their reformation is made void, their sanctification is stopped and hindered. Rebellion is mixed in it, because they have mixed what God has said, with what they like. So, God is not in those places. Yes, they have his word, they profess his Son and profess walking in the Spirit. But God's prescriptions are thrown out. They have in essence thrown out God. God speaking, "He said furthermore unto me, Son of man, seest thou what they do? even the great abominations that the house of Israel committeth here, that I should go far off from my sanctuary?" (Ezek. 8:6). God leaves and deserts deserters who first desert him, and continue to desert him, in their false profession. He abandons such places as those who break his covenant and do not reform their lives. If rebellion is in your reformation, it will be a hindrance for you. It is a daring God to judge you. How many times has God's church dared him? Do not dare God in your sin, i.e. let us not by our provoking sins dare God, try his patience, whether he will make good his threats on us against our sin. When you act in that way, you act as all proud sinners do, all covenant offenders, which are said to weary him in their service. "I am weary to bear them," (Isa. 1:14). "Wherefore doth the wicked condemn God? he hath said in his heart, Thou wilt not require it," (Psa. 10:13). They do not fear him. They deny his providence. They wish there was no God to trouble them. Open sins, sins that are still thriving in you, are a dare to God and they defy him; they are covenant-breaking sins. Taken to its logical extreme, to continue in sin, to continue without sorrow and remorse and repentance, to continue in a course, even with so great providences surrounding us today, in such strange time as they are, is to dare God even to damn you. God is quite serious about his covenant. God is quite serious about his Christ. God is quite serious that we put off all sin and put on the Lord Jesus Christ, and that speedily. What will the church ultimately do? What will God ultimately do? I end with this final statement as a cliff hanging warning: The church's obstinance in continuing in covenant breaking sins dares God to do his worst against them; do you?

Appendix:
Obedience in the Little Things

"As for the sons of Merari, thou shalt number them after their families, by the house of their fathers; From thirty years old and upward even unto fifty years old shalt thou number them, every one that entereth into the service, to do the work of the tabernacle of the congregation. And this is the charge of their burden, according to all their service in the tabernacle of the congregation; the boards of the tabernacle, and the bars thereof, and the pillars thereof, and sockets thereof, And the pillars of the court round about, and their sockets, and their pins, and their cords, with all their instruments, and with all their service: and by name ye shall reckon the instruments of the charge of their burden. This is the service of the families of the sons of Merari, according to all their service, in the tabernacle of the congregation, under the hand of Ithamar the son of Aaron the priest," (Num. 4:29-33).

What a day it would have been when Israel was released from 400 years of bondage. They had great preparations for worship. This is why God released them from captivity, to bring them into the desert to worship him. The Father seeks worshippers to worship him in Spirit and truth. They had in this release, which was a type of sin and salvation, a preparation for the journey and worship. Keep in mind from bondage to worship was 400 years. An in this preparation into the wilderness and mountain of God, God appointed certain duties to the priests. At this point in Numbers, the tabernacle was made, and the priests were assigned various duties in and for it. Such duties were in fact for God. They all had a "charge," they were all given a burden in this appointment, according as God appointed their burdens, (Num. 4:25, 31, 36). There was a burden of work and carrying items for the tabernacle. Some of them were appointed by God to carry the parts of the tabernacle as God led them through their wilderness wanderings.

God took great care in specifically setting down all things for the tabernacle, how it was to be constructed, and a great care in the way it would be set up. The tabernacle is the meeting place for God and the people. It was, in fact, a shadow of the full picture of Christ and the greater tabernacle/temple that the Savior is High Priest in heaven. This is the place, at the time, where the sacrifices for sin took place, for the church. The day of atonement, Yom Kippur. How Levitical sacrifice would hold back the wrath of God until the Christ would fulfill all things. God was very specific about what he wanted accomplished for his worship. God directed his people and these men were to obey – all things pertaining to his worship were regulated by him, even the manner in which the tabernacle, again at this time, was set up, even carried in service to him. There was no consensus on anything in this way pertaining to sustaining God's worship. There were directives, and there was obedience.

Now, in this passage is found the charge, the appointment the burden of the sons of Merari. This is the second mention of their appointed duties. Merari is the third son of Levi, (Gen. 46:11). The Levites were specifically set as a tribe in service to God for matters of worship.

They were to be numbered, "Number them..." Such a numbering was written down, and recorded, much like a heavenly inventory of things. This was as if God was saying, who do I have to work with? I want them to know I know. God leaves no details undone. He is precise and orderly. All through the life of the congregation the Spirit gifts men for certain tasks. "And under the custody and charge of the sons of Merari shall be the boards of the tabernacle, and the bars thereof, and the pillars thereof, and the sockets thereof, and all the vessels thereof, and all that serveth thereto, And the pillars of the court round about, and their sockets, and their pins, and their cords," (Num. 3:36-37).

Verse 31, "This is what they must carry..." This was not up for debate. They were under obligation or charge from the Almighty God. This was not opportunity for service. This was not opportunity for ministry. The Hebrew idea (*Mishmeret*) to watch, guard, keep over, with great care over, is to have a great attention to be paid to the obligations.

Verse 32 "and you shall assign to each man by name the items he must carry." God knew each person by name and had a task for each man; and each hand in particular! "Service..." it has connotation of fighting, or to render service for in a total dedication and careful watchfulness over a specific task. *Yahweh Sebaot* – the Lord of Hosts, the Lord of the armies of heaven and earth commanded these men to serve him in a very particular manner.

What exactly did the sons of Merari do? They were to carry boards, pegs, sockets, and poles. Their service was manual labor. Who told them to do this? God did. Yes, but not exactly. The sons of Aaron told them. It went from God to Moses to Aaron to the sons, and the sons told them. Gershonites and Merarites under the care of Ithamar (verses 28, 33). What did the sons of Merari do when they heard this from Aaron's son? Did they murmur? It seems, from the text, and other texts regarding them, that, all in all, they did not. They demonstrated exemplary obedience in their calling, in their obligation, in their burden. A wonderful example of contented obedience.

DOCTRINE: Christians ought to be obedient to God and Christ in all things commanded of them.

The sons of Merari obeyed God, in this instance, without challenge, without excuse and without delay. Do Christians generally do this? The Lord Jesus questions his followers in Luke 6:46, "And why call ye me, Lord, Lord, and do not the things which I say?" Christians are to act and serve God, serve Christ, in a particular manner.

Without challenge. What could the sons of Merari have said? Do we have to? This would have shown a great deal of discontentedness. Can't the animals do it? This would have shown they despised the service of God as something abhorred. Is it necessary for a Levite to do this kind of work? Was such service to God beneath them? Christians often say the same kinds of things. Can't we find someone better qualified to do it? I don't think that kind of work is for me. I would like more important work. What about the simplified basics of what Christ commands the Christian? The spiritual work of fundamental Christian duty? Will God give Christians more duties to do if they are not able to do what God requires of them in simple things? Is this not the very reason, at least one of the very reasons, why Paul's list for elder qualifications revolve around practical qualifications? How his house is maintained. Whether his children serve him in all submission and reverence. He cannot be a novice and must exemplify practical outworkings of his Christianity. Is this not the same for deacons too, and the wives of both? Will God lavish more service, which he loves, on those that cannot fulfill the simple basics of Christian experience and service? Or what about Christians generally speaking? Daily personal devotions, daily family worship, meeting at the appointed times for the Lord's Day for public worship, prayer meetings, fellowship with the saints. It seems, at some point in some way Christians tend to challenge God often, and regularly. They are often like young children that test to see how far the parent will allow them to go. They push an inch and then try to take a yard. But Christians are to do what God requires without challenge as the sons of Merari did, even in the little things.

Without Excuse. All things done for the Kingdom of God are important; the sons of Merari knew this, even in just carrying tent poles and pegs and such. From entering into the Holy of Holies and offering up the sacrifice, to carrying the sockets of the Tent. Was it a menial task? They could have given a number of excuses. This is too far to carry these things. We've walked too far. It's too hot and we are overburdened in this wilderness. We are too tired with having just come out of slavery in Egypt. This task is not important enough for us to do. Is this the way Christians often think about the work of the church? Even in the repairs of a church building, the cleaning of the rest rooms; the manual labor to keep up what God has given as good stewards; all these kinds of little things are important; but are they really little to God? Christians tend to give a great number of excuses before they engage in spiritual service to God. I'm not patient enough to visit shut ins. I'm not spiritual enough to do such spiritual works. Isn't the minister supposed to do all those things? Aren't I just merely supposed to come to church and fill this seat here in the pew? It's the elder's job to do all those things. It's their job to attend the things of the tabernacle, not mine. Whenever the commandment is broken, to honor superiors and inferiors in the 5th commandment, for those are annexed to it, at some point, in mind, or heart, everyone tends to give excuses, but as the sons of Merari did, they ought to do as well without excuse.

Without Delay. What do the sons of Merari do after they are appointed to carry the boards, pegs, sockets and poles? After the law is given, they set out, and they carried their burden. Make no mistake, it was a burden – it was hard! God said it was! He called it mas-saw a load, a burden to lift up. Christians too, though, should carry their "burdens" without delay; it literally makes them a disciple or not. Shall they halt between two opinions or serve God? Spiritual Sacrifices and trials and tribulations are burdensome. But, Christians, to be Christians, are required to carry their crosses. Matthew 16:24, "Then said Jesus unto his disciples, If any man will come after me, let him deny himself, and take up his cross, and follow me." This was stated in a very direct manner by the Lord. To be a Christian is to be a cross bearer, to be a burden bearer. To be serviceable is to carry the boards, pegs sockets and poles if needs be, spiritually speaking. Cross bearing is required by all Christians. Are God's people often in service without delay, or by delay? At this point the sons of Merari did not complain, at all. Not even a "murmur" is transcribed in these places and these texts about carrying the boards, pegs, sockets and poles.

God has work to be done by appointed workers. God knows who is fitted for the task. God requires them to pick up their burdens as he sees them fit. God requires Christians to pick up all their spiritual burdens, all their cross burdens without delay. The Spirit assigns Christians spiritual and physical tasks according to the gifts Christians bear. What are one's gifts? That's to be considered. Why are they gifted but for service to God and Christ? Christians ought to be obedient to Christ in all things he commands of them.

And yet, what does God command the Christian? This is to press the importance of God's revealed word and all its practical works in their life. It is interesting that God did not speak to the sons, but to Moses, and Moses did not speak to the sons, but to Aaron, and Aaron did not speak to the sons, but to Ithamar, and Ithamar spoke to the sons of Merari. God's word, at the time, was orally sent. Did they murmur at the words of the minister who brought them the truth of God? Did they mumble against God's mouthpiece? Or is it to their praise that they did not disparage the word of the Lord that was sent to them? Provided that Ithamar had things right, and he was charged to speak on behalf of God, this is why Hebrews says "Obey them that have the rule over you, and submit yourselves: for they watch for your souls, as they that must give account, that they may do it with joy, and not with grief: for that is unprofitable for you," (Heb. 13:17). Do Christians heed the word in this way as the sons of Merari did?

How will one know what the Lord says, if he is not familiar with, what the Lord says? For the Christian, John says these commandments should not be burdensome, "For this is the love of God, that we keep his commandments: and his commandments are not burdensome," (1 John 5:3). But how will Christians know if they do not spend time in the word of God, which Christians have far more of today than the sons of Merari did. Christians have the Christ in his fulness.

Jesus did all things without challenge, without excuse and without delay. All Christ's covenant work was without challenge, "not my will, but thine be done." All Christ's covenantal work was without excuse. John 10:17-19, "Therefore doth my Father love me, because I lay down my life, that I might take it again. No man taketh it from me, but I lay it down of myself. I have power to lay it down, and I have power to take it again. This commandment have I received of my Father." All Christ's covenantal work was without delay. Even from the beginning, Jesus as a boy was teaching in the temple, "I must be about my Father's business." Mark's Gospel is filled with Christ's work under the central word, "immediately;" straightway, forthwith. Christ was the covenanted God-man sent by the Father to fulfill the counsel of peace, and to usher into time the covenant of grace to save sinful men. He was, truly, a man with a mission, and yet he did all he did without murmuring, without complaining, without making excuses for its difficulty; and what a difficulty it was; to be the sin-bearer. He did all he did before God in service to the Father with eager joyfulness. Psalm 1:2, "but his delight is in the law of the Lord." Jesus delighted to do the Father's will with fullness of joy, "...Jesus the author and finisher of our faith; who for the joy that was set before him endured the cross, despising the shame, and is set down at the right hand of the throne of God," (Heb. 12:2).

Sinners ought to serve God without challenge, without excuse and without delay. But this is problematic because sinners are lost. They must first look the Christ, look to him and be saved, and they ought to do it in the same threefold manner.

Without challenge. Sinners who challenge Christ do not love Christ nor want Christ. They are content to sin and that into the grave and then into judgment. They find that their works are somewhat good. They are not contrite. They do not mourn over sin. They are not burdened by sin. They are full of themselves. They see other religions, and think Christianity is challenged by them; which is a horrid and indefensible argument to assert; simply because they want to hide their sin and continue in it. Sinners who do not challenge Christ, rely in and on him alone for salvation. All those things that hinder the sinner to come to Christ are cast away. They no longer rely on themselves, or the world, or desire to serve their previous father the devil. They take away all those deceiving crutches and lean on Jesus. They go to the promises of God. "Look unto me, and be ye saved, all the ends of the earth: for I am God, and there is none else," (Isa. 45:22).

Without excuse. They are supposed to serve God without excuse, but sinners have so many excuses. I am too old a sinner. I am too young a sinner and want to serve my flesh. I am not worthy. I do not know if Christ will take me. I do not have time right now, maybe later; there is time to spare. I haven't thought all this through well enough, let me have more time to think about it. I need to bury my father first, one told Jesus. I have great possessions, another said. I love the world more, was Demas' ultimate plea. Contrite, humble and broken sinners come with no excuses. Lord, be merciful to me a sinner. And such a one goes away justified.

Without delay. Sinners who don't love Christ don't come to Christ. They delay and put off as much as they can because they regard the things of the world more important than God's will or Christ's work. They listen to the devil and his whispers. You don't need that right now. You can go to him if needs be at any time. Contrite sinners come to a Christ they need speedily; without delay. They know the end is at any moment. They may have a heart attack. They may have an aneurism. They may be hit by a car. They may suffer and die under a strange new virus. Sinners come to Christ speedily. "And when Jesus came to the place, he looked up, and saw him, and said unto him, Zacchaeus, make haste, and come down; for today I must abide at thy house. And he made haste, and came down, and received him joyfully," (Luke 19:5-6). Salvation comes to such houses as this man's with haste, speedily and without delay. We take this idea that Christians ought to be obedient to God and Christ in all things commanded of them.

How do you serve God? Are you obedient even in the little things – the common things? Christians ought to be obedient to Christ in all things he commands of them without challenge, without excuse and without delay.

Things of the bible and the closet. Prayer, Study, bible reading, godly meditation It's a foolish thing to offer up to God the least of our time instead of the most of our time, the choice of our time. Was Jesus ever negligent of these things?

Things of the home. Family worship, home provision, discipline for the children, guidance for the family, helpmeet for the husband, honor to the parents; study of the word, when you rise up and when you lie down, when you come in and when you go out. Was Jesus negligent in these things?

Things of the church. Gathering together at the appointed meetings; using gifts, ministry to one another, worship with the whole being; singing so hard it hurts; bearing one another's burdens. Was Jesus ever negligent of these things? If you are negligent, repent, look to Christ for forgiveness and stop murmuring whether by your actions (which is outwardly with your tongue (which is deplorable). Or, stop blaspheming the name of Christ and Christianity in the eyes of the world by your horrid lifestyle and witness. If you are not a Christian, stop *pretending* to be one. Christ commands you repent and be saved; look to him and make amendment of life, reformation of life, transformation of life. He never commands hypocrisy in such things. He gets very tired of your challenges, and your excuses and your constant delays. He looks for compliance, resolve and haste in your

271

life in all things he commands. "I made haste, and did not delay To keep Your commandment," (Psa. 119:60). He had to know them to keep them.

Things as a church. The marks of a biblical church: strong biblical oversight of the flock, sound doctrine in preaching and teaching, the right administration of the sacraments, biblical church discipline and biblical worship. Should any church be blessed by God in greater things if they are not obedient in the little things, the common things, of the church and life of the church in godliness?

Christians must stop acting like wicked servants that hide their talents in the dirt (Luke 19:21ff). God will never bless a church with that which is greater, if they cannot be faithful in those things which are lesser. We would be sorely mistaken to believe otherwise.

Consider all the providences of God in your church. Consider both collectively and individually – even weekly in light of the Lord's Supper, and judge whether you have been faithful even in the little things... Are you obedient in the little things God gives you to do? Do you do them without challenge, without excuse and without delay? Luke 16:10, "He who is faithful in what is least is faithful also in much; and he who is unjust in what is least is unjust also in much."

The sons of Merari exemplified the true soldier in Christ's ranks at this point in their life. They are a very fine picture of a soldier. Like the English guards, professional soldiers who are never distracted from what they are doing, even in little things when people try to distract them from their duty. Hypocrites are always in it for the uniform, but never for the service.

God did not ask the sons of Merari what they wanted to do; he does not ask you. He has commanded you what needs to be done and now its high time to be serious Christians to do all that he requires. Obedience is your responsibility. He has, in fact, Ephesians 2:10, "prepared works in advance for us to do..." Do them well, even in the little things. Never by way of hypocrisy.

Consider the apostle Judas...Judas heard all of Christ's sermons. Some of you are like Judas. You think because you hear a sermon or go to a church that such things makes you a Christian—as much as it makes Judas a true disciple. Look at the sons of Merari. Later in the Scriptures we see that they are given other duties to fulfill, keeping the gates in 1 Chronicles 26:10-19. God chose three key Levitical leaders to help Ezra after the return from the exile, one of which was a son of Merari (Ezra 8:18-19). Those faithful in little will be given more to be faithful in much.

Look at the pattern of Jesus Christ! Exemplary obedience in everything as he served God in his life and death, then he is given "...all authority..." exalted to the right hand of the Father.

Take a moment, consider your life in light of this brief exhortation, that you too would be obedient to God in all the little things he has given you to do, and all the big things he looks to give you to do. May we all serve Christ as he so commands us, even in the little things, without challenge, without excuse and without delay.

Other Helpful Works by C. Matthew McMahon from Puritan Publications

Joseph's Resolve and the Unreasonableness of Sinning Against God

How much do you hate sin? Joseph was resolved to cast off all wickedness as he lived before the face of God. Do you?

Walking Victoriously in the Power of the Spirit

Are you walking victoriously in the Spirit? Are you baptized by the Spirit, indwelt by the Spirit, walking abundantly in Jesus Christ by the Spirit? Do you even regularly talk this way?

5 Marks of Biblical Reformation

Everybody loves to claim the magisterial reformation for their own! Everyone wants to be a reformer in that way. But take God's principles of a Biblical Reformation and apply them to the church in practical daily living, then that's a different story all together.

5 Marks of Biblical Commitment to the Visible Body of Christ

Are you a member of Christ's church? Are you a covenanter? Do you support your church? Are you committed to it? How do you show it?

5 Marks of a Biblical Disciple

What is a disciple? A disciple has "5 Marks" outlined in Scripture which demonstrate a Spirit-filled walking with Jesus Christ in newness of life.

5 Marks of a Biblical Church

What are the marks of a biblical church? There are 5 marks that demonstrate the church as the pillar and ground of the truth.

Seeing Christ Clearly

How did Jesus view himself in the Gospels? Who is this divine Son of Man who comes down out of heaven? Do you see Christ clearly?

The Wickedness, Humiliation, Restoration and Reformation of Manasseh

Why study the life of Manasseh who was such a wicked and deplorable man? God, in his great mercy, saved him, converted him, and caused him to start a reformation of religion.

The Lord's Voice Cries to the City: A Biblical Guide for Hearing the word of God Preached -

Is the preacher doing what he is supposed to in his preaching in order for you to do what you are commanded to do in your duty to hear the word of God rightly?

The Reformed Apprentice Volume 4: A Workbook on Private Devotions

In this 4th volume to the Reformed Apprentice Series, the workbook covers private devotions. Its aim is to draw closer to Christ in communion with him in an interactive workbook filled with Reformed Theology and Puritan directions to the three important spiritual disciplines of bible reading, godly meditation and prayer.

The Two Wills of God Made Easy

What is God's will for my life? Does God love everyone? Is God's will ever frustrated? Does God change his mind? This newly abridged version gives the Christian the proper hermeneutical tools to define "God's will" and how his will functions in and through redemptive history. It solves critical questions surrounding God's nature, demonstrating that proper biblical interpretation is the key to understanding the will of God in an easy to understand format.

John 3:16

Do you know of any other Bible verse more quoted than John 3:16? And yet, even though this verse is known by everyone, it is often the most misunderstood verse in the Bible. McMahon is not only faithful exegetically, to the Biblical text, but he also extensively quotes the major theologians and writers of church history to find out what the consensus is on this most beloved passage.

A Practical Guide to Primeval History

Where did sin come from? Or for that matter, all the people on the face of the earth after Adam and Eve? What do you know about primeval history? Whatever your question is about the early history of the world, from a biblical perspective, this work will help you understand these first 11 chapters of Genesis and God's plan for the ages thereafter, both doctrinally and practically.

Sophia and the Umbrella: A Children's Book on Justification

What does it mean to be justified by faith alone? It is not "just as if I'd never sinned," as so many trendy evangelicals believe. So what then? In this easy to understand and fully illustrated children's story we find Sophia who lives in the city of Drown, and who is constantly soaking wet. She is looking to find a way to get dry but cannot do it on her own. Then, she meets a stranger on the corner of a street who has a special gift just for her to help her get out of the rain. It is a story centering around 1 John 1:7, "...and the blood of Jesus Christ his Son cleanseth us from all sin."

Umiko and the Mask

Reformed children's books are hard to find. Fully Illustrated Reformed Children's books are even harder. Here is the first by Puritan Publications on how to teach the doctrine of regeneration and conversion to little children through the adventure of Umiko.

The Reformed Apprentice Volume 3: A Workbook on the Doctrine of God

This one-of-a-kind workbook series (this is the third volume) teaches the student of theology about Reformed Theology. In this workbook, students will learn about the Doctrine of God in order to bring them into a more intimate relationship with Jesus Christ. It covers God's divine attributes, the Trinity, the divinity of the Son and Holy Spirit, and the decrees of God.

John Calvin's View of God's Love and the Doctrine of Reprobation

Everyone wants Calvin on "their side" when it comes to theological matters. What did Calvin actually teach concerning God's love and the reprobation of the wicked? Are these two ideas compatible?

Gradual Reformation Intolerable

Is there a need for a biblical reformation today? The answer on that is a Bible-thumping YES! But should it happen slowly and gradually? Was this the method Christ used in preaching, or the Reformers? McMahon and Anthony Burgess (1600-1663) team up to give the thoughtful Christian a biblical foundation to promote current reformation in their church and in their homes.

The Children's Shorter Catechism

Do you spend time each day training up your children in godliness? This new version of the Children's Shorter Catechism is an extremely effective way in teaching young children the basic principles of the Bible, and the Reformed Faith. It updates some poor theological language and some antiquated language from the previous version published in the past. It follows the *1647 Westminster Shorter Catechism*, and also has added Bible references for study.

Psalm 96: A Theology of Praise

We often hear about prayer, but we hear very little about praise. We know how to ask God for things we think we need, but how often do we take time to praise him for who he is and what he has done? Psalm

96 not only answers those questions, but it gives us a complete theology of praise. It tells us how we should praise God and why we should praise God.

The Reformed Apprentice Volume 2: A Workbook on the Doctrine of Scripture and Biblical Interpretation

When someone asks you why you believe the Bible to be the word of God, what do you tell them? When you come across a passage that is hard to understand, what do you do to interpret it? This workbook will guide you through answering questions around the Doctrine of Scripture, as well as the science of Hermeneutics, the art of biblical interpretation. This is the second volume in the workbook series.

The Reformed Apprentice: A Workbook on Reformed Theology

This one-of-a-kind workbook teaches the student of theology about Reformed Theology. They are, in fact, apprenticed under Master Theologians throughout the history of the church in order to bring them into a more intimate relationship with Jesus Christ.

Bah Humbug: How Christians Should Think About the Christmas Holiday

Do you celebrate the Christmas holiday? Is Jesus the Reason for the Season?" Did you know the church throughout history outlawed Christmas? So, can Christians partake in Christmas? Or not?

Augustine's Calvinism: The Doctrines of Grace in Augustine's Writings

Did Augustine believe and teach the doctrines of grace? Or were these doctrines formulated later? This work is a survey of Augustine's writings with the conclusion that Augustine was no doubt, a Calvinist.

The Reformation Made Easy

Read about the sovereignty of God in action during the greatest revival and recovery of the Gospel of Jesus Christ in church history, the Reformation...and all of it MADE EASY.

Systematic Theology Made Easy

Do you love theology? Sometimes it's hard to wade through thousands of pages in giant tomes exhausting every possible subject. Don't you wish there was an EASY systematic theology book? There is....

Historical Theology Made Easy

Everyone needs to understand where their beliefs came from in the history of the church. This work in the "made easy" series, covers all you need to know about Historical Theology in an easy to understand format!

How to Live Every Day in the End Times

So many Christians live a life devoid of true joy. Did you know that you are living in the end times and that your life should be marked with joy as a result? Do people think you are a joyful Christian? In this study of Philippians see what God has said about being joyful in these end times.

Eternity Weighed in the Balance

These chapters are so important that I even decided to use this book to create a video series on heaven, hell and salvation (coming soon). This work is a great tool in understanding three key ingredients in salvation, the doctrine of heaven, the doctrine of hell and the, manner in which we gain one or the other.

Overcoming Lust in a Sex-crazed World

In our day pornographic material is everywhere on the internet, in the grocery store magazines, on television, on billboards, in the movies EVERYWHERE. Is it in your home? Do you struggle with lust? If you are struggling with your thoughts, this book is for you and will help you strive for godliness and purity in honoring Christ with your body and mind.

A Simple Overview of Covenant Theology

When dealing with Covenant Theology "simple" is a good thing. After the Bible, this work is the FIRST that you should read, or one that you should introduce to a friend if they are struggling with covenant concepts.

How Faith Works: Rescuing the Gospel from Contemporary Evangelicalism

What is the Biblical Gospel? Are you content to call yourself an "Evangelical?" Is the Evangelical Gospel the same Gospel of the Protestant Reformation? Is an Evangelical today the same as an evangelical during the time of Luther, Calvin or the Puritans? If the magisterial Reformers suddenly walked into your church today, would they be pleased with the Gospel that is being preached from its pulpit? This work covers the "Gospel" of the contemporary church and the remedy found in the Gospel of Jesus Christ.

Covenant Theology Made Easy

This book takes Covenant Theology and MAKES IT EASY. Really? YES. This is McMahon's second work on the subject. His "Simple Overview of Covenant Theology" has received high acclaim and now this work continues to advance the student in the next step in an easy to understand manner.

The Two Wills of God: Does God Really Have Two Wills?

Does God have two wills? It sure does seem like he does when on the one hand, "our God is in the heavens He doth whatsoever He pleases," and then "God repenteth that He made man..." What do we make of this and other seemingly difficult passages in the bible about God's will? This work will lay to rest the tension between orthodox Calvinism, and deviant Arminianism.

A Heart for Reformation

How much do you love being "Reformed?" What does God require of you as a Reforming Christian at home, at work, in church, as a parent, as a child and as a friend? How does "being a covenanted Reformed Christian" work? Do you have a heart for true biblical reformation?